365 Homemade Chocolate Candy Recipes

(365 Homemade Chocolate Candy Recipes - Volume 1)

Shani Moore

Copyright: Published in the United States by Shani Moore/ © SHANI MOORE

Published on October, 12 2020

All rights reserved. No part of this publication may be reproduced, stored in retrieval system, copied in any form or by any means, electronic, mechanical, photocopying, recording or otherwise transmitted without written permission from the publisher. Please do not participate in or encourage piracy of this material in any way. You must not circulate this book in any format. SHANI MOORE does not control or direct users' actions and is not responsible for the information or content shared, harm and/or actions of the book readers.

In accordance with the U.S. Copyright Act of 1976, the scanning, uploading and electronic sharing of any part of this book without the permission of the publisher constitute unlawful piracy and theft of the author's intellectual property. If you would like to use material from the book (other than just simply for reviewing the book), prior permission must be obtained by contacting the author at author@bisquerecipes.com

Thank you for your support of the author's rights.

Content

365 AWESOME CHOCOLATE CANDY RECIPES 8

1. 1881 Chocolate Caramels Recipe 8
2. 3 Muskateers Recipe 8
3. 4 Chip Fudge Recipe 9
4. APRICOT ALMOND CHOCOLATE CHEWS Recipe 9
5. AZTEC Chocolate Bark Recipe 10
6. Addicting Chocolate Pecan Saltine Delights Recipe 10
7. Adorable Christmas Mice Recipe 10
8. Almond Bark Pink Peppermint Patties Recipe 11
9. Almond Coated Dark Chocolate Peanut Butter Balls Recipe 11
10. Almond Ganache Cups Recipe 11
11. Almond Joy Bars Recipe 12
12. Almond And Chocolate Clusters Recipe .. 12
13. Almond Filled Chocolate Covered Cherries Recipe 13
14. Amazing Candy Recipe 14
15. Apricot White Chocolate Fudge Recipe 14
16. Assembly Of Chocolates Recipe 14
17. Awesome Chocolate Truffles Recipe 15
18. BAILEYS SNOWBALL TRUFFLES Recipe 15
19. Baileys Irish Cream Chocolate Truffles Recipe 15
20. Barfing Pumpkin Candy Recipe 16
21. Belgian Chocolats For Kids Recipe 16
22. Bing Bars Recipe 17
23. Blueberry Clusters Recipe 17
24. Boognish Brown Mix Recipe 18
25. Bourbon Balls Recipe 18
26. Bread Chocolate Recipe 18
27. Brigadeiro Recipe 19
28. Brigadeiros Recipe 19
29. BuckEye Balls Recipe 19
30. Buckeye Peanut Butter Candy Recipe 20
31. Buckeys Peanut Butter Chocolate Candy Recipe 20
32. Butterfinger Candy Bars Recipe 21
33. Butterscotch Chocolate Divinity Recipe ... 21
34. CHERRY MASH CANDY Recipe 22
35. CHOCOLATE COVERED CHERRIES Recipe 22
36. CHOCOLATE MARZIPANS Recipe 22
37. CREAMY CHOCOLATE FUDGE Recipe 23
38. Caggiune E Caggiunitte Recipe 23
39. California White Chocolate Fudge Recipe 24
40. Canadian Chocolate Fruit Roll Recipe 24
41. Candi Style Cookie Dough Bites Recipe ... 24
42. Candied Orange Slices Dipped In Chocolate Recipe 25
43. Caramel Chocolate Rolo Pretzels Recipe .. 25
44. Carmel Chocolate Green Apple Mess Recipe 26
45. Charlie Chaplin Candy Recipe 26
46. Cheerio Candy Recipe 26
47. Chelseas Candy Bars Recipe 27
48. Cherry White Chocolate Fudge Recipe 27
49. Chewy Chocolate Nut Candies Recipe 27
50. Chewy Chocolates Recipe 28
51. Chex Muddy Buddies Recipe 28
52. Chinese Noodle Candy Recipe 28
53. Chocolate Billionaires Recipe 29
54. Chocolate Almond Toffee Recipe 29
55. Chocolate And Peanut Butter Candy Recipe 29
56. Chocolate Anise Truffles Recipe 30
57. Chocolate Bonbons Recipe 30
58. Chocolate Bourbon Truffles Recipe 30
59. Chocolate Butter Crunch Toffee Recipe ... 31
60. Chocolate Butter Toffee Recipe 31
61. Chocolate Buttercream Cherry Candies Recipe 32
62. Chocolate Cappuccino Candy Recipe 32
63. Chocolate Caramel Apples Wcandy Bars Recipe 33
64. Chocolate Caramel Apples With Salted Pretzels Recipe 33
65. Chocolate Caramel Graham Crackers Recipe 34
66. Chocolate Caramel Popcorn Recipe 34
67. Chocolate Caramel Squares Recipe 35
68. Chocolate Caramel Walnut Fudge Recipe .35
69. Chocolate Cherries Cookies Mix In A Jar Recipe Recipe 36
70. Chocolate Cherries Recipe 37

71. Chocolate Cherry Creams Recipe 37
72. Chocolate Cherry Pistachio Fudge Recipe 37
73. Chocolate Cherry Sweets Recipe 38
74. Chocolate Coated Coconut Balls Recipe .. 38
75. Chocolate Coated Macaroon Balls Recipe 38
76. Chocolate Covered Almond Apricot Tassies Recipe 39
77. Chocolate Covered Butter Crunch Toffee Recipe 39
78. Chocolate Covered Cherries Recipe 40
79. Chocolate Covered Easter Eggs Recipe 40
80. Chocolate Covered Peanut Butter Balls Recipe 41
81. Chocolate Covered Worms Recipe 41
82. Chocolate Cranberry Cashew Bark Recipe 41
83. Chocolate Cream Cheese Fudge Recipe ... 42
84. Chocolate Creams Recipe 42
85. Chocolate Crunch Recipe 43
86. Chocolate Dipped Apricots Recipe 43
87. Chocolate Dipped Caramallows Recipe 43
88. Chocolate Dipped Caramel Apples Recipe 44
89. Chocolate Dreams Recipe 45
90. Chocolate Fleur De Sel Bonbons Recipe .. 45
91. Chocolate Fruit And Nut Truffles Recipe 45
92. Chocolate Fudge Recipe 46
93. Chocolate Fudgies Recipe 46
94. Chocolate Ganache Truffles Recipe 47
95. Chocolate Hazelnut Sticks Recipe 47
96. Chocolate Honey Fudge Recipe 48
97. Chocolate Marshmallow Cashew Fudge Recipe 48
98. Chocolate Marshmallow Nut Clusters Recipe 49
99. Chocolate Marshmallow Pizza Recipe 49
100. Chocolate Marshmallow Popcorn Balls Recipe 49
101. Chocolate Marshmello Fudge Lite Recipe 50
102. Chocolate Mint Candy Recipe 50
103. Chocolate Mint Fudge Recipe 50
104. Chocolate Mint Truffles Recipe 51
105. Chocolate Nut Chews Recipe 51
106. Chocolate Nut Clusters Recipe 52
107. Chocolate Nut Drops Recipe 52
108. Chocolate Orange Truffles Recipe 52
109. Chocolate Peanut Butter Fudge Recipe 53
110. Chocolate Peanut Butter Rocky Road Clusters Recipe 53
111. Chocolate Peanut Butter Squares Recipe .. 53
112. Chocolate Peanut Popcorn Crunch Recipe 54
113. Chocolate Peanut Sweeties Recipe 54
114. Chocolate Pecan Candy Recipe 55
115. Chocolate Potato Candy Recipe 55
116. Chocolate Pretzel Rings 55
117. Chocolate Pretzel Rings Recipe 56
118. Chocolate Raspberry Truffles Recipe 56
119. Chocolate Roses Recipe 56
120. Chocolate Truffle Meringues Recipe 57
121. Chocolate Truffles 58
122. Chocolate Truffles Recipe 58
123. Chocolate Truffles With Rum And Raisins Recipe 59
124. Chocolate Turtle Bars Recipe 59
125. Chocolate Walnut Toffee Candy Recipe ... 60
126. Chocolate [Turds] Drops Recipe 60
127. Chocolate And Butterscotch Fudge Recipe 60
128. Chocolate Butterscotch Pecan Fudge Ala Easy Recipe 61
129. Chocolate Candy With Dates And Peanuts Recipe 61
130. Chocolate Popcorn Recipe 61
131. Chocolate Covered Peanut Butter Crisp Squares Recipe 62
132. Chocolate Macadamia Caramels Recipe 62
133. Chocolate Peanut Butter Truffles Recipe .. 62
134. Chocolate Coconut Candiesmounds Like Recipe 63
135. Chocolate Coconut Truffles Recipe 63
136. Chocolate Dipped Peanut Butter Balls Recipe 64
137. Christmas Bon Bons Recipe 64
138. Christmas Crack Recipe 65
139. Christmas Cracker Candy Recipe 65
140. Christmas Sweet Treats Recipe 65
141. Cobblestone Candy Recipe 66
142. Coconut Bon Bons Recipe 66
143. Coconut Macadamia Truffles Recipe 66
144. Coconut Mounds Recipe 67
145. Coconut Patties Recipe 67
146. Coconut Almond Candy Bars Recipe 68
147. Coffee Chocolate Truffles Recipe 68
148. Cognac Truffles Recipe 69

149. Cool Whip Candy Recipe 69
150. Copy Cat Chunky Bars Recipe 69
151. Cranberry Nut Chocolate Bark Recipe 70
152. Cranberry Orange Almond Bark Recipe ... 70
153. Cranberry Orange White Chocolate Fudge Recipe 70
154. Cranberry White Chocolate Fudge Recipe 71
155. Creamy Chocolate Fudge Recipe 71
156. Crispy Chocolate Peanut Butter Bars Recipe 71
157. Crock Pot Candy Recipe 72
158. Crock Pot Chocolate Fritos Candy Recipe 72
159. Crockpot White Chocolate Candy Recipe 72
160. Darianas Easy Chocolate Truffles Recipe 73
161. Dark Chocolate ButterCrunch Recipe 73
162. Dark Chocolate Cococans Recipe 74
163. Dark Chocolate Fudge With Almonds Recipe 74
164. Decadent Fudge Recipe 75
165. Deep Fried Candy Bars Recipe 75
166. Deep Fried Candy Bars Recipe 75
167. Delicious Copycat Almond Joy Bars Recipe 76
168. Delicious Homemade Creme Filled Chocolate Candy Recipe 77
169. Deviled Egg Candy Recipe 77
170. Diabetic Chocolate Candy Recipe 77
171. Dipped Chocolate Graham Sticks Recipe 78
172. Dressed Up Chocolate Bark Recipe 78
173. EASY CHOCOLATE CLUSTERS Recipe 79
174. Eagle Brands Rocky Road Candy Recipe Recipe 79
175. Earl Grey Tea Chocolate Recipe 80
176. Easiest Chocolate Candy Recipe 80
177. Easiest Chocolate Candy With Flavors Recipe 80
178. Easy Bark Cookies Recipe 81
179. Easy Breezy Fudge Recipe 81
180. Easy Chocolate Cashew Clusters Recipe .. 81
181. Easy Chocolate Dipped Coconut Creams Recipe 82
182. Easy Chocolate Mint Covered Pretzils Recipe 82
183. Easy Chocolate Mint Truffles Recipe 82
184. Easy Chocolate Truffles Recipe 83

185. Easy White Chocolate Popcorn Recipe..... 83
186. Edible Chocolate Body Paint For Romantics Recipe 84
187. English Toffee Recipe 84
188. Erins Mini Squares Recipe 84
189. Fairy Or Sponge Candy Recipe 85
190. Famous Chocolate Bourbon Balls Recipe. 85
191. Fancy Coffee Cup Truffles Recipe 85
192. Flat Truffles Recipe 86
193. Fluted Kisses Cups With Peanut Butter Filling Recipe 86
194. Frozen Peppermint Patties Recipe 87
195. Fruit And Nut Chocolate Chunk Candy Recipe 87
196. Ganache Recipe 88
197. Georgia Cookie Candy Recipe 89
198. Ghost Candies Recipe 89
199. Gold Brick Candy Recipe 89
200. Goo Goo Bars Recipe 90
201. Goo Goo Clusters Recipe 90
202. Graham Break Aways Recipe 90
203. Grand Marnier And Chocolate Truffles Recipe 91
204. Grownup Smores Recipe 91
205. HAYSTACKS Recipe 91
206. Harvest Moon Lollipops Recipe 92
207. Hazelnut Truffles Recipe 92
208. Hob Nobs Recipe 92
209. Homade Peanut Butter Cups Recipe 93
210. Home Made "mozart Kugel" Recipe 93
211. Homemade "ferrero Rocher" Recipe 94
212. Homemade Butterfinger Bars Recipe 94
213. Homemade Melt In Your Mouth Dark Paleo Chocolate Recipe 95
214. Homemade Peanut Butter Cups Recipe.... 95
215. Homemade Snickers Bars Recipe 95
216. Homemade Snickers Recipe 97
217. Homemade Tootsie Rolls Recipe 97
218. Indoor S'more Bites Recipe 98
219. Italian Chocolate Almond Truffles Recipe 98
220. Itsa Chocolate Pizza Recipe 98
221. Kahlua Balls Recipe 99
222. Kamikazes Recipe 99
223. Kids Chews Chocolate Recipe 99
224. Krafts Chocolate Peanut Butter Snowballs Recipe 100
225. LONG STEMMED Chocolate Covered

CHERRIES SUPREME Recipe 100
226. Light Cranberry Fudge Recipe 101
227. Low Fat Truffles Recipe 101
228. MARSHMALLOW PUFFS Recipe 102
229. Make Your Own Chocolate Kiss Recipe 102
230. Mandies Candies Recipe 103
231. Marshmallow Butterscotch Chocolate Fudge Recipe 103
232. Marshmallow Chocolate Cookie Lollipops Recipe 104
233. Martha Washington Balls Recipe 104
234. Mels Valentine Truffles Recipe 104
235. Mendiants Recipe 105
236. Mile High Chocolate Marshmallow Squares Recipe 105
237. Milky Way Delights Recipe 105
238. Million Dollar Fudge Recipe 105
239. Mint Chocolate Snacks Recipe 106
240. Mint Cookie Candies Recipe 106
241. Mint Meltaways Recipe 106
242. Mint Thins Recipe 107
243. Mint Chocolate Almond Fudge Recipe ... 107
244. Mock Ferrero Rochers Recipe 108
245. My Favorite Fudge Recipe 108
246. My First Chocolate Fudge Recipe 108
247. No Bake Peanut Butter Bars Recipe 109
248. No Bake Peanut Butter Cups Recipe 109
249. No Bake Marshmallow Chip Clusters Recipe 109
250. Noir Chocolate Spread Recipe 110
251. Nut Goodie Bars Recipe 110
252. Nut Goody Candy Bars Recipe 110
253. Nutchos Recipe 111
254. Nutty Buddies Recipe 111
255. Nutty Chocolate Mint Fudge Recipe 112
256. Nutty Chocolate Rum Truffles Recipe 112
257. Ohio Buckeyes Balls Recipe 112
258. Ohio Buckeye Bars Recipe 113
259. Orange Cappuccino Creams Recipe 113
260. Oreo Balls Recipe 114
261. Oreo Truffle Balls Recipe 114
262. Oven Off Chocolate Chip Divinity Cookies Recipe 115
263. PERFECT CHOCOLATE TRUFFLES Recipe 116
264. Peanut Butter Pretzel Bites Recipe 117
265. Peanut Butter Balls 1 Recipe 117

266. Peanut Butter Bon Bons Recipe 117
267. Peanut Butter Bonbons Recipe 118
268. Peanut Butter Chocolate Balls Recipe 118
269. Peanut Butter Chocolate Fudge Easiest Recipe 118
270. Peanut Butter Chocolates Recipe 119
271. Peanut Butter Coconut Fudge Balls Recipe 119
272. Peanut Butter Cup Squares Recipe 120
273. Peanut Butter Cups Recipe 120
274. Peanut Butter Date Candy Recipe 121
275. Peanut Butter Easter Eggs Recipe 121
276. Peanut Butter Nerds Recipe 121
277. Peanut Butter Crispy Eggs Recipe 122
278. Peanut ButterChocolate Caramel Apples With Honey Peanuts Recipe 122
279. Peanut Buttery Chocolate Balls Recipe .. 122
280. Peanut Clusters Recipe 123
281. Peanutty Chocolate Truffles Recipe 123
282. Pecan Caramel Spiders Recipe 123
283. Pecan Clusters Recipe 124
284. Peppermint Patties Recipe 124
285. Peppermint Pattys Peppermint Patties Recipe 125
286. Perfect Chocolate Fudge Recipe 125
287. Pistachio Truffles Recipe 126
288. Potato Chocolate Fudge Recipe 126
289. ROLLO PRETZELS Recipe 127
290. Raisin Cashew Chocolate Fudge Recipe . 127
291. Raisin Cashew Drops Recipe 128
292. Raisin Peanut Clusters Recipe 128
293. Raspberry Chocolate Chips Recipe 128
294. Raspberry Fudge Balls Recipe 129
295. Red Velvet Popcorn Recipe 129
296. Reese's Peanut Butter Pumpkin Spider Recipe 129
297. Reindeer Belly Buttons Recipe 130
298. Rich Chocolate Pumpkin Truffles Recipe 130
299. Rocky Road Balls Recipe 130
300. Rocky Road Bars Recipe 131
301. Rocky Road Candy Recipe 131
302. Rocky Road Recipe 131
303. SALTINE CHOCOLATE CRUNCH Recipe 132
304. SOFT TORRONE Italian Candy Recipe 132

305. Salted Chocolate Caramels Recipe 132
306. Saltine Candy Recipe 133
307. Salty Chocolate Pecan Candy Recipe....... 133
308. Sea Salted Smoky Almond Chocolate Bark Recipe 134
309. Sees Candy Recipe 134
310. Semi Sweet And White Chocolate Peanut Butter Cups Recipe 135
311. Slacker Jacks Recipe 135
312. Snickers Bars Recipe 135
313. Somewhat Sophisticated Chocolate Chews Recipe 136
314. Squidgy Chocolate Bars Recipe 136
315. St Patricks Day Layered Mint Chocolate Fudge Recipe 137
316. Starlight Sugar Cookies Cookie Mix Recipe Recipe 137
317. Sugar Cookie Chocolate Crunch Fudge Recipe 138
318. Sugar Free Chocolate Fudge Recipe 138
319. Sweet And Savory Munch Mix Recipe 139
320. Sweet Cocoa Flax Truffles Recipe 139
321. Sweet, Salty, Frito Candy Recipe 140
322. THREE CHOCOLATE FUDGE WITH PECANS Recipe 140
323. Taras Candy Recipe 141
324. The Best Darned Peanut Butter Filling For Buckeyes Or Easter Eggs Recipe 141
325. Tias Treats Recipe 141
326. Tiger Butter Recipe 142
327. Tiger Stripes Recipe 142
328. Toasted Almond Truffles Recipe 143
329. Triple Chocolate Sour Cherry Fudge Recipe 143
330. Truffles With Chocolate Raspberry And Hazelnuts Recipe 143
331. Upside Down Peanut Butter Cups Recipe 144
332. White Chocolate Cherry Fudge Recipe ... 144
333. White Chocolate Cherry Pistachio Bark Recipe 145
334. White Chocolate Cranberry Bark Recipe 145
335. White Chocolate Cranberry Pistachio Bark Recipe 145
336. White Chocolate Crunch Mix Recipe 146
337. White Chocolate Fruit And Nut Clusters Recipe 146
338. White Chocolate Fudge Recipe 146
339. White Chocolate Hazelnut Apricot Truffles Recipe 147
340. White Chocolate Hazelnut Crunch Recipe 147
341. White Chocolate Macadamia Fudge Recipe 147
342. White Chocolate Marshmallow Drops Recipe 148
343. White Chocolate Party Mix Recipe 148
344. White Chocolate Peppermint Meltaways Recipe 149
345. White Chocolate Truffles Recipe............. 149
346. White Chocolate Walnut Decadent Saltines Recipe 149
347. White Christmas Jewel Fudge Recipe 150
348. White Trash Recipe 150
349. White Or Chocolate Eggnog Fudge Recipe 150
350. Candy Haystacks Recipe 151
351. Chocolate Chip Oatmeal Bars Recipe..... 151
352. Chocolate Leaves Recipe............................ 151
353. Chocolate Truffles Recipe.......................... 151
354. Ciocolata De Casa Home Chocolate0 Recipe 152
355. Easy Chocolate Cranberry Truffles Recipe 152
356. Easy Tipsy Turtle Bark Recipe 152
357. Easy Chocolate Fudge Recipe 153
358. Easy Chocolate Nougat Recipe................. 153
359. Nutty Chocolate Clusters Recipe 154
360. Pecan Bark Recipe....................................... 154
361. Pistachio Chocolate Apples Recipe 154
362. Rocky Road Bites Recipe 155
363. True Love Truffles Recipe 155
364. White Chocolate Cranberry Cashew Truffles Recipe 155
365. White Chocolate Truffles Recipe............. 156

INDEX 158
CONCLUSION 160

365 Awesome Chocolate Candy Recipes

***

1. 1881 Chocolate Caramels Recipe

Serving: 50 | Prep: | Cook: 20mins | Ready in:

Ingredients

- 3 tablespoons unsalted butter, plus more for greasing the baking dish
- 4 1/2 ounces bittersweet chocolate, chopped (about 1 cup)
- 1 cup whole milk
- 1 cup molasses
- 1 cup sugar
- 1 teaspoon vanilla extract
- Softened butter, for cutting the caramels.

Direction

- Butter an 8-by-8-inch baking dish. Clip a candy thermometer to the side of a medium, heavy saucepan. Combine the butter, chocolate, milk, molasses and sugar in the pan and cook over medium heat, stirring constantly, until the mixture reaches 248 degrees on the thermometer. Do this slowly, scraping the bottom of the pan with a silicon spatula (or a wooden spoon) so the mixture doesn't stick and burn.
- Wearing an oven mitt, remove the pan from the heat and add the vanilla to the hot mixture. Give it a quick stir, then pour the mixture into the buttered baking dish.
- As soon as the caramel is cool enough to handle, transfer it to a cutting board and use a buttered chef's knife (or scissors) to cut the caramel into ¾-inch-wide strips, and then crosswise into ¾-inch pieces.
- When the caramels are completely cool, wrap them individually in wax paper, or layer in parchment paper in an airtight container. Store in a cool, dry place for up to 1 month. Makes about 100 pieces.

2. 3 Muskateers Recipe

Serving: 14 | Prep: | Cook: 60mins | Ready in:

Ingredients

- 3 cups granulated sugar
- 3/4 cup light corn syrup
- 3/4 cup water
- 1/8 teaspoon salt
- 3 egg whites
- 1/3 cup semisweet chocolate chips
- 2 bags milk chocolate chips (12-ounce bags)

Direction

- In a large saucepan over medium heat, combine the sugar, corn syrup, water, and salt. Heat, stirring, to boiling, then continue to cook using a candy thermometer to monitor the temperature.
- Beat the egg whites until they are stiff and form peaks. Don't use a plastic bowl for this. When the sugar solution comes to 270 degrees F, or the soft-crack stage, remove from the heat and pour the mixture in thin streams into the egg whites, blending completely with a mixer set on low speed. Continue to mix until the candy begins to harden to the consistency of dough. This may take as long as 20 minutes. At this point add the semisweet chocolate chips. Remember that the candy must already be at the consistency of dough when you add

the chocolate; the nougat will thicken no more after the chocolate is added.
- When the chocolate is thoroughly blended and the nougat has thickened, press it into a greased 9x9-inch pan. Refrigerate until firm, about 30 minutes. With a sharp knife, cut the candy in half down the middle of the pan. Then cut across into 7 segments to create a total of 14 bars.
- Melt the milk chocolate chips in the microwave for 2 minutes on half power, stirring halfway through the heating time. Melt completely, but be careful not to overheat. Resting a bar on a fork dip each bar into the chocolate to coat completely and place on wax paper.
- Cool until firm at room temperature, 1 to 2 hours. Makes 14 candy bars.

3. 4 Chip Fudge Recipe

Serving: 15 | Prep: | Cook: 15mins | Ready in:

Ingredients

- * 3/4 cup butter or margarine
- * 14 ounces sweetened condensed milk
- * 3 tablespoons milk
- * 12 ounces package semi-sweet chocolate morsels
- * 11 1/2 ounces package milk chocolate morsels
- * 10 ounces package peanut butter flavored morsels
- * 1 cup butterscotch flavored morsels
- * 7 ounces jar marshmallow cream
- * 1 1/2 teaspoons vanilla extract
- * 1/2 teaspoon almond extract
- * 1 pound walnuts, coarsely chopped

Direction

- Melt butter in a heavy 4 quart saucepan over low heat; stir in sweetened condensed milk and milk.
- Add all morsels, stirring constantly, until mixture is smooth.
- Remove from heat; stir in marshmallow cream and flavorings.
- Stir in walnuts.
- Pour into a buttered 15" x 12" pan or two 9" x 9" pans.
- Chill.
- Cut into squares.
- Store in refrigerator.

4. APRICOT ALMOND CHOCOLATE CHEWS Recipe

Serving: 60 | Prep: | Cook: | Ready in:

Ingredients

- 60 whole almonds, blanched or unblanched, toasted
- 60 dried Turkish apricots (approximately one pound)
- Approximately 1/2 pound of bittersweet chocolate, the best quality you can find, and the darker the better

Direction

- Find the slit in each apricot where the pit was removed, or make one with a small paring knife.
- Gently push one whole toasted almond into each apricot.
- Squeeze the apricot closed around the almond.
- Break up the chocolate and heat on full power in microwave or over very low heat until melted. Stir until smooth.
- Line a cookie sheet with waxed paper.
- One at a time, drop the apricots into the melted chocolate, turn to coat completely and lift out with a fork.
- Tap the excess chocolate off and place apricots on the waxed paper lined cookie sheet.
- Refrigerate until completely set.
- Store in airtight container, in the refrigerator.

5. AZTEC Chocolate Bark Recipe

Serving: 6 | Prep: | Cook: 4mins | Ready in:

Ingredients

- * 1/2 cup of hulled, unsalted pumpkin seeds
- * 1/4 teaspoon of cayenne pepper, plus a dash extra
- * 3/4 teaspoon of cinnamon, plus a dash extra
- * 3/4 teaspoon of ancho chili powder, plus a dash extra
- * 12 oz. of bitter or semi-sweet chocolate
- .

Direction

- 1 Place the pumpkin seeds in a skillet over medium-low heat. Toast the pumpkin seeds for about 5 minutes, they'll pop and jump a bit as they release their oils and moisture. Allow to cool.
- 2 Melt the chocolate according to the manufacturer's directions. (Or Microwave) Once melted add the cinnamon, cayenne pepper, Ancho chili powder, and most of the pumpkin seeds saving some to decorate the top with.
- 3 Spread onto a flat baking pan lined with a Silpat or wax paper. Sprinkle over and press into the chocolate the last few pumpkin seeds and sprinkle on a dash more of the spices for color and taste. Place in the freezer for 5 minutes or until hardened. Break into pieces and serve or store in the fridge in an airtight container. Best consumed in one or two days

6. Addicting Chocolate Pecan Saltine Delights Recipe

Serving: 24 | Prep: | Cook: 10mins | Ready in:

Ingredients

- 24 saltine crackers
- 1 cup light brown sugar
- 1/2 cup unsalted butter
- 6 ounces chocolate chips
- 1/2 cup chopped pecans

Direction

- Lay saltines side by side on a cookie sheet.
- Heat brown sugar and butter until dissolved then pour over saltines and bake at 450 for 5 minutes.
- Cover with chocolate chips and spread.
- Sprinkle with pecans and allow to sit at room temperature for at least an hour.

7. Adorable Christmas Mice Recipe

Serving: 20 | Prep: | Cook: 2mins | Ready in:

Ingredients

- 1 jar cherries with stems on
- 1 package chocolate bark
- 20 Hershey kisses
- almond slices
- gel tubes of black and red
- 20 Oreo cookies (white chocolate covered, or an opened cookie)
- Directions

Direction

- Melt chocolate bark until creamy. Dip cherry into chocolate while holding the stem (completely cover cherry, but not stem) place cherry on its side on top of the cookie (the stem of the cherry is the mice tail). Press a Hershey kiss to the opposite side of the cherry (mice head). Place two almond slices in-between the cherry and the kiss (ears). I use the gel tubes of decorating frosting to make a nose (black) and two eyes (red or black). You can even decorate the cookie next to the mouse to make it more festive, I generally will make little holly leaves and a couple red dots.

8. Almond Bark Pink Peppermint Patties Recipe

Serving: 30 | Prep: | Cook: 20mins | Ready in:

Ingredients

- 1 pkg(24oz) White almond Bark chocolate Flavored Coating(melting chocolate)
- 2 boxes(12ct) standard peppermint flavored candy canes

Direction

- In a double boiler, on low-medium heat, melt entire package of Almond Bark Chocolate, until all is melted and smooth with no lumps.
- In the meantime while melting chocolate, unwrap plastic from candy canes. Break into pieces. Place candy canes in a food processor. Pulse and grind the candy in processor until in tiny pieces. You may have powder and small chunks but is okay, it's what gives the candy its pink color. Remove from processor and pour into the melted chocolate, stir thoroughly until well combined. This will make it thick, wet and somewhat lumpy, normal and will turn pink.
- 2-different ways for the next step---Choice is up to you: 1) Take 2 tsp. size spoons and spoon out peppermint mixture on to a parchment lined pan (like spooning cookie dough) Spacing dropfuls 1 inch apart from each other onto pan. When cooled remove from pan and store in Ziploc type bags. Makes 30 + medallions OR 2) Pour mixture onto a jelly roll lined baking pan with foil. Covering bottom and edges of pan. Spread peppermint mixture evenly. When cooled, turn over pan, remove foil and break into huge pieces. And store Ziploc type bags.

9. Almond Coated Dark Chocolate Peanut Butter Balls Recipe

Serving: 48 | Prep: | Cook: 10mins | Ready in:

Ingredients

- 1 pound smooth peanut butter
- 1 stick softened butter
- 1 pound powdered sugar
- 3-1/2 cups Rice Krispies
- 1/4 teaspoon salt
- 1 teaspoon vanilla extract
- 1 pound dark chocolate melted
- 2 cups chopped almonds

Direction

- Mix all ingredients except chocolate and almonds together until well blended.
- Roll into balls then dip in chocolate then roll in nuts and place on cookie sheet in refrigerator until hardened.

10. Almond Ganache Cups Recipe

Serving: 60 | Prep: | Cook: 10mins | Ready in:

Ingredients

- 8 ounces (226 grams) bittersweet or semisweet chocolate, coarsely chopped
- 3/4 cup (180 ml) heavy whipping cream
- 1 tablespoon alcohol (brandy, Grand Marnier, rum or bourbon) or 1 teaspoon pure vanilla extract (optional)
- 2/3 cup (100 grams) almonds, toasted and finely ground plus 60 whole almonds to be used for garnish

Direction

- Preheat oven to 350 degrees F (177 degrees C). Bake the almonds for 10 - 15 minutes or until the nuts are fragrant. Remove from oven. Let cool. Remove 60 almonds to be used as garnish and then place the remaining cooled almonds in a food processor and process until finely ground. Set aside.
- Coarsely chopped the chocolate and place in a heatproof bowl.
- In a small saucepan bring the cream to a boil. Immediately, remove from heat and pour over the chopped chocolate. Gently stir the mixture until smooth and then add the alcohol (or vanilla extract) and finely ground almonds. Cover with plastic wrap and refrigerate the mixture until thick but not solid (about 30 minutes).
- Transfer the mixture to a pastry bag fitted with a large plain tip and pipe the ganache into small candy cups until they are 3/4 full. Place a toasted almond on top of each cup. Chill the ganache cups until they are firm (about 1 hour).
- Store in an airtight container in the refrigerator for several weeks or they can be frozen for a few months. Best served at room temperature.
- Makes about 60 1-inch (2.54 cm) ganache cups.

11. Almond Joy Bars Recipe

Serving: 26 | Prep: | Cook: 10mins | Ready in:

Ingredients

- 4 c (8 1/2-oz) shredded coconut
- 1/4 c light corn syrup
- 1 pk (11 1/2-oz) milk chocolate pieces
- 1/4 c vegetable shortening
- 26 Whole natural almonds (1-oz)

Direction

- Line two large cookie sheets with waxed paper. Set large wire cooling rack on paper; set aside.
- Place coconut in large bowl; set aside.
- Place corn syrup in a 1-cup glass measure. Microwave on high (100%) 1 minute or until syrup boils. Immediately pour over coconut. Work warm syrup into coconut using the back of a wooden spoon until coconut is thoroughly coated.
- This takes a little time, and yes, there is enough syrup.
- Using 1 level measuring tablespoon of coconut, shape into a ball by squeezing coconut firmly in palm of one hand, then rolling between both palms. (HINT: Measure out all of the coconut then roll into balls.) Place 2 inches apart on wire racks. Let dry 10 minutes. Reroll coconut balls so there are no loose ends of coconut sticking up.
- Place milk chocolate and shortening in a 4-cup glass measure or 1 1/2 quart microwave-safe bowl. Microwave on high 1 to 2 minutes or until mixture can be stirred smooth and is glossy; stirring once or twice.
- Working quickly, spoon 1 level measuring tablespoon of the chocolate over each coconut ball, making sure chocolate coats and letting excess chocolate drip down onto waxed paper. While chocolate coating is still soft, lightly press whole almond on top of each. Let stand to set or place in refrigerator. Store in a single layer in airtight container.
- Keeps best if refrigerated. Makes 26.

12. Almond And Chocolate Clusters Recipe

Serving: 24 | Prep: | Cook: 15mins | Ready in:

Ingredients

- 1/2 cup (about 3 ounces) toasted slivered almonds
- 24 individually wrapped caramel candies (about 6 ounces)

- 1 cup (about 6 ounces) bittersweet chocolate chips
- 4 to 6 tablespoons cream, room temperature, divided
- 1 cup (about 6 ounces) white chocolate chips
- Special equipment: 2 mini muffin tins

Direction

- Preheat the oven to 350 degrees F.
- Lightly grease the mini-muffin tins with vegetable oil spray.
- Place 1 teaspoon of slivered nuts in each of the muffin cups.
- Unwrap the caramel candies, cut each candy into quarters and place 4 quarters (1 candy) in each of the muffin cups on top of the nuts in a single layer.
- Bake in the oven until the caramel is just melted and beginning to spread, about 8 minutes.
- Be careful not to over melt the caramel or it will bubble, burn, and become too hard.
- Place the mini muffin tins in the refrigerator for 5 minutes to cool.
- Remove the nut clusters from the tins and set aside.
- Meanwhile, melt the bittersweet chocolate in a double boiler over low heat.
- Wisk 2 to 3 tablespoons of cream into the chocolate to slightly thin the chocolate for coating the clusters.
- Dip half of the nut clusters in the bittersweet chocolate and place on a parchment paper-lined baking sheet.
- Return the clusters to the refrigerator to harden, about 30 minutes.
- Melt the white chocolate in a double boiler over low heat.
- Wisk 2 to 3 tablespoons of cream into the chocolate to slightly thin the chocolate for coating the clusters.
- Dip remaining half of the nut clusters in the white chocolate and place on the parchment paper-lined baking sheet with the other chocolate-covered clusters.
- Return the clusters to the refrigerator to harden, about 30 minutes.

13. Almond Filled Chocolate Covered Cherries Recipe

Serving: 30 | Prep: | Cook: |Ready in:

Ingredients

- 1/2-7 oz box Odense marzipan or almond paste
- 1-16 oz jar maraschino cherries with stems, drained
- 1-12 oz bag semi-sweet mini chocolate chips
- (You can use white chocolate chips or dark choco chips)

Direction

- Pat cherries dry between layers of paper towel. With a sharp knife, slit from bottom of cherry to stem, without cutting completely in half.
- Pinch off small pieces of Marzipan (about the size of a large pea) and roll into balls. Fill cavities of cherries with Marzipan. Round out shape using a paper towel to soak up any extra syrup.
- Heat 1 cup chocolate chips on high in microwaveable container for 1 minute and stir, then at 15 second intervals (stirring between each) until smooth and melted. Make sure chocolate does not come into any contact with water (on bowl or spoon) or it will seize (harden).
- Holding stem, dip filled cherries into melted chocolate and place on wax paper or directly into paper bonbon cups to dry. Melt additional chocolate as needed.
- Note
- This recipe uses less than 1/2 roll of Marzipan and can be easily doubled. Otherwise, double wrap Marzipan (in plastic wrap or foil) and freeze for future use. Color white chocolate

pink or for a marbled effect, swirl red color into white then dip cherry.

14. Amazing Candy Recipe

Serving: 30 | Prep: | Cook: 8mins | Ready in:

Ingredients

- unsalted saltine crackers
- 1/2 lb butter
- 1 cup sugar
- 1 large pkg chocolate chips
- 1 cup crushed walnuts

Direction

- Line a baking sheet with aluminum foil and butter foil well.
- Place crackers on baking sheet in a single layer.
- Melt butter and sugar in a sauce pan and boil for 3 minutes.
- Pour over crackers.
- Bake in 400 degree oven for 5 minutes.
- Sprinkle and smooth chocolate chips over crackers immediately upon removing from oven.
- Top with crushed walnuts.
- Refrigerate for at least four hours.
- Break or cut into pieces.
- Serving size will vary depending on how big you make the pieces.

15. Apricot White Chocolate Fudge Recipe

Serving: 12 | Prep: | Cook: 10mins | Ready in:

Ingredients

- 2-1/2 cups powder sugar
- 2/3 cup milk
- 1/4 cup butter
- 12 ounces white chocolate coarsely chopped
- 1/2 teaspoon almond extract
- 3/4 cup dried apricots
- 3/4 cup toasted almond slices

Direction

- Line square pan with foil then grease foil.
- Mix powder sugar and milk in a heavy saucepan.
- Over medium heat add butter and stir constantly and bring to boil.
- Without stirring boil constantly for 5 minutes.
- Over low heat add chocolate and almond extract.
- Stir then whisk until chocolate melts and mixture is smooth.
- Stir in dried apricots and toasted almonds then pour mixture into prepared pan.
- Refrigerate 2 hours until firm then invert pan and peel off foil then cut into squares.

16. Assembly Of Chocolates Recipe

Serving: 7 | Prep: | Cook: 2mins | Ready in:

Ingredients

- 100 g white chocolate melted
- 100 g glace ginger
- 100 g dark chocolate melted
- 100 g dried mixed fruits or raisins , sultanas or toasted chopped nuts (almonds , macadamia etc)

Direction

- Add the ginger to the slightly cooled white chocolate.
- Add the dried fruits/nuts into slightly cooled dark chocolate.
- Spoon the mixture into small paper cups.
- Leave to set.
- Store in an air tight container.

17. Awesome Chocolate Truffles Recipe

Serving: 60 | Prep: | Cook: 30mins | Ready in:

Ingredients

- One whole package Oreos (reg size package)
- 1 cup cream cheese
- chocolate chips small bag
- Try different Oreo flavors for a great taste treat.
- I have used mint Oreos, peanut butter, and the vanilla Oreos.
- I have also used dark chocolate, milk chocolate, white chocolate
- I am going to try chocolate filled Oreos.
- You can use double stuffed Oreos the very same way.

Direction

- Grind whole package of Oreos in blender.
- Mix with 1 cup softened Cream Cheese.
- Chill in fridge for about 30minutes.
- Roll into 1" balls-melon baller works great.
- Melt Chocolate Chips in Microwave-slowly, 30 seconds at a time.
- Stir chocolate every 30 seconds-this will take 3 or 4 times.
- Using a fork, dip each ball in melted chocolate.
- You can put sprinkles, chopped nuts, coconut, etc. on top.
- Place on wax paper and chill in fridge for 30 minutes.
- Store in covered plastic container.
- Get ready for the compliments!
- Vanilla (golden) Oreos make beautiful White Chocolate Truffles.
- OMG these are good and very easy.

18. BAILEYS SNOWBALL TRUFFLES Recipe

Serving: 60 | Prep: | Cook: 30mins | Ready in:

Ingredients

- 1 1/4 LLB white chocolate
- 3/4 CUP heavy cream
- 1/4 CUP BAILETS irish cream
- 1/4 CUP unsalted butter SOFTENED
- sliced almonds, CRUSHED
- CONFECTIONERS sugar

Direction

- COARSELY CHOP CHOCOLATE, SET ASIDE.
- COMBINE CREAM BAILEYS IN SAUCEPAN AND BRING TO A BOIL.
- REMOVE FROM HEAT AND STIR IN CHOCOLATE UNTIL MELTED.
- STIR IN BUTTER UNTOL MELTED.
- CHILL THE CHOCOLATE MIXTURE.
- SPOON OUT CHOCOLATE MIXTURE.
- SHAPE INTO 1 INCH BALLS.
- ROLL YOUR BALLS INTO CRUSHED ALMONDS.
- DUST YOUR BALLS WITH SUGAR.
- KEEP YOUR BALLS REFRIGERATED UNTIL READY TO SERVE.
- EAT YOUR BALLS.

19. Baileys Irish Cream Chocolate Truffles Recipe

Serving: 35 | Prep: | Cook: 480mins | Ready in:

Ingredients

- 1/4 cup Bailey's irish cream
- 12 oz semisweet chocolate chips
- 1/4 c heavy cream
- 1 T butter
- 2 egg yolks

Direction

- Melt chocolate over very low heat. Stir in Bailey's and cream.
- Beat egg yolks, stir a small amount of chocolate mixture into eggs, and then slowly add the eggs to the chocolate mixture. Mixture will thicken. Add butter.
- Refrigerate overnight, or several hours (I usually leave it in for 6-7 hours)
- Using two large spoons or a small ice cream scoop, form small balls.
- Roll in powdered sugar, then cocoa. The brand of cocoa with chocolate bits works nicely.

20. Barfing Pumpkin Candy Recipe

Serving: 12 | Prep: | Cook: 10mins | Ready in:

Ingredients

- 2 lbs. white chocolate
- 1 cup or more M&Ms - Halloween colors if you can find them
- 1/2 c. craisins
- 2 c, candy corn
- 1 1/2 c. broken small pretzels
- 1/2 c. cashews
- Plus extra of all of the above to sprinkle on afterward.

Direction

- Melt white chocolate according to package directions. In the meantime, spray Pam on 2 cookie sheets and then sprinkle evenly all of the above ingredients, but the white chocolate.
- Once white chocolate is melted, pour evenly over both sheets. Using a small plastic bag, insert your hand into and butter the palm of your hand on the outside of the bag. Moving quickly, mix the white chocolate and the other ingredients together and spread evenly on pans.
- Once it is spread out well, sprinkle additional M&Ms, Craisins, candy corn, pretzels, and cashews over the top and press lightly into the still-soft white chocolate. Let sit until the candy is completely set. Break up to serve. Store in sealable plastic bag.
- For a fun presentation, carve a craft pumpkin into a barfing pumpkin face and serve.
- Happy Halloween!

21. Belgian Chocolats For Kids Recipe

Serving: 45 | Prep: | Cook: 20mins | Ready in:

Ingredients

- chocolate FILLING
- 4 3/8 ounce (125 gr) brown cooking chocolate (this already has sugar inside, so it is not the pure chocolate, yet again, it is what was available in the shop next door)
- 2 fluid ounce (60 ml) double cream (40+ % fat)
- 1 fluid ounce (30 ml) Kahlua (a coffee liquor)
- 1/2 ounce (15 gr) non liquid honey
- 1 egg yolk
- chocolate COVER (outer layer)
- 2 5/8ounce (75 gr) of the same brown cooking chocolate
- 1 ounce (30 gr) real cocoa powder (no sugar added here!)
- butter as needed to make a chocolate paste (1/2 ounce (15 gr) in our case, depending on how much fat already is in the brown cooking chocolate)

Direction

- CHOCOLATE FILLING
- To fasten things up, we grated the chocolate.
- Do chocolate, cream and honey in the top pot, let the chocolate melt and stir until all is mixed.
- Take the pot out of the au bain marie and add the egg yolk and Kahlua.

- Beat until you get a chocolate mixture that is not very liquid, yet not hard. (An electrical mixer could fasten things up again!)
- Put this chocolate filling or ganache in a cling wrap covered pan so you get at least a 1/2 inch (1.25cm) thick chocolate mixture.
- Put the chocolate ganache in the freezer (1/2 hour or so)
- CHOCOLATE COATING
- Again in a warm water bath: melt the chocolate and add in the cocoa powder. When the whole mixture becomes to dry, add in some butter and stir again. Add more butter until you just get a paste. Again an electrical mixer can help you out very well.
- HOW TO MAKE BELGIAN CHOCOLATES
- Take the ganache out of the freezer and cut into squares. (This is why it is practical to have your chocolate on cling wrap, as you can easily transfer it on a flat cutting board for easy cutting.)
- Now get dirty: the kids loved it and it is not smart to let them wear white T-shirts in this stage of the chocolate making. So take out one square of the ganache, put it in the coating mixture, turn them around until they are completely coated and put them on another cling wrap.
- Repeat this for each square of the ganache.
- If you have too much ganache, just coat the left-overs with cocoa powder.
- If you have too much of the chocolate coating, you can start coating nuts with it. Or freeze it in for another day of making chocolates or with chocolate: anything can.

22. Bing Bars Recipe

Serving: 16 | Prep: | Cook: 60mins | Ready in:

Ingredients

- 12 ounces chocolate chips
- 3/4 cup chunky peanut butter
- 12 ounces fine ground Spanish peanuts
- 1 can sweetened condensed milk
- 12 large marshmallows
- 1/2 cup real butter
- 1 teaspoon cherry extract
- 6 ounces cherry chips
- 1/2 cup chopped maraschino cherries, well drained

Direction

- Melt together chocolate and peanut butter; stir in peanuts and spread half of mixture into a 9x13 inch pan reserving the rest for later.
- In very heavy saucepan combine condensed milk, marshmallows and butter. Bring to a boil carefully (scorches easily), and boil for 5 minutes, watching closely.
- Add cherry extract and cherry chips; stir to melt the chips and then stir in cherries. Spread over chocolate in pan, then top with remaining mixture.
- Chill to set but remove from fridge before serving.

23. Blueberry Clusters Recipe

Serving: 36 | Prep: | Cook: 10mins | Ready in:

Ingredients

- 2 cups milk chocolate morsels
- 1/4 cup shortening
- 3 doz 1 1/4 in. candy liners
- 2 cups fresh blueberries washed and dried

Direction

- Combine over hot water (not boiling) chocolate and shortening, stir until morsels melt and mixture is smooth.
- Remove from heat.
- Place 1 tsp. chocolate in candy liners.
- Add 6 to 8 blueberries.
- Top with 2 tsp. chocolate making sure berries are well coated.

- Chill for 20 to 30 minutes until chocolate is set.
- ~@~
- Makes about 2 1/2 to 3 dozen clusters.
- ~@~
- Blueberry clusters may be kept at room temp up to 1 hour. If chocolate becomes sticky, return to fridge.

24. Boognish Brown Mix Recipe

Serving: 20 | Prep: | Cook: 30mins | Ready in:

Ingredients

- 7 Cups Rice Chex (Gluten Free!)
- 1/4 C butter
- 12 oz. chocolate chips
- 1/4 C sweetened shredded coconut
- 1/2 C almond butter
- 1 Tb. agave
- 1 Tb. coconut oil
- 1/2 tsp. vanilla
- 1/4 C. confectioner's sugar
- parchment paper

Direction

- Melt chocolate, almond butter, and butter in a stockpot on low heat, stirring occasionally. Once all melted and smooth add agave, coconut oil, and vanilla, mix well. Stir in rice Chex, toss in shredded coconut and mix well to coat.
- Line two cookie pans with parchment paper, spread chocolate/Chex mix in as thin of a layer as possible. Sprinkle with confectioners' sugar. Cool in fridge, break apart pieces, and store in airtight container in the fridge--if you have ANY leftovers.

25. Bourbon Balls Recipe

Serving: 12 | Prep: | Cook: | Ready in:

Ingredients

- 3 cups vanilla wafers, rolled to powder consistency
- 3 Tbsp corn syrup
- 1 cup confectioners' sugar
- 1/2 cup cocoa powder
- 1 cup very finely chopped pecans
- 1/2 tsp vanilla extract
- 1/2 cup bourbon

Direction

- Mix all ingredients together.
- Roll into small 3/4 inch balls.
- Roll balls in confectioners' sugar, cocoa or shredded coconut.
- Makes about 3 dozen.

26. Bread Chocolate Recipe

Serving: 2 | Prep: | Cook: 5mins | Ready in:

Ingredients

- bread pieces - 1 cup
- jaggery - 1 cup
- ghee - 1/2 cup

Direction

- 1) Make small pieces of breads and keep aside.
- 2) Heat oil in the pan, add the bread pieces and fry till it becomes light brown. Keep aside.
- 3) Heat a separate pan, put jaggery and stir well it till it is fully melted. Add ghee and fried bread pieces and stir for a minute. Freeze the pieces for 5 minutes in freezer.

27. Brigadeiro Recipe

Serving: 6 | Prep: | Cook: 30mins | Ready in:

Ingredients

- 1 can sweetened condensed milk
- 3 egg yolks
- 3 tablespoons Nestle quick chocolate powder
- 1 tablespoon butter
- chocolate sprinkles

Direction

- In medium sauce pan cook all ingredients except sprinkles over medium heat.
- STIR CONSTANTLY (15-25 minutes).
- Mix until it gets hard to stir.
- Let it cool just a bit.
- Butter fingers.
- Make a ball on a spoon and roll in chocolate sprinkles.

28. Brigadeiros Recipe

Serving: 2 | Prep: | Cook: 20mins | Ready in:

Ingredients

- 2 cans of condensed milk
- 1 stick of butter
- 1 cup chocolate powder (sweetened)
- 1 cup of chocolate sprinkles
- Mini cupcake holders or similar packaging.

Direction

- In a saucepan, melt half of the butter. When melted, add the condensed milk and chocolate powder and mix well and simmer over low heat for about 15 minutes until the mix achieves the right consistency (this happens when you pass the spoon across the middle of the pan and the space you created stays for a few seconds). Turn off the heat and set aside.
- Prepare your work station. We recommend covering a table surface with newspaper. On this place a large plate or tray and a bowl.
- Fill the bowl with the chocolate sprinkles.
- Also, put the remaining butter on a small plate which provides easy access.
- When the chocolate mixture has cooled for about ten minutes and is warm enough to handle, bring the saucepan to your work station. Butter your hands thoroughly. Pick out a small bit of the mixture from the pan using your thumb, forefinger and middle finger. Roll this into a ball using both hands and toss into the bowl of sprinkles. Roll the ball in the sprinkles until it is coated and then place into one of the mini-cupcake holders or directly onto your tray or plate.
- Repeat until you've finished the mixture buttering your hands as often as necessary to prevent the mixture from sticking to them.
- Allow them to sit for about one hour at room temperature (if you refrigerate they will get hard and very sticky, like toffee).
- Serves all the people who need some loving.
- Note:
- (Women) If you have just been dumped, I recommend you save your sprinkles and eat the whole mixture straight out of the pan with a wooden spoon while sitting in front of the TV watching "Gone with the Wind" or a Meg Ryan movie on your VCR.
- (Men) Clint Eastwood in "Play Misty for Me"

29. BuckEye Balls Recipe

Serving: 20 | Prep: | Cook: 15mins | Ready in:

Ingredients

- 1 lb powered sugar
- 3 c. rice crispies cereal
- 2 cups creamy peanut butter (cruncy works too)
- 1 stick softened butter not melted

- 12-16 oz semi sweet chocolate chips
- 1/2 block paraffin wax
- wax paper
- tooth picks

Direction

- In large mixing bowl add softened butter, powdered sugar and peanut butter first mix well.
- Add rice krispies and fold into the mix.
- Use your hands to roll into tablespoon balls or a little bigger.
- Set balls on to wax paper.
- Once done put in freezer for about an hour 2 harden so they won't fall apart.
- After that melt chocolate in a sauce pan on low heat.
- Shave the wax into it until all is melted
- Use a toothpick to dip the peanut rice krispies balls into chocolate, place back on wax paper dry pretty quickly.
- Then enjoy your little chocolate peanut butter ball treats. Buckeye balls...

30. Buckeye Peanut Butter Candy Recipe

Serving: 40 | Prep: | Cook: 30mins | Ready in:

Ingredients

- 2 cups peanut Buttter, smooth (for best results, don't use natural, organic for this)
- 2 sticks of butter, softened
- 22 oz powdered sugar
- 1 - 12 oz bag semisweet chocolate chips (you make want to have another bag on hand just in case - my family tends to like them double dipped in chocolate for a thicker chocolate crust)

Direction

- Mix well all 3 ingredients until evenly incorporated. Line a baking sheet or tray with waxed paper to place the peanut butter balls.
- Make balls the size of walnuts or smaller. If mixture is too wet to roll into balls, you can add more powdered sugar, though this will make the balls denser and not as creamy in texture. I put them on a tray and in freezer for an hour or so until they are firm and ready to roll. You can use a melon-baller to make the job of rolling easier.
- Place rolled balls on tray and refrigerate overnight or in freezer for a few hours. This will make them easier for dipping.
- Melt chocolate chips in double boiler. Dip the balls in melted chocolate and place on lined cookie sheet. I use toothpicks to dip the balls in chocolate. Cover about 3/4 of the ball in chocolate. YOU WANT SOME OF THE PEANUT BUTTER FILLING TO SHOW. This makes them look like the buckeye nuts.
- Place back in refrigerator or freezer until chocolate sets.
- Enjoy!

31. Buckeys Peanut Butter Chocolate Candy Recipe

Serving: 1 | Prep: | Cook: | Ready in:

Ingredients

- peanutBUTTER MIXTURE:
- 1 lb. of butter (not margarine), cut into pieces
- 2 lbs. of peanut butter
- 3 lbs. of confectioners sugar
- chocolate DIP:
- 2 - 12 oz. packages of semi-sweet chocolate chips
- 1/4 bar of Para-Wax, i USE butter IF CHOCOATE EVER SEIZES or THIN WITH VEGGIE oil

Direction

- PEANUT BUTTER MIXTURE:
- Place ingredients in large bowl. Mix with knives, then hands.
- Mixture will be crumbly like pie dough.
- When well mixed, take large handfuls and knead.
- Pinch off small amount and roll into small balls.
- Place on waxed paper on cookie sheet.
- Chill in refrigerator.
- CHOCOLATE DIP:
- Chip or grate Para-Wax into chocolate chips and melt in double boiler.
- Mix thoroughly.
- Remove from stove or leave on low heat.
- Stick toothpick in ball & dip each ball leaving small area around pick free of dip.
- Place on waxed paper on cookie sheet & refrigerate.
- (If you want the easy way out of the chocolate mixture, use chocolate flavored Almond Bark, or Melting Chocolate for Candy.)
- MAKES 6 LBS. OF BUCKEYES!

32. Butterfinger Candy Bars Recipe

Serving: 8 | Prep: | Cook: 30mins | Ready in:

Ingredients

- 1 Cup peanut butter
- 1/3 cup light corn syrup
- 1 cup sugar
- 1/3 cup water
- Melted milk chocolate

Direction

- Cook syrup, sugar, and water to 310 F. Remove from heat.
- Stir in warmed peanut butter (warm slightly in microwave) until well blended. Pour into a greased (buttered) 8" X 8" pan.
- Score mixture into desired size bars.
- When COMPLETELY cool, dip in melted milk chocolate (use a double boiler to SLOWLY melt) and set on wax paper until chocolate has hardened.

33. Butterscotch Chocolate Divinity Recipe

Serving: 36 | Prep: | Cook: 30mins | Ready in:

Ingredients

- 2 cups sugar
- 1/3 cup light corn syrup
- 1/3 cup water
- 2 egg whites
- 1/8 teaspoon cream of tartar
- 1 teaspoon vanilla
- 1/2 cup milk chocolate chips
- 1/2 cup butterscotch chips
- 1/2 cup chopped nuts

Direction

- Line 2 or 3 baking sheets with buttered waxed paper; set aside.
- Combine sugar, corn syrup and water in a medium saucepan.
- Cook over medium heat, stirring constantly, until sugar dissolves and mixture comes to boil; washing down the sides of the pan frequently with pastry brush dipped in hot water to remove sugar crystals.
- Add candy thermometer, careful to not let bulb touch bottom of the pan.
- Continue to cook until mixture reaches the hard ball stage (225 degrees).
- Meanwhile, beat egg whites and cream of tartar with electric mixer until stiff but not dry.
- Slowly pour hot syrup into egg whites beating constantly.
- Add vanilla; beat until candy forms soft peaks and starts to lose its gloss.
- Stir in both kinds of chips and nuts.

- Immediately drop tablespoons full of candy in mounds on prepared baking sheets.
- Store in refrigerator in airtight container between layers of waxed paper or freeze up to 3 months!

34. CHERRY MASH CANDY Recipe

Serving: 12 | Prep: | Cook: 20mins | Ready in:

Ingredients

- 1 cup sugar
- 2 Tbsp butter
- 1/4 tsp.salt
- 1/2 cup evaporated milk
- 20 marashmallows
- 1 cup cherry chips or 1/2 cup chopped marischino cherries
- 1/2 cup peanut butter
- 1 cup salted peanuts, chopped or smashed with the side of a meat pounder or hammer (this is also stress therapy...)

Direction

- Combine sugar, butter, salt and milk in saucepan.
- Boil over medium heat for 5 minutes, stirring occasionally.
- Stir in marshmallows and cherry chips.
- Spread in 8 or 9 inch square pan lined with waxed paper.
- Melt chocolate chips with peanut butter in small saucepan over low heat, stirring constantly.
- Stir in chopped peanuts.
- Spread over cherry layer.
- Cool and cut into squares.

35. CHOCOLATE COVERED CHERRIES Recipe

Serving: 10 | Prep: | Cook: | Ready in:

Ingredients

- 1/2 CUP butter
- 1/2 CUP heavy whipping cream
- 2 PKGS powdered sugar
- 1 LARG 9 OZ JAR maraschino cherries
- 3 CUPS CHOPPED nuts
- 3 6OZ PKGS chocolate chips
- 1/3 BLOCK paraffin wax
- 1 TBLS butter

Direction

- MIX TOGETHER BUTTER AND CREAM.
- ADD POWDERED SUGAR AND MIX.
- PUT IN REFRIGERATOR OR FREEZER UNTIL FIRM.
- TAKE SMALL PIECE OF DOUGH.
- PAT FLAT.
- PRESS AROUND CHERRY.
- ROLL INTO BALL.
- PUT INTO FREEZER UNTIL HARD.
- MELT BUTTER, CHOCOLATE CHIPS AND PARRIFIN WAX IN DOUBLE BOILER.
- TAKE COVERED CHERRIES FROM FREEZER AND USE TOOTHPICKS TO DIP IN MELTED CHOCOLATE.
- ENJOY.

36. CHOCOLATE MARZIPANS Recipe

Serving: 30 | Prep: | Cook: 5mins | Ready in:

Ingredients

- 500 grams / 1 pound of good quality bought marzipan
- 1/3 cup very finely chopped candied cherries
- 1 ounce preserved ginger, very finely chopped

- 1/4 cup no-need-to-soak dried apricot, very finely chopped
- 12 ounces dark chocolate
- 1 ounce white chocolate
- confectioner's sugar to dust

Direction

- Line a baking sheet with parchment paper.
- Divide the marzipan into three, kneading each piece to make it soft.
- To the first piece add the cherries, on a surface lightly dusted with the icing sugar, set aside.
- To the second piece add the ginger, in the same way, set aside.
- To the third piece add the apricots, in the same way, set aside.
- Form each flavoured portion into tiny balls, keep them separately.
- Melt the dark chocolate in a double boiler.
- Dip one of each flavored ball into the melted chocolate, using a toothpick, allow the extra chocolate to drip into pot.
- Carefully place in clusters of three, using one of each flavour, on baking tray.
- Chill until set.
- Melt the white chocolate and drizzle on.
- Dust with edible gold dust / icing sugar and munch!

37. CREAMY CHOCOLATE FUDGE Recipe

Serving: 1 | Prep: | Cook: 5mins | Ready in:

Ingredients

- 1 jar (7 1/2 to 13 oz.) marshmallow cream
- 1 1/2 c. sugar
- 2/3 c. evaporated milk
- 1/4 c. butter
- 1/2 tsp. salt
- 1 (12 oz.) pkg. Nestles' Toll House Semi sweet chocolate Morsels
- 1/2 c. chopped nuts
- 1 tsp. vanilla
- Makes 2 1/4 pounds candy.

Direction

- In medium saucepan, combine marshmallow crème, sugar, evaporated milk, butter and salt. Bring to full boil stirring constantly over moderate heat. Boil 5 minutes, stirring constantly over medium heat. Remove from heat. Add chocolate morsels; stir until mixture is smooth. Stir in nuts and vanilla. Pour into foil lined 8 inch square pan. Chill until firm.

38. Caggiune E Caggiunitte Recipe

Serving: 10 | Prep: | Cook: 30mins | Ready in:

Ingredients

- 1/3 cup goat's milk (or whole cow's milk)
- 2 cups boiled chick peas, pureed
- ¾ cup + 2 tbsp honey
- ½ cup sugar
- 3.5 oz unsweetened chocolate
- 3 tbsp finely chopped pine nuts
- 1 cup sweet white wine
- 2-3 tbsp simple syrup
- 1 recipe fresh pasta dough (forgive me, it doesn't say how much)

Direction

- Cook the milk, chick peas, honey, sugar, chocolate and pine nuts in a pan on a lively heat.
- Stir continuously with a wooden spoon, without interruption.
- After 20 minutes of the above operation, add the white wine.
- 20 minutes after adding the wine, add simple syrup and cook 10 minutes longer.
- By now the mixture should be creamy and have a distinct perfume.

- Roll out pastry thinly, and cut dough into 8cm diameter circles.
- Pour spoonful of the chickpea blend on each in a strip along the middle.
- Close each circle firmly, pinching between thumb and forefinger.
- Deep fry in a spacious pan of half canola, half olive oil.

39. California White Chocolate Fudge Recipe

Serving: 24 | Prep: | Cook: 14mins | Ready in:

Ingredients

- 1 1/2 cups sugar
- 3/4 - cup sour cream
- 1/2 - cup butter12- ounces white chocolate , coarsely chopped
- 1- (7 ounce) jar of kraft marshmallow creme
- 3/4- cup chopped walnuts
- 3/4- cup chopped dried apricots

Direction

- In a heavy saucepan 3-4 quart size, bring sugar, sour cream and butter to a full rolling boil over medium heat, stirring constantly.
- Continue boiling 7 minutes or until candy thermometer reaches 234 degrees stirring constantly.
- Stir in remaining ingredients until well blended.
- Pour into a greased 9 inch square pan cool until set.
- Cut into squares and enjoy.
- Makes about 2 1/2 pounds of candy.
- Try it with macadamia nuts. I made it like that it was truly heavenly.

40. Canadian Chocolate Fruit Roll Recipe

Serving: 8 | Prep: | Cook: 5mins | Ready in:

Ingredients

- 3/4 lb semi sweet chocolate chips
- 1/4 cup sugar
- 2 oz butter
- 1/2 cup chocolate cookie crumbs
- 1 1/2 cups chopped dried fruit
- 1/2 cup chopped asorted nuts (walnuts, pecans, almonds setc)
- 3/4 cup raisins

Direction

- Melt chocolate with butter and sugar.
- Blend in all remaining ingredients.
- Spread mixture flat on parchment paper.
- Shape mixture into a cylinder using the parchment to help roll it.
- Chill well.
- When well chilled, slice and serve along with pound cake, strawberries and cream.

41. Candi Style Cookie Dough Bites Recipe

Serving: 2030 | Prep: | Cook: 135mins | Ready in:

Ingredients

- 1/2 cup butter, softened
- 3/4 cup packed brown sugar
- 2 cups all-purpose flour
- 1 (14oz) can Eagle Brand sweetened milk
- 1 tsp vanilla
- 1/2 cup peanut butter chips
- 1.5 lbs chocolate almond bark

Direction

- Cream butter and brown sugar till fluffy.

- Add flour, milk, and vanilla.
- Mix well.
- Stir in peanut butter chips.
- Shape into 1 inch balls.
- Place on wax paper lined cookie sheet.
- Place in fridge for 1 to 2 hours or until firm.
- Melt almond bark in microwave till smooth.
- Dip balls in almond bark.
- Place on wax paper lined cookie sheet.
- Place in fridge till firm, about 15 minutes.
- **if desired, melt leftover peanut butter chips and drizzle over chocolate coated balls before placing in fridge**
- ***store in fridge***

42. Candied Orange Slices Dipped In Chocolate Recipe

Serving: 6 | Prep: | Cook: 90mins | Ready in:

Ingredients

- 4 valencia oranges
- 2 cups water
- 3 1/2 cups granulated sugar
- 3 cups granulated sugar, as needed for coating
- 2 lbs semisweet chocolate, chopped into small pieces (reserve a 2-ounce chunk)

Direction

- Cut the oranges in half lengthwise.
- With the cut side down, slice the oranges crosswise into 1/4-inch slices. DO NOT peel. Discard the stem ends.
- In a 10-inch sauté pan combine the water and the 3 1/2 cups of sugar.
- Stir to blend, then bring to a boil over medium heat.
- Add the orange slices, separating them, and simmer them gently for 1 hour uncovered. Occasionally dunk any floating slices.
- **NOTE: When cooking the orange slices DO-NOT STIR. If someone is helping you make sure they do not stir, just let them push down on the orange slices as recipe says.
- Remove from heat and cool to room temperature.
- Remove the orange slices, with a slotted spoon and transfer to a cooling rack set over a baking sheet to let drain and dry for 24 hours.
- Cut the slices in half again after cooking.to make thinner slices.
- NOTE; I dried them in my oven. Preheat to 350F and then turn off heat, or if oven has a pilot light, this works great if it is a damp day.
- After drying the slices, toss them in the granulated sugar and set them aside. Do not stack them because they will stick together.
- While you are coating the orange slices with the sugar, have the chocolate melting slowly in the top of a double boiler over boiling water, or chocolate can be melted in the microwave.
- When all the chocolate is melted and creamy and registers 100C/212F on a candy thermometer, remove the top section from the double boiler.
- Add the 2-ounce of chocolate and gently stir until the thermometer reads 88C/190F to 91C/196F, then remove what remains of the chunk of chocolate.
- Dip the orange slices 2/3 of the way into the chocolate.
- Gently scrape off excess chocolate against the side of the pan.
- Place the orange slices on a sheet of wax paper to set.
- Work quickly with the slices.
- **If the chocolate becomes too thick for dipping place it over the boiling water again until it reaches 88 /190Fto 91/196F degrees.

43. Caramel Chocolate Rolo Pretzels Recipe

Serving: 48 | Prep: | Cook: 20mins | Ready in:

Ingredients

- 48 Rold Gold Classic Twist pretzels
- 48 Rolo caramel Chocolate candies (unwrapped)
- 48 pecan halves

Direction

- Preheat oven to 275.
- On a cookie sheet spread out 3 rows of 4 pretzels about 2 inches apart.
- Place Rolo candy in center of pretzel.
- Put on lowest rack of oven for around 8-10 minutes.
- DO NOT let candy completely melt flat. You ONLY want it softened.
- Remove cookie sheet from oven and smoosh 1 pecan into the center of the Rolo candy.
- Place back in oven and bake just long enough to roast the pecan around another 8-10 minutes.
- Allow to cool and then remove and place in an airtight container.
- They won't last long!

44. Carmel Chocolate Green Apple Mess Recipe

Serving: 4 | Prep: | Cook: 5mins | Ready in:

Ingredients

- 4 granny smith apples
- Cool Whip
- 2 king size nutragous bars

Direction

- Core the apples and cut into bite size pieces.
- Cut up the NutRageous bar into bite size pieces.
- Mix together with CoolWhip and store in fridge!
- This is really good! Kids love making it too!

45. Charlie Chaplin Candy Recipe

Serving: 1 | Prep: | Cook: | Ready in:

Ingredients

- Two pounds of milk chocolate bars - regular Hershey Bars or whatever you like
- Two pounds of large marshmallows
- Half a pound of cashews, chopped
- Half a pound of toasted coconut flakes
- One stick of real butter, unsalted
- Half a can of Milnot
- sea salt

Direction

- Butter a large cookie sheet;
- In double boiler or microwave, melt the chocolate bars, the butter and the Milnot;
- In a large bowl, put the marshmallows, nuts, and coconut;
- Pour the melted chocolate over the mixture in the bowl;
- Stir until coated;
- Pour it all out onto the buttered cookie sheet;
- Press the mixture down with the back of a spoon;
- Sprinkle lightly with sea salt;
- Cover and refrigerate at least two hours;
- Cut into squares.

46. Cheerio Candy Recipe

Serving: 6 | Prep: | Cook: | Ready in:

Ingredients

- 2 pounds white chocolate
- 1 cup creamy peanut butter
- 4 cups Cheerios
- 2 cups miniature marshmallows
- 2 cups peanuts

Direction

- Melt chocolate in pan. Add peanut butter; blend well. Add Cheerios, marshmallows and peanuts. Drop onto wax paper-lined cookie sheet.

47. Chelseas Candy Bars Recipe

Serving: 8 | Prep: | Cook: 10mins | Ready in:

Ingredients

- 4-5 scoops of peanut butter
- 1-3 Hershey Bars
- about half of the bag of honey nut Cheerios
- sprinkles
- **Editor's Note**
- Chelsea originally told me she had used honey Nut Cheerios -- for the sake of accuracy, I am annotating here that the recipe she gave me to post had just plain old Cheerios. Forgive me Chelsea, I like the honey nut idea better ;-)

Direction

- Melt together the sprinkles, peanut butter, and chocolate in the microwave for about 1 ½ minutes.
- Put the Cheerios in any size pan, then put the mixture on top of that.
- Freeze for about 1 to 1 ½ hours.

48. Cherry White Chocolate Fudge Recipe

Serving: 12 | Prep: | Cook: 10mins | Ready in:

Ingredients

- 2-1/2 cups powder sugar
- 2/3 cup milk
- 1/4 cup butter
- 12 ounces white chocolate coarsely chopped
- 1/2 teaspoon almond extract
- 3/4 cup dried cherries
- 3/4 cup toasted almond slices

Direction

- Line square pan with foil then grease foil.
- Mix powder sugar and milk in a heavy saucepan.
- Over medium heat add butter and stir constantly and bring to boil.
- Without stirring boil constantly for 5 minutes.
- Over low heat add chocolate and almond extract.
- Stir then whisk until chocolate melts and mixture is smooth.
- Stir in dried cherries and toasted almonds then pour mixture into prepared pan.
- Refrigerate 2 hours until firm then invert pan and peel off foil then cut into squares.

49. Chewy Chocolate Nut Candies Recipe

Serving: 24 | Prep: | Cook: 30mins | Ready in:

Ingredients

- 1 1/2 cups candy corn
- 1 tbsp chocolate fudge frosting
- 1 1/2 tbsp nutella
- 1/4 cup smooth peanut butter
- 1 tbsp salted butter
- Optional:
- Add 1/4 cup crushed Rice Krispies cereal to the freshly melted dough mixture and knead in for "crispy" candy

Direction

- In a bowl, combine the candy corn, frosting, Nutella and peanut butter.

- Microwave until everything is melted together, about 2 minutes, stirring halfway through.
- Stir in the butter until smooth.
- Press into chocolate / candy moulds or a 9" square pan.
- If in the square pan, let sit 2 minutes then score with a bench scraper or sharp knife. Let cool completely.
- If desired, coat in chocolate after they have set completely.

50. Chewy Chocolates Recipe

Serving: 24 | Prep: | Cook: 10mins | Ready in:

Ingredients

- 3/4 cup pecan halves
- 12 dates, cut in half
- 1/2 pound soft caramels
- 2 tablespoons heavy cream
- 1/2 package semi sweet chocolate melted and slightly cooled. (4 squares)

Direction

- Place 2 pecan halves and a date half in clusters on lightly buttered baking sheet.
- Melt caramels in cream in a saucepan over very low heat, stirring constantly until smooth.
- Spoon caramel mixture over clusters, leaving ends uncovered.
- Let stand until set, about 30 minutes.
- Spread chocolate over caramel mixture.
- Makes about 2 dozen.

51. Chex Muddy Buddies Recipe

Serving: 18 | Prep: | Cook: | Ready in:

Ingredients

- 1 cup semisweet chocolate chips
- 1/2 cup peanut butter
- 1/4 cup butter
- 1 teaspoon vanilla
- 9 cups chex cereal
- 1 1/2 cups powdered sugar

Direction

- In one quart micro wave bowl, mix chocolate chips, peanut butter and butter; microwave uncovered on high 1 minute; stir; microwave 30 seconds longer or until mixture can be stirred smooth.
- Stir in vanilla.
- In a large bowl, place cereal.
- Pour chocolate mixture over cereal, stirring until evenly coated.
- Pour into a 2 gallon food storage plastic bag.
- Add powdered sugar; seal bag and shake until well coated.
- Spread on wax paper to cool.

52. Chinese Noodle Candy Recipe

Serving: 12 | Prep: | Cook: 30mins | Ready in:

Ingredients

- 1 (6-ounce) package chocolate chips
- 1 (6-ounce) package butterscotch chips
- 1 (3-ounce) can chow mein noodles
- 1 cup broken nuts

Direction

- Instructions
- Melt chocolate and butterscotch chips over hot water, stirring until smooth. Fold in chow mein noodles and nuts. Let mixture cool about 1/2 hour, and then drop clusters onto waxed paper; let set.

53. Chocolate Billionaires Recipe

Serving: 28 | Prep: | Cook: 5mins | Ready in:

Ingredients

- 1- package caramels unwrapped (about 14 ounces)
- 3- tablespoons water
- 1 1/2 - cups of chopped pecans
- 1- cup crisp rice cereal....like (Rice Krispies)
- 3- cups milk chocolate chips
- 1 1/2 - teaspoons shortening

Direction

- Line 2 baking sheets with waxed paper, grease the paper and set aside.
- In a large heavy saucepan, combine the caramels and water, cook and stir over low heat until smooth.
- Stir in pecans and rice cereal until all is coated.
- Drop by teaspoonsfuls onto prepared pans.
- Refrigerate for 10 minutes or until firm.
- Meanwhile melt chocolate chips and shortening, stir until smooth.
- Dip candy into chocolate coating entire candy and place back onto waxed paper.
- Refrigerate until set.
- Then store in airtight containers.
- Yields approx. 2 pounds.

54. Chocolate Almond Toffee Recipe

Serving: 212 | Prep: | Cook: 10mins | Ready in:

Ingredients

- 6 oz sliced almonds
- About 60 saltine crackers
- 1 1/2 cup sugar
- 3/4 lbs butter
- 2 T light corn syrup
- 1/2 lb bittersweet chocolate chips

Direction

- Preheat oven to 350. Toast almonds until golden.
- Butter 12x17 baking sheet. Arrange crackers in a single layer on the bottom of the baking sheet.
- In a medium saucepan combine sugar, butter, corn syrup. Cook over low heat until the sugar is melted. Continue to cook over moderate heat without stirring until it starts to brown around the edges. Stir with a wooden spoon until honey colored and temperature reaches 300 degrees.
- Pour the caramel over the crackers covering evenly. Cool for a couple of minutes and then sprinkle the chocolate chips on top and spread evenly as they melt.
- Freeze the toffee until it sets, about 15 minutes or so.
- Break into shards and serve.

55. Chocolate And Peanut Butter Candy Recipe

Serving: 0 | Prep: | Cook: 30mins | Ready in:

Ingredients

- 1 cup peanut butter, melted
- 1 cup butter, melted
- 1 lb. powdered sugar
- 2 8-oz. chocolate bars

Direction

- Mix together peanut butter, butter and powdered sugar until smooth.
- Spread onto a cookie sheet. Chill.
- Melt chocolate bars and spread on top of peanut butter.
- Freeze until ready to use, then cut into pieces and eat.

56. Chocolate Anise Truffles Recipe

Serving: 48 | Prep: | Cook: 10mins | Ready in:

Ingredients

- 1/4 cup Anise liqueur
- 1/2 cup butter
- 12 ounces semisweet chocolate
- 2 cups pulverized anisette cookies
- confectioners' sugar or powdered chocolate

Direction

- In double boiler melt chocolate constantly stirring with a wooden spoon.
- When chocolate has melted add butter and slowly stir it into the chocolate as it melts.
- Continue to stir for another minute until it is well mixed and smooth.
- Add in liqueur and stir until well mixed then sprinkle in pulverized cookies a little at a time.
- When you have thoroughly mixed in anisettes rest top of your double boiler in a bucket of ice.
- Whisk truffle mixture slowly until it has cooled about 15 minutes.
- Do not stop whisking or the butter and rum will separate out of the chocolate-anisette.
- When the sauce is completely cooled it should have a soft but solid consistency.
- Spoon out and form into balls and coat with confectioners' sugar or chocolate powder.

57. Chocolate Bonbons Recipe

Serving: 30 | Prep: | Cook: 10mins | Ready in:

Ingredients

- 1 14oz can of sweetened condensed milk
- 1/4 cup sifted baking cocoa
- 1 Tbsp butter
- 1/4 tsp salt
- 1/2 -3/4 cup multi-colored or chocolate sprinkles
- cooking spray
- wax paper

Direction

- *put wax paper on a cookie sheet and set aside
- *In a medium saucepan, put condensed milk and cocoa in and put on medium-low heat. Stir constantly for about 10 to 15 minutes or until the mixture starts to pull from the sides (it took me a little longer than 20 minutes, but I was scared of burning the mixture).
- *Remove from the burner and add the butter and salt, stir until thoroughly mixed. At this stage, you can add some kind of flavor extract like hazelnut, almond, mint, whatever. Let this mixture cool for about 20 minutes.
- *with a teaspoon or a small melon baller, start scooping out the mixture (about an inch in size) and place on the prepared cookie sheet. Place in the refrigerator and cool for 30 minutes.
- *Get a small bowl and put sprinkles in it. Spray hands with the cooking spray then shape the bonbons, you might have to respray a few times. Roll them in the sprinkles or whatever you would like (chopped nuts, powdered sugar, whatever).
- You can keep these for about 5 days in an airtight container, but why they would last that long is beyond me.
- Makes about 2 1/2 dozen, give or take.

58. Chocolate Bourbon Truffles Recipe

Serving: 26 | Prep: | Cook: 15mins | Ready in:

Ingredients

- 1 can (14 ounces) sweetened condensed milk
- 3 cups semisweet chocolate chips
- 1 Tablespoon vanilla extract

- 2 Tablespoons bourbon (if you don't like bourbon you can substitute it with Frangelico, Bailey's Irish Creme, Kahlua coffee liqueur, Cointreau, Grand Marnier, creme de menthe or any other liqueur.)
- 1/2 to 3/4 cup pecans, finely chopped
- granulated sugar, unsweetened cocoa, or very finely chopped pecans

Direction

- Combine chocolate chips and sweetened condensed milk in a saucepan over low heat.
- Heat, stirring, until melted and smooth.
- Remove from heat.
- Stir in the vanilla, bourbon, and 1/2 to 3/4 cup pecans.
- Transfer to a small bowl.
- Cover and chill for 3 to 4 hours, or until mixture is firm.
- Working with fingertips, shape into 1-inch balls.
- Roll in finely chopped pecans, sugar, coconut or unsweetened cocoa.
- Place on a tray or baking sheet, cover loosely, and chill for at least 1 hour.
- If desired, put each truffle in a decorative fluted paper or foil cup and keep in tightly covered container in the refrigerator until giving or serving.
- Keep these refrigerated, tightly covered.

59. Chocolate Butter Crunch Toffee Recipe

Serving: 8 | Prep: | Cook: 20mins | Ready in:

Ingredients

- 1/2 pound unsalted butter
- 1 cup granulated sugar
- 3 teaspoons water
- 1 teaspoon vanilla
- 8 small milk chocolate bars
- 1 cup chopped pecans

Direction

- Stir butter, sugar and water well and bring to rapid boil stirring constantly.
- Remove from fire and add vanilla then pour into shallow buttered pan.
- Place chocolate bars on top and spread with spatula.
- Sprinkle with pecan then cool and break into pieces.

60. Chocolate Butter Toffee Recipe

Serving: 15 | Prep: | Cook: 30mins | Ready in:

Ingredients

- 1 - cup (2 sticks) butter. (margarine is never a good thing for (humans.) hahaha........ In addition, for this recipe, it will not work................
- 1 - c upsugar
- 1 - cup semi sweet chocolate chips
- 1/4 - cup finely chopped toasted almonds

Direction

- Cook butter and sugar in a heavy 2 quart saucepan over medium heat, stirring occasionally until small amount of mixture dropped into ice water forms brittle globs or candy thermometer reaches 300 degrees – about 25-30 minutes.
- If stirred too often, the toffee may separate.
- Spread quickly into 15x10x1 inch pan.
- Sprinkle chocolate chips over hot candy.
- Let stand for 5 minutes.
- Spread melted chocolate over candy, then sprinkle with almonds. Cool and break into pieces

61. Chocolate Buttercream Cherry Candies Recipe

Serving: 48 | Prep: | Cook: |Ready in:

Ingredients

- Buttercream:
- About 48 maraschino cherries with stems, well drained
- 1/4 cup (1/2 stick) butter, softened
- 2 cups powdered sugar
- 1/4 cup cocoa
- 1 to 2 tablespoons milk, divided
- 1/2 teaspoon vanilla extract
- 1/4 teaspoon almond extract
- White Chip Coating (recipe follows)
- chocolate Chip Drizzle (recipe follows)
- White Chip Coating:
- 1 (12 oz.) pkg. white chocolate chips
- 2 tbsp. vegetable oil
- chocolate Chip Drizzle:
- 1/4 C. chocolate chips
- 1/4 tsp. shortening (do not use butter, margarine, spread or oil)

Direction

- Buttercream Cherries:
- 1. Cover tray with wax paper. Lightly press cherries between layers of paper towels to remove excess moisture.
- 2. Beat butter, powdered sugar, cocoa and 1 tablespoon milk in small bowl until well blended; stir in vanilla and almond extract. If necessary, add remaining milk, one teaspoon at a time, until mixture will hold together but is not wet.
- 3. Mold scant teaspoon mixture around each cherry, covering completely; place on prepared tray. Cover; refrigerate 3 hours or until firm.
- 4. Prepare White Chip Coating. Holding each cherry by stem, dip into coating. Place on tray; refrigerate until firm.
- 5. About 1 hour before serving, prepare Chocolate Chip Drizzle; with tines of fork drizzle randomly over candies. Refrigerate until drizzle is firm. Store in refrigerator.
- White Chip Coating:
- Place White Chips in small microwave-safe bowl; drizzle with vegetable oil. Microwave at HIGH (100%) 1 minute; stir. If necessary, microwave at HIGH an additional 15 seconds at a time, stirring after each heating just until chips are melted and mixture is smooth. If mixture thickens while coating, microwave at HIGH 15 seconds; stir until smooth.
- Chocolate Chip Drizzle:
- Place Chocolate Chips and teaspoon shortening in another small microwave-safe bowl. Microwave at HIGH (100%) 30 seconds to 1 minute; stir until chips are melted and mixture is smooth.

62. Chocolate Cappuccino Candy Recipe

Serving: 0 | Prep: | Cook: 15mins |Ready in:

Ingredients

- 1 TBSP. instant coffee granules.... get a good coffee
- 1 TBSP. hot water
- 2 cups sugar
- 1 cup evaporated milk
- 1/2 cup butter
- 1 (12-ounce) bag of semisweet chocolate morsels
- 1 (7-ounce) jar marshmallow cream
- 1 cup chopped pecans
- 1 TBSP. finely grated orange rind
- 2 teasp. orange or orange extract
- 2 teasp. brandy extract

Direction

- Combine the coffee granules and the water.
- Stir until the granules are dissolved. Set aside.
- Combine the sugar, milk, and butter in a large saucepan.

- Cook over medium heat until mixture comes to a boil, stirring constantly.
- Boil 10 minutes, stirring constantly. Remove from heat after the 10 minutes.
- Add chocolate morsels and the marshmallow cream. Stirring until melted.
- Stir in coffee mixture, pecans, orange rind and the orange and brandy extracts. Mix well.
- Spread mixture evenly in a well-buttered 13 x 9 x 2-inch pan.
- Cover and chill.
- Cut into squares.
- Store in refrigerator.
- Yields: 2 3/4 pounds

63. Chocolate Caramel Apples Wcandy Bars Recipe

Serving: 4 | Prep: | Cook: 75mins | Ready in:

Ingredients

- *Cook time is actually CHILL TIME.
- 4 ripe apples
- 4 wooden skewers
- 14 ounces (1 bag) soft caramel candy
- 2 tbsp water
- 10 ounces semi-sweet chocolate chips
- 2 tbsp shortening
- 2 cups chopped candy bars, chocolate, or nuts

Direction

- 1. Prepare a baking sheet by lining it with aluminum foil and spraying the foil with non-stick cooking spray.
- 2. Wash and dry the apples carefully. Remove the stems, and stick the skewers firmly in the stem ends.
- 3. Place the unwrapped caramels and the water in a microwave-safe bowl. Microwave for 1 minute, then stir, then microwave for and additional minute or until completely melted. The caramel should be smooth and liquid by the end.
- 4. Hold an apple by the skewer and dip it in the caramel, tilting the bowl at an angle and rotating the apple to cover it completely with a smooth, even layer. Bring it out of the caramel and twirl it upside down to remove excess, then set it on the prepared baking sheet. Repeat with remaining apples.
- 5. Place the caramel-covered apples in the refrigerator to set for at least 30 minutes.
- 6. Combine the chocolate and the shortening in a microwave-safe bowl and microwave until melted, stirring every 45 seconds.
- 7. Dip the caramel-covered apple in the chocolate. If necessary, spoon some chocolate over the top to ensure the apple is completely covered with chocolate. While the chocolate is still wet, dip the bottom half in the chopped candy bars and roll until the bottom half is covered. Place back on the baking sheet and repeat with remaining apples.
- 8. Chill apples in refrigerator until completely set, about 45 minutes. Always store apples in the refrigerator.

64. Chocolate Caramel Apples With Salted Pretzels Recipe

Serving: 8 | Prep: | Cook: 20mins | Ready in:

Ingredients

- For the apples:
- ----
- 8 large granny smith apples, at room temperature
- bittersweet chocolate Ganache
- 8 craft sticks or chopsticks
- -----
- For the coating:
- --------------
- 3 cups crushed salted pretzel twists
- 1 3/4 cups heavy cream
- 2 cups packed light brown sugar
- 3/4 cup dark corn syrup

- 2 tablespoons unsalted butter (1/4 stick)
- 2 teaspoons kosher salt

Direction

- For the apples:

65. Chocolate Caramel Graham Crackers Recipe

Serving: 30 | Prep: | Cook: 15mins | Ready in:

Ingredients

- 12 (4 3/4- by 2 1/2-inch) graham crackers
- 1-1/2 sticks (3/4 cup) unsalted butter, cut into pieces
- 1/2 cup packed light brown sugar
- 1/8 teaspoon salt
- 1-1/2 cups semisweet chocolate chips (9 1/2 oz)
- 1 cup walnuts, pecans, or almonds (3 to 4 oz), toasted and chopped

Direction

- Preheat oven to 375°F.
- Line a 15- by 10- by 1-inch baking pan with foil, leaving a 2-inch overhang at each end.
- Line bottom of pan with graham crackers (it will be a tight fit).
- Melt butter in a 1 1/2- to 2-quart heavy saucepan over moderately low heat, then add brown sugar and salt and cook, whisking, until mixture is smooth and combined well, about 1 minute.
- Pour butter/sugar mixture over crackers, spreading evenly.
- Bake in middle of oven until golden brown and bubbling, about 10 minutes.
- Scatter chocolate chips evenly over crackers and bake in oven until chocolate is soft, about 1 minute.
- Remove pan from oven and gently spread chocolate evenly over crackers with offset spatula.
- Sprinkle nuts evenly over chocolate and cool crackers in pan on a rack 30 minutes.
- Freeze until chocolate is firm, 10 to 15 minutes.
- Carefully lift crackers from pan by grasping both ends of foil, then peel foil from crackers. Break crackers into serving pieces.
- Cooks' note:
- • Crackers keep, chilled and layered between sheets of wax paper in an airtight container, 2 weeks.

66. Chocolate Caramel Popcorn Recipe

Serving: 1 | Prep: | Cook: 45mins | Ready in:

Ingredients

- 2 bags microwave popcorn (yield: 24 cups popped popcorn)
- 4 tbsp (1/2 stick) butter, cut into pieces
- 1 cup packed brown sugar
- 1/2 cup light corn syrup
- 2/3 cup sweetened condensed milk
- 1 tsp vanilla extract
- 12 ounce bag of semi-sweet chocolate chips

Direction

- Pop both bags of microwave popcorn, and empty them into a large roasting pan, or two 9x13 pans. You should have approximately 24 cups of popped corn. Remove as many unpopped kernels as you can. Turn the oven to 250 degrees, and place the popcorn in the oven to keep warm.
- 2. Place the butter, sugar, and corn syrup in a medium saucepan over medium heat. Stir until the sugar melts, and continue to cook, stirring, until the butter is melted and the candy begins to boil.

- 3. Stir in the condensed milk, and insert a candy thermometer. Continue to cook the mixture, stirring occasionally, until the candy reaches 238 degrees. Remove it from the heat, and stir in the vanilla.
- 4. Take the popcorn out of the oven and pour the caramel over the popcorn, stirring it so that the pieces are evenly coated.
- 5. Return the popcorn to the oven, and bake it for about 45 minutes, stirring every 10 minutes. If you use multiple pans and your popcorn is in a single layer, the cooking time will be closer to 25 minutes. It is done when the caramel mixture darkens and bubbles all over the pan.
- 6. Remove the popcorn from the oven and allow it cool completely at room temperature before breaking it into pieces by hand.
- 7. Place the chocolate chips in a large microwave-safe bowl and microwave until melted, stirring after every minute to prevent overheating. Pour the chocolate over the caramel corn and stir to coat the pieces. Put the chocolate-covered corn in the refrigerator to quickly set the chocolate for about 15 minutes.
- 8. Once set, break up the chocolate caramel popcorn into pieces, and store it in an airtight container in a cool, dry place.

67. Chocolate Caramel Squares Recipe

Serving: 16 | Prep: | Cook: 10mins | Ready in:

Ingredients

- 12 ounces milk chocolate chips
- 1/2 cup butterscotch chips
- 3/4 cup creamy peanut butter
- 1/4 cup butter
- 1 cup granulated sugar
- 1/4 cup evaporated milk
- 1-1/2 cups miniature marshmallows
- 1 teaspoon vanilla
- 1-1/2 cups chopped peanuts
- 14 ounces caramels
- 1/4 cup whipping cream

Direction

- Combine 6 ounces milk chocolate chips, 1/4 cup butterscotch chips and 1/4 cup peanut butter.
- Melt over low heat then pour into rectangular baking dish and refrigerate until set.
- In another pan melt butter then add sugar and bring to a boil stirring for 5 minutes.
- Remove from heat and add milk, marshmallows, 1/4 cup peanut butter, vanilla and peanuts.
- Stir well then spread over first layer.
- Combine caramels and whipping cream over low heat until melted.
- Spread over second layer and let set.
- Melt remaining chocolate chips, butterscotch chips and peanut butter over low heat.
- Spread over third layer then place in refrigerator until cool.

68. Chocolate Caramel Walnut Fudge Recipe

Serving: 1 | Prep: | Cook: 5mins | Ready in:

Ingredients

- Yield: 2 pounds
- 3 cups semisweet chocolate morsels
- 1 14-ounce can condensed milk
- 1/8 teaspoon salt
- 1 cup chopped walnuts
- 1/2 cup caramel ice cream topping
- 1-1/2 teaspoons vanilla extract

Direction

- Line an 8x8-inch baking pan with aluminum foil; spray lightly with non-stick vegetable spray.
- In a large saucepan, combine chocolate morsels, condensed milk, and salt. Heat, stirring constantly, until chocolate melts. Remove from heat. Stir in walnuts, caramel topping, and vanilla. Spread evenly in prepared baking pan. Chill for 2 hours or until firm.
- Invert onto a cutting board; peel off foil. Cut into squares.

69. Chocolate Cherries Cookies Mix In A Jar Recipe Recipe

Serving: 20 | Prep: | Cook: 10mins | Ready in:

Ingredients

- 3/4 cup granulated sugar
- 1/3 cup baking cocoa
- 1/2 cup firmly packed brown sugar
- 1 1/2 cups dried cherries
- 1 cup semi-sweet or milk chocolate chips
- 1 3/4 cups all-purpose flour
- 1 teaspoon baking powder
- 1/2 teaspoon baking soda
- Other Supplies:
- 1 wide mouth quart size canning jar per child
- Rings and flat lids
- Colorful print fabric to cut in 6-inch circles
- Dry measuring cups
- paper, pencils, color markers to make labels
- Tape or yarn to attach labels

Direction

- 1. Whisk together the flour, baking powder and baking soda.
- 2. In a wide mouth quart jar, layer ingredients in order listed. Press after each layer before adding next ingredient.
- 3. Prepare the label instructions
- Tips for Packing Mix Jars
- -Use dry measuring cups and measure accurately
- -Do not assume a pasta sauce or mayonnaise jar is a quart.
- -Blend the flour, baking powder, soda and salt with a wire whisk
- -Pack layers tightly in the order they are listed so all the ingredients will fit and won't get mixed up
- -If you want to keep two layers separate, cut a circle of wax paper and lay between.
- -If baking cocoa is in the middle, wipe down the inside of the jar with paper towel to prevent streaking.
- -Place lid on to pack tightly the last layer.
- -Lay fabric ring over lid and screw on the ring portion of the lid.
- Attach ingredient list and directions with tape or punch a hole and tie it on with yarn or ribbon.
- Attach the following recipe on a gift label:
- Chocolate Cherry Cookies
- Makes 3 dozen
- Preheat oven to 375 degrees F.
- Empty jar of cookie mix into a large mixing bowl. Thoroughly blend the mix ingredients. Add 3/4 cup butter or margarine, softened, 1 large egg, slightly beaten, and 1 teaspoon vanilla extract. Mix until completely blended – it will be a very stiff mix and may require hand mixing.
- Grease or line baking sheets with parchment paper.
- Shape dough in to balls the size of walnuts. Place 2 inches apart on baking sheets.
- Bake 12 to 15 minutes. Cool 5 minutes on a baking sheet. Remove to racks to finish cooling.
- Recipe ingredients: Dried cherries, enriched wheat flour, chocolate chips, butter, granulated and brown sugars, whole egg, cocoa, baking powder, vanilla extract, and baking soda
- Nutrition Facts: One of 36 cookies (1.1 ounces each) provides approximately: 131 calories, 1 g protein, 20 g carbohydrate, 1 g fiber, 5 g total

fat (2 g saturated), 6 mg cholesterol, 10 mcg folate, 1 g iron, 72 mg sodium

70. Chocolate Cherries Recipe

Serving: 12 | Prep: | Cook: | Ready in:

Ingredients

- 8 ounces of your favorite chocolate, melted
- 1 jar of maraschino cherries with the stem on!
- 2 ounces of white chocolate melted OR candy sprinkles or glitter

Direction

- Drain the cherries well and dry lightly with paper towels. They have to be dry!
- Pick up three cherries and hold them together by the stems.
- Dip the cherries into the chocolate and let excess fall off.
- Place dipped cherries on to wax paper or "Release" aluminum foil to try.
- Once these have dried, you can melt white chocolate and drizzle over the cherries OR sprinkle with cake sprinkles cake glitter.
- I serve these with a vanilla or lemon mousse. Delicious!
- * I couldn't find cherries with the stem intact one day so I bought a bag of small pretzel sticks and stuck them in the dried cherries. I dipped them one at a time and served them that way. They were good! You can always dip the cherries individually and then hold three together and redip them. They're larger in size. More chocolate for your guests!

71. Chocolate Cherry Creams Recipe

Serving: 12 | Prep: | Cook: | Ready in:

Ingredients

- 1 6 oz package semi-sweet chocolate bits
- 1/2 cup evaporated milk
- 2 1/2 cups powdered sugar
- 1/3 cup chopped nuts
- 1/3 cup cut-up and drained maraschino cherries (12)
- 2 cans coconut

Direction

- Put chocolate bits and milk in heavy 2 quart pan. Stir over low heat until chocolate melts. Remove from heat. Stir in sugar, nuts and cherries until well mixed. Chill until firm enough to handle, about one hour. Roll teaspoonful of mixture in coconut. Chill until firm, and store in refrigerator. Can be frozen.

72. Chocolate Cherry Pistachio Fudge Recipe

Serving: 30 | Prep: | Cook: | Ready in:

Ingredients

- 1 ½ cups granulated sugar
- 1 cup evaporated milk
- 2 T butter
- ¼ tsp fleur de sel
- 2 cups marshmallows
- 2 oz 85% cocoa chocolate, chopped
- 8 oz bittersweet chocolate, chopped
- ¼ cup pistachios, chopped
- ¼ cup pecans, chopped
- ½ cup dried cherries

Direction

- Line and 8 inch square baking pan with foil.
- Combine sugar, evaporated milk, butter and salt in a medium, heavy bottomed saucepan. Bring to a full rolling boil over medium heat,

stirring constantly. Boil, stirring constantly, for 5-6 minutes. Remove from heat.
- Stir in everything that's leftover until marshmallows and chocolate are melted. Pour into prepared baking pan. Refrigerate for 2 hours or until firm. Lift from pan, remove foil, cut into pieces.
- Stores well in wax paper in a zip lock.

73. Chocolate Cherry Sweets Recipe

Serving: 24 | Prep: | Cook: 240mins | Ready in:

Ingredients

- 1 cup semi-sweet chocolate chips
- 1/3 cup evaporated milk
- 1 1/2 cups sifted powdered sugar
- 1/3 cup chopped nuts
- 1/3 cup chopped maraschino cherries, well drained
- 1 1/4 cups coconut or chopped nuts

Direction

- Melt chocolate and milk over low heat.
- Remove from heat.
- Stir in powdered sugar, nuts and cherries, mix well.
- Chill until cool enough to handle.
- Shape into 1-inch balls and roll in nuts or coconut.
- Chill at least 4 hours.
- Keep chilled till time to serve.

74. Chocolate Coated Coconut Balls Recipe

Serving: 40 | Prep: | Cook: 60mins | Ready in:

Ingredients

- 1 can (14-15 oz.) sweetened condensed milk (NOT evaporated milk)
- 1 stick butter or good quality margarine
- 1 teaspoon vanilla extract
- 2 1 lbs boxes confectioners sugar
- 15 - 16 oz. flaked coconut
- 2 cups chopped pecans
- 12 oz. package semi-sweet chocolate chips
- 1 block Gulf paraffin wax

Direction

- Mix milk, butter and vanilla.
- Add confectioners' sugar.
- Then add pecans and coconut. Mix well. (It will be necessary to mix with washed hands as mixture maybe quite stiff)
- Chill 15 minutes.
- Form into balls the size of walnuts and insert a tooth pick in center of each ball.
- Chill again.
- Melt chocolate chips and paraffin wax in top of double boiler.
- Remove from heat.
- Dip each candy ball in chocolate.
- Remove quickly and place on wax paper.
- Use a spoon dipped in chocolate to smooth over hole left from toothpick.
- Refrigerate candy balls.
- Enjoy!

75. Chocolate Coated Macaroon Balls Recipe

Serving: 54 | Prep: | Cook: 5mins | Ready in:

Ingredients

- BALLS:
- 2 1/2 cups powdered sugar
- 2 1/2 cups flaked coconut
- 3 tablespoons milk
- COATING:
- 1 cup chocolate chips

- 1/4 cup corn syrup
- 2 tablespoons shortening

Direction

- In large bowl, combine powdered sugar and coconut. Gradually stir in milk.
- Knead mixture on powdered sugar-dusted surface for 1-2 minutes or until smooth.
- Roll mixture into 3/4" balls.
- Refrigerate balls while preparing coating.
- In small saucepan over low heat, melt coating ingredients, stirring constantly. Remove from heat.
- Set saucepan in pan of warm water to maintain dipping consistency.
- Insert toothpick in ball; dip in melted chocolate. Place balls on waxed paper-lined cookie sheet or insert toothpicks in piece of Styrofoam.
- Refrigerate balls 15 minutes or until chocolate is set. Place in candy cup papers. Store in fridge.
- Makes 54.

76. Chocolate Covered Almond Apricot Tassies Recipe

Serving: 60 | Prep: | Cook: |Ready in:

Ingredients

- 2 cups (about 60 wafers) vanilla wafer crumbs , crushed
- 1 cup finely chopped almonds
- 1/3 cup HERSHEY'S cocoa
- 1 can (14 oz.) sweetened condensed milk (not evaporated milk)
- 1 package (8 oz.) dried apricots, chopped
- 1/2 cup chopped candied cherries
- 1/4 teaspoon almond extract
- 2 cups (11.5-oz. pkg.) HERSHEY'S milk chocolate chips
- 4 teaspoons shortening (do not use butter, margarine, spread or oil)

Direction

- 1. Line small muffin cups (1-3/4 inches in diameter) with paper bake cups.
- 2. Combine crumbs, almonds and cocoa in large bowl. Add sweetened condensed milk, apricots, cherries and almond extract; mix well. Refrigerate 30 minutes. Roll mixture into 1-inch balls; press into prepared muffin cups.
- 3. Place chocolate chips and shortening in medium microwave-safe bowl. Microwave at HIGH (100%) 1-1/2 minutes; stir. If necessary, microwave at HIGH an additional 15 seconds at a time, stirring after each heating, just until chips are melted when stirred. Spoon 1 teaspoonful melted chocolate over each filled cup.
- 4. Refrigerate until chocolate is set. Store, covered, in refrigerator. About 6 dozen candies.

77. Chocolate Covered Butter Crunch Toffee Recipe

Serving: 6 | Prep: | Cook: 30mins |Ready in:

Ingredients

- 1 lb butter
- 2 cups granulated sugar
- 1/4 cup water
- 2 Tbsp white syrup
- frosting
- 1 (6 oz bag milk or dark chocolate chips, melted
- 1/4 cup finely chopped nuts

Direction

- In a 2-quart saucepan, melt butter and sugar.
- Add water and syrup.
- Cook over low heat to 300 degrees F (crack stage).
- Pour into lightly oiled jellyroll pan.
- Cool.

- Spread with chocolate frosting, let frosting set and break into pieces.

78. Chocolate Covered Cherries Recipe

Serving: 24 | Prep: | Cook: 5mins | Ready in:

Ingredients

- 2 cups powdered sugar
- 1/4 cup butter
- 1/4 cup sweetened condensed milk
- 1 teaspoon vanilla or 1/2 teaspoon almond extract
- 1 pinch salt
- 10 ounce jar of maraschino cherries, drained
- 12 ounce bag chocolate chips

Direction

- Combine the first 5 ingredients until well blended and smooth and place in fridge until firm.
- Meanwhile spread out the drained cherries on a cookie sheet and freeze for at least 1 hours.
- Scoop out about 1-2 teaspoon of filling and form into a ball, flatten it and form around a cherry.
- Place on a wax paper lined cookie sheet and freeze for 1 hr. after you have formed them all.
- Melt chocolate and using a small fork dip each cherry placing it on a wax paper or foil lined cookie sheet and chill in fridge until chocolate is solid.
- Remove cherries carefully as not to break them open and lose the center.
- Place in an airtight plastic container and keep in a cool dry place for up to 1 month.

79. Chocolate Covered Easter Eggs Recipe

Serving: 48 | Prep: | Cook: 150mins | Ready in:

Ingredients

- ·1/2 cup butter, softened
- ·1 teaspoon vanilla extract
- ·1 (8 ounce) package cream cheese, softened
- ·2 1/2 pounds confectioners' sugar
- ·1 cup creamy peanut butter (optional)
- ·1 cup flaked coconut (optional)
- ·1 cup unsweetened cocoa powder (optional)
- 1 cup chopped dried cherries (optional)
- ·2 cups semisweet chocolate pieces
- ·2 tablespoons shortening or vegetable oil (optional)

Direction

- In a large bowl, mix together the butter, vanilla, and cream cheese. Stir in confectioners' sugar to make a workable dough. For best results, use your hands for mixing.
- Divide the dough into four parts. Leave one of the parts plain. To the second part, mix in peanut butter. Mix coconut into the third part, and cocoa powder into the last part. Roll each type of dough into egg shapes, and place on a waxed paper lined cookie sheet. Refrigerate until hard, at least an hour.
- Melt chocolate chips in a heat-proof bowl over a pan of simmering water. Stir occasionally until smooth. If the chocolate seems too thick for coating, stir in some of the shortening or oil until it thins. Dip the chilled candy eggs in chocolate, and return to the waxed paper lined sheet to set. Refrigerate for 1/2 hour to harden.

80. Chocolate Covered Peanut Butter Balls Recipe

Serving: 30 | Prep: | Cook: 10mins | Ready in:

Ingredients

- 2 cups peanut butter-I use Jiffy
- 3 cups powdered sugar
- 1 stick melted butter
- 3 cups Rice Krispies cereal
- 2 pkg. chocolate chips-I use Giradelli semi sweet
- 1/2 bar paraffin wax- Gulf Wax household paraffin wax for canning.

Direction

- In double broiler melt wax and chocolate.
- While that heats up mix together peanut butter and melted butter. Add powder sugar then the Rice Krispies. I usually end up using my hands to mix the peanut butter mixture.
- Make balls about the size of a ping pong ball and place on wax paper on a cookie sheet.
- Dip each ball in chocolate with a fork tap to remove excess chocolate.
- Place back on wax paper.
- Place in freezer for about 10-15 minutes or until the balls remove easily from the wax paper.
- You can find the wax at the grocery store in the baking aisle by the canning stuff, it is called Gulf Wax household paraffin cooking wax for canning.
- If you do not have a double broiler take a sauce pan fill 1/3 with water in another sauce pan add chocolate & wax place on top of pan with water, heat on stove about med. low heat.
- I keep it on the heat while I am dipping the balls.
- Do not cook chocolate at too high of heat it will ruin it.
- If you have chocolate left over you can cover the pan and reuse within 3-4 days.

81. Chocolate Covered Worms Recipe

Serving: 24 | Prep: | Cook: 10mins | Ready in:

Ingredients

- 1 Bag of Choc chips
- 1 Bag of butterscotch chips
- 1 Stick of Butter
- 2 bags of chow mein noodles (the crunchy kind)

Direction

- Melt choc chips, butterscotch chips and butter in a pan on low heat.
- Add the chow mein noodles until all covered.
- Take a cookie sheet and spoon out servings about the side of a small ball.
- I put them in the freezer to form and then take them out and put in a container for when ready to serve.
- Soooo good!

82. Chocolate Cranberry Cashew Bark Recipe

Serving: 1216 | Prep: | Cook: 1mins | Ready in:

Ingredients

- 1 1/2 cups semi sweet chocolate chips
- 1 1/2 cups white chocolate chips
- 2/3 cup dried cranberries
- 2/3 cup toasted cashews coarsley chopped

Direction

- Line a rimmed cookie sheet with aluminum foil (I like the quick release).
- In a small bowl, set aside 1/4 c semi-sweet chocolate, 1/4 c white chocolate, 1/3 c cranberries and 1/3 c cashews.

- In a medium microwave safe bowl, place the remaining 1 1/4 c semisweet chocolate and microwave until melted, stirring every 45 seconds. Do not overheat.
- In the melted chocolate stir the remaining 1/3 cup cranberries and 1/3 cup cashews.
- Pour the mixture on the prepared cookie sheet and using an offset spatula or knife spread as thinly as possible trying to cover most of the sheet.
- In another microwave safe bowl melt the remaining 1/1/2 cups white chocolate until melted stirring every 45 seconds being careful not to overheat.
- Drop spoonfuls of the melted white chocolate evenly over the chocolate on the cookie sheet.
- Use the tip of a knife to swirl the white chocolate through the semi-sweet, being careful not to overdo it so that looks muddy.
- While the chocolate it still wet sprinkle the reserved chips, nuts and fruit over the top and press gently so they stick.
- Place in the refrigerator for about 30 minutes to firm up the chocolate.
- Once firm peel the foil away from the candy and break into pieces by hand
- This can be stored in an airtight container in the refrigerator for about 1 week

83. Chocolate Cream Cheese Fudge Recipe

Serving: 14 | Prep: | Cook: 20mins | Ready in:

Ingredients

- 4 squares unsweetened chocolate
- 8 oz. cream cheese
- 4 cups confectioners' sugar
- 1-1/2 tsps. vanilla extract
- Note: Instead of vanilla extract I add liqueur ie. Baileys or Frangelico or whatever.
- 1/2 cup pecans or walnuts, chopped

Direction

- Melt chocolate in microwave, then cool to room temperature.
- With cream cheese at room temperature, mix cream cheese with melted chocolate.
- Add confectioners' sugar and vanilla extract.
- Pour into an 8 x 8 inch pan.
- Refrigerate for a couple of hours before cutting.
- If you want to add a peanut butter flavour, add 1/2 cup peanut butter and increase sugar to 5 cups.

84. Chocolate Creams Recipe

Serving: 25 | Prep: | Cook: 10mins | Ready in:

Ingredients

- 1 package semi sweet chocolate (8 squares)
- 1 cup sifted confectioners sugar
- 1 egg well beaten
- 1 tablespoon milk
- Assorted decorations

Direction

- Melt chocolate in a saucepan over very low heat, stirring constantly.
- Remove from heat.
- Add sugar, egg and milk and beat until smooth.
- Chill until firm enough to handle, about 30 minutes.
- Shape into 1/2 inch balls, ovals or logs.
- Roll in decorations.
- Makes about 5 dozen.
- Decorations:
- Flake coconut
- Chocolate or colored decors
- Colored sugar crystals
- Chopped almonds

85. Chocolate Crunch Recipe

Serving: 16 | Prep: | Cook: | Ready in:

Ingredients

- 4 ounces milk chocolate
- 4 ounces white chocolate
- 1 stick butter
- 1/2 cup whipping cream
- 1 cup chopped pecans
- 2/3 cup chopped dates
- 1/2 pound ladyfingers coarsely crushed

Direction

- Line bottom of a round cake pan with parchment paper then butter or spray with baking spray.
- Break chocolate into small pieces.
- Place milk chocolate in one bowl and white chocolate in another.
- Add 4 tablespoons butter to each.
- Stand bowls over pans of hot water until chocolate and butter have melted stirring occasionally.
- Place bowls on counter and stir half the cream, nuts, dates and crushed cookies into each.
- Spoon darker chocolate mixture into pan and spread level with back of a spoon.
- Push mixture down into the corners then top with white chocolate mixture.
- Cover with foil or plastic wrap and chill until set.
- Remove from pan and serve cut into slices.

86. Chocolate Dipped Apricots Recipe

Serving: 24 | Prep: | Cook: 15mins | Ready in:

Ingredients

- 1/2 cup sugar
- 1-1/2 cups water
- 1 lb. dried apricots
- 4 ounces bittersweet chocolate, coarsely chopped (or semisweet)
- 1 tablespoon chopped pecans

Direction

- Line a cookie sheet with parchment paper and put a wire rack on top.
- Combine sugar and water in a small saucepan; bring to a boil, stirring to dissolve the sugar. Reduce the heat to medium and simmer for 3 minutes. Add apricots and gently simmer 5 minutes. Transfer the apricots with a slotted spoon to the rack. Let cool completely. They should not be wet when dipping them.
- Melt chocolate in a double boiler of simmering water. Dip half of a poached apricot in the chocolate, letting excess drip off. Sprinkle with chopped pecans over the chocolate half and return the apricot to the rack. Repeat with the remaining apricots. (You will have some melted chocolate left over.) Refrigerate until the chocolate has set, about 20 minutes.

87. Chocolate Dipped Caramallows Recipe

Serving: 70 | Prep: | Cook: | Ready in:

Ingredients

- FOR THE caramel LAYERS
- vegetable oil cooking spray
- 4 cups heavy cream
- 4 cups sugar
- 2 cups light corn syrup
- 6 ounces (1 1/2 sticks) unsalted butter
- 1 1/2 teaspoons salt
- 1 teaspoon pure vanilla extract
- FOR THE marshmallow LAYER
- 2 1/2 teaspoons unflavored gelatin (one 1/4 ounce envelope)

- 1/3 cup plus 1/4 cup cold water
- 1 cup sugar
- salt
- FOR FINISHING candies
- Tempered chocolate
- White nonpareils, for sprinkling

Direction

- Make first caramel layer: Coat a rimmed baking sheet with cooking spray. Line with parchment, leaving a 2-inch overhang on 2 sides, then coat parchment with spray.
- Place 2 cups cream, 2 cups sugar, 1 cup corn syrup, and 6 tablespoons butter in a large pot. Bring to a boil, stirring until sugar dissolves and butter melts, about 5 minutes. Cook over medium heat, stirring often, until mixture registers 245 degrees on a candy thermometer, about 20 minutes. Remove pot from heat, and stir in 3/4 teaspoon salt and 1/2 teaspoon vanilla. Pour into prepared pan without scraping bottom of pot. Let stand.
- Make the marshmallow layer: Sprinkle gelatine over 1/3 cup water in a mixer bowl, and let soften, about 5 minutes.
- Mix sugar and remaining cup water in a small saucepan over medium-high heat, stirring until sugar dissolves. Wash down sides of pan with a wet pastry brush to prevent sugar crystals from forming. Cook, undisturbed, until mixture registers 238 degrees on a candy thermometer, about 10 minutes. (You may have to tilt pan to get an accurate read.) Remove pan from heat, and whisk sugar syrup and a pinch of salt into gelatine. Pour into a mixer bowl, and whisk on medium-high until cool and thick, about 10 minutes. Spread marshmallow evenly over caramel to cover, and let stand for 30 minutes.
- Prepare second caramel layer with remaining ingredients as in step 2. Pour over marshmallow layer, covering entire surface, and let stand, uncovered, until set, about 8 hours.
- Using a 1 1/4-inch round cutter, cut out 70 rounds. Using a fork, dunk each round in chocolate. Scrape bottom of fork against edge of bowl to remove excess, and place dipped candies on a parchment-lined baking sheet. Sprinkle nonpareils on top, and let stand until set. Caramallows will keep, covered and refrigerated, for up to 5 days
- Helpful Hint
- These indulgent treats include two caramel layers, and each layer must be made separately at different times. Start the second one after the marshmallow layer has set on top of the caramel.

88. Chocolate Dipped Caramel Apples Recipe

Serving: 5 | Prep: | Cook: 51mins | Ready in:

Ingredients

- 5 medium apples, washed, well dried
- 1 pkg. (14 oz.) caramels
- 3/4 cup chopped salted peanuts
- 1 pkg. (4 oz.) sweet chocolate
- 1 tsp. butter or margarine

Direction

- INSERT 1 wooden pop stick (from bag of caramels) into stem end of each apple.
- MICROWAVE caramels and 2 Tbsp. water in deep microwavable bowl on HIGH 2 to 3 minutes or until caramels are completely melted, stirring after each minute. Dip apples into hot caramel mixture; turn until well coated. Scrape excess caramel mixture from bottoms of apples. Roll bottom halves in peanuts. Place on greased tray. Refrigerate at least 15 minutes.
- MICROWAVE chocolate and butter in deep microwavable bowl on HIGH 2 to 3 minutes until chocolate is almost melted, stirring after each minute. Stir until chocolate is completely melted. Drizzle chocolate generously over apples or dip bottom of apple into melted

chocolate. Let stand on wax paper-lined tray until chocolate is firm.
- NOTE:
- If the apples you purchase are waxed, be sure to wash the wax off completely before dipping in caramel.

89. Chocolate Dreams Recipe

Serving: 15 | Prep: | Cook: 5mins | Ready in:

Ingredients

- 2 cups sugar
- 1/4 cup butter
- 1 teaspoon vanilla
- 1 cup chucky peanut butter
- 1 cup chopped pecans
- 14 large marshmellows
- 1/2 cup milk
- 1/4 cup cocoa
- 1/8 teaspoon salt

Direction

- Mix sugar, milk and butter in a medium size saucepan.
- Boil, stirring constantly, for 1 minute.
- Add remaining ingredients; stir well.
- Drop by teaspoon onto waxed paper or pour into a buttered pan and cut into bars when cooled.

90. Chocolate Fleur De Sel Bonbons Recipe

Serving: 0 | Prep: | Cook: 45mins | Ready in:

Ingredients

- 1 pound good quality dark chocolate (70% cocoa)
- 2 tbsp fleur de sel
- 30 bonbon cups

Direction

- Chop the chocolate.
- Place the chocolate in a double boiler (water bath) and let it melt.
- Line a plastic tray with the bonbon cups.
- Put the melted chocolate in a piping bag and pour a small amount on each cup.
- Let the chocolate set for 10 minutes and then sprinkle each bonbon with a tiny amount of fleur de sel.
- Put the tray in the fridge until the chocolate is fully set.
- These chocolates, nicely wrapped, make a wonderful gift.

91. Chocolate Fruit And Nut Truffles Recipe

Serving: 30 | Prep: | Cook: 15mins | Ready in:

Ingredients

- 9 ounces bittersweet chocolate
- 2 tablespoons heavy cream
- 2 tablespoons cognac or rum
- 1 1/4 cups apricots, finely chopped
- 1/2 cup hazelnuts, finely chopped
- 2 tablespoons crystallized ginger, minced
- 2 tablespoons confectioners sugar, sifted
- 30 hazelnut halves

Direction

- Step 1:
- Line a large baking sheet with baking parchment or aluminum foil.
- Step 2:
- In the top of a double boiler over low heat, stir 4 ounces of the chocolate until melted.
- Step 3:
- Remove from the heat and beat in the cream and cognac. Blend in the apricots, chopped

hazelnuts, ginger, and confectioners' sugar. Stir well to combine.
- Step 4:
- Chill the mixture, if necessary, until firm enough to handle. Form into 1-inch balls and set aside on a sheet of wax paper.
- Step 5:
- In the top of a double boiler over low heat, stir the remaining 5 ounces of chocolate until melted. Remove from the heat.
- Step 6:
- Using a fork, dip each truffle into the melted chocolate, allowing any excess to run off. Place the truffles on the prepared baking sheet. Top each with a hazelnut half and chill.
- Step 7:
- When the chocolate has set, the truffles can be stored in an airtight container in the refrigerator for up to 1 month.

92. Chocolate Fudge Recipe

Serving: 10 | Prep: | Cook: 20mins | Ready in:

Ingredients

- 1 1/2 sticks butter
- 3 cups sugar
- 5 oz evaporated milk
- 12 oz semi-sweet chocolate chips
- 6 oz marshmallow creme
- 1 tsp vanilla
- toppings as desired

Direction

- Butter a 9X13 inch pan. Smaller pan can be used for thicker fudge.
- Melt butter in a large heavy saucepan.
- Add milk and sugar.
- Bring to a boil over medium heat, stirring occasionally.
- Cook at a rolling boil for 5 minutes, still stirring only occasionally but don't let the bottom burn.
- Remove from heat and add marshmallow crème.
- Add chocolate chips gradually, stirring constantly and making sure the chocolate melts evenly.
- Add vanilla and any nuts if desired.
- Pour into pan.
- At this time you can add another layer if you want, I like to use the Hershey's mint chocolate kisses and just drop them on top of the fudge and let them melt, then spread around evenly. You can also add nuts on top, crushed candy cane or toffee, etc.
- Cool for at least 4 hours. The fudge will be soft and is easier to cut if you put it into the fridge about 30 minutes before you want to cut it.

93. Chocolate Fudgies Recipe

Serving: 60 | Prep: | Cook: 3mins | Ready in:

Ingredients

- 2 cups (12 oz. pkg.) milk chocolate chips * see note below
- 1 cup (6 oz. pkg.) semi-sweet chocolate chips
- 1/4 cup butter
- 1, 14 oz. can of condensed milk (Not evaporated milk!)
- 1/4 tsp of salt
- 2 cups coarsely chopped pecans or 2 cups of chopped walnuts
- 2 teaspoons vanilla extract
- pecan halves / walnut halves
- *Note: Using top quality chocolate chips will make a better candy. Taste the chips. If they don't melt well in your mouth and are flavorless and sandy in texture, do not use them in this recipe.

Direction

- Melt the chocolate chips, butter, condensed milk and salt in a glass bowl in your microwave on High for 2 minutes.

- Take the bowl out and stir well until the mixture is creamy and well-blended.
- Stir in chopped nuts and vanilla.
- DROP by teaspoonfuls onto wax paper, Non-stick aluminum foil or a silicone mat.
- Top with pecan or walnut halves.
- Chill in your refrigerator until firm or let sit overnight out on your counter if your kitchen temperature is cool.

94. Chocolate Ganache Truffles Recipe

Serving: 100 | Prep: | Cook: 5mins | Ready in:

Ingredients

- 2 pounds bittersweet or semisweet chocolate, chopped into small pieces
- 16 ounces heavy cream
- 4 ounces (1 stick) butter, cut into small pieces
- ½ c. liqueur, such as brandy, Frangelico, or Amaretto (optional)
- toasted hazelnuts, almonds, pistachios, chocolate jimmies, cocoa, or cocoa nibs for garnish

Direction

- 1. Put the chopped chocolate in a medium-size stainless-steel bowl.
- 2. Heat cream to scalding in a small saucepan. (When you see bubbles form around the edge of the cream in the pan, it's ready.)
- 3. Pour the hot cream over the chocolate in the bowl. Make sure cream is covering all of the chocolate. You can shake the bowl a little to settle the chocolate and get the cream to cover it. Let this mixture rest for 3 to 4 minutes.
- 4. Add the butter to the bowl and whisk the chocolate mixture until it's smooth.
- 5. Stir in the liqueur, if using.
- 6. Pour the chocolate ganache into a 9-by-13-inch dish and chill until set. (The ganache can be made at least a day in advance.)
- 7. Once set, use a ½-ounce cookie scoop to make chocolate balls, placing them on a parchment-lined sheet pan.
- 8. Roll the truffles in toasted nuts, chocolate jimmies, cocoa powder, or cocoa nibs and place on a separate parchment-lined sheet pan. When finished, place the truffles in a tightly sealed container, separating layers with waxed paper, and store in the refrigerator.

95. Chocolate Hazelnut Sticks Recipe

Serving: 48 | Prep: | Cook: 10mins | Ready in:

Ingredients

- a package of the long thin, plain Italian breadsticks
- 1 cup meltable chocolate wafers or chocolate bark
- 2 heaping tablespoons nutella
- very finely chopped hazelnuts
- sea salt

Direction

- 1. Line a cookie sheet with parchment paper or waxed paper.
- 2. Melt chocolate in the microwave, stopping every 30 seconds to stir and check on it. Stop microwaving it when the wafers start to look shiny.
- Trust me, you do not want to scorch the chocolate - I've said it before, let me say it again: Burned chocolate is an abomination.
- 3. Add the Nutella and stir well until it melts in with the chocolate.
- 4. Break the breadsticks in half and dip the broken half in the chocolate/Nutella mixture, swirling around and building up a lush and lovely coating of chocolate.
- 5. Lay them on the lined cookie sheet and sprinkle with chopped nuts.
- 6. Grind some fresh sea salt over the top.

- 7. Put the cookie sheet in the freezer and let them harden before removing to a plate or packaging in cellophane bags.

96. Chocolate Honey Fudge Recipe

Serving: 24 | Prep: | Cook: 15mins | Ready in:

Ingredients

- 2 tbsp butter
- 2 squares unsweetened chocolate
- 1 cup milk
- 2 3/4 cup sugar
- 1/2 cup honey
- 1/8 tsp salt
- 1 tsp vinegar
- 1 tsp vanilla
- 1/2 cup chopped nuts

Direction

- Melt butter and chocolate with milk in pan. Beat to blend. Add sugar, hone and salt. Bring to a boil. Cover and boil two minutes. Uncover and cook without stirring until a small amount of mixture dropped in cold water forms a soft ball. Remove from heat and add vinegar. Let stand until lukewarm and add vanilla. Beat until thick. Add nuts and turn onto a buttered plate. Let stand until cool enough to handle, then knead for five minutes. Shape into two rolls about two inches in diameter. Wrap in wax paper and store in a cool place until ready to serve. Slice and enjoy.

97. Chocolate Marshmallow Cashew Fudge Recipe

Serving: 6 | Prep: | Cook: 40mins | Ready in:

Ingredients

- 2 cups sugar
- 4 Tbsp cocoa powder
- 1 cup milk
- 1 Tbsp butter
- Dash of salt (not needed if you use salted cashews)
- 1 tsp vanilla essence
- 10 large or 25 miniature marshmallows (white or colored)
- 4 oz cashews, crushed into large pieces
- veg oil

Direction

- Oil a cookie sheet with the veg oil (for thin fudge) or a square jelly roll or cake pan (for thicker fudge)
- In a saucepan combine the sugar, cocoa powder and milk
- Cook to the soft ball stage*
- *Bring to a rapid boil, stirring occasionally. Boil until the mixture becomes the thickness of thin pudding. The mixture will be foamy. Put a drop on a cold saucer and wait for a few minutes. When mixture on plate is shiny and doesn't stick to your finger, it's ready. Don't give up. Keep boiling! It will be thin for a while but will thicken up eventually. Be patient!
- Turn down the heat to very low and stir in the butter. This will immediately cut the foam and make the mixture shiny.
- Stir in the salt (if you are using unsalted nuts) and vanilla.
- Stir in the marshmallows. You can melt them completely or not. It's up to you. I melt the large ones, but don't melt the miniatures.
- Stir in the nut pieces.
- Turn off the heat and pour QUICKLY into the prepared pan. Make sure you use a wooden spatula to scrape and spread the fudge.
- Allow to cool before cutting or breaking into squares.

98. Chocolate Marshmallow Nut Clusters Recipe

Serving: 8 | Prep: | Cook: 10mins | Ready in:

Ingredients

- 1 can Eagle Brand milk
- 1 (12 oz.) pkg. chocolate chips
- 1 1/2 c. peanuts (roasted work great)
- 3 c. miniature marshmallows

Direction

- Combine Eagle Brand milk and chocolate chips in large saucepan.
- Allow chips to melt over very low heat, stirring constantly until chips are melted and mixed completely. Let cool until lukewarm, gradually fold in nuts and marshmallows until covered with chocolate.
- Spoon onto waxed paper (lightly spread some butter on the wax paper, so no sticking) in small clusters.
- Let stand at room temperature, then chill in refrigerator to set.

99. Chocolate Marshmallow Pizza Recipe

Serving: 12 | Prep: | Cook: | Ready in:

Ingredients

- 1-12oz. package semi-sweet chocolate chips
- 1 lb. white almond bark, divided
- 2 C. miniature marshmallows
- 1 C. crisp rice cereal
- 1 C. peanuts
- 1- 6oz. jar red maraschino cherries, drained & quartered
- 1/3 C. angel flake coconut
- 1 tsp. oil

Direction

- Melt chips and 14 oz. of the almond bark in large saucepan over low heat, stirring until smooth, remove from heat.
- Stir in marshmallows, cereal, and peanuts.
- Pour onto greased 12" pizza pan
- Top with cherries and sprinkle on coconut.
- Melt remaining 2 oz. bark with oil stirring until smooth. Drizzle over coconut.
- Refrigerate until firm.

100. Chocolate Marshmallow Popcorn Balls Recipe

Serving: 10 | Prep: | Cook: 15mins | Ready in:

Ingredients

- 8 ounces marshmallows
- 3/4 cup butter
- 1/8 teaspoon salt
- 1/2 teaspoon vanilla extract
- 12 cups popped popcorn
- 1-1/2 pounds sweet dark chocolate chopped
- 3 tablespoons whipping cream

Direction

- Combine marshmallows, 1 stick of the butter and salt in medium saucepan.
- Cook over medium heat stirring often until marshmallows and butter are melted.
- Remove from heat then stir in vanilla.
- Pour over popcorn in large bowl then toss to combine.
- Form popcorn mixture into small 1" balls and place on baking sheet covered with wax paper.
- Let sit until completely dry.
- Melt chocolate, remaining 1/4 butter and cream in medium saucepan over medium low heat.
- Roll popcorn balls in chocolate one at a time to completely cover then let harden on wax paper.

101. Chocolate Marshmello Fudge Lite Recipe

Serving: 36 | Prep: | Cook: 5mins | Ready in:

Ingredients

- Points 2
- 1 2/3 cup sugar
- 2/3 cup fat-free evaporated milk
- 2 Tbsp light margarine
- 12 oz semisweet chocolate, chopped
- 1 cup miniature marshmallows
- 2 tsp. vanilla extract

Direction

- Coat an 8- x 8-inch pan with cooking spray. Stir together sugar, evaporated milk and margarine. Bring to a boil in a sauce pan, reduce heat to medium-low and cook 3 mins stirring constantly. Stir in chocolate and marshmallows. Remove from heat and stir until smooth. Pour into pan and refrigerate until firm, about 2 hours. Cut into 36 squares and serve. (Leave fudge in refrigerator or freezer for a firmer consistency.)
- Nutrition Info per serving: 91 Cal., 3g. Fat, 0g. Fiber

102. Chocolate Mint Candy Recipe

Serving: 12 | Prep: | Cook: 10mins | Ready in:

Ingredients

- 10 squares of semi-sweet chocolate baking bar (1oz each)
- 1 can of Eagle Brand sweetened condensed milk
- 2 Tsp of vanilla extract
- 1 package of White baking chocolate 170 grams
- 1 TB peppermint extract
- 4-6 drops of green food coloring

Direction

- Melt the semi-sweet chocolate chips with one cup of the Eagle Brand milk in the microwave for one minute, stir to blend.
- Remove from microwave and stir in vanilla extract
- Spread half of the mixture into a parchment paper-lined 8 inch square pan.
- Chill in the refrigerator until firm for 10 minutes.
- Keep the remaining semi-sweet chocolate at room temperature!
- Melt the white chocolate in remaining Eagle Brand in microwave for one minute. Stir to blend.
- Stir in Peppermint extract and food coloring. You can add more color if you want a deeper green color. The color is up to you!
- Spread over the chilled semi-sweet chocolate layer.
- Chill for 10 minutes in the refrigerator.
- Spread the reserved semi-sweet chocolate over the mint layer.
- Chill again but for 2 full hours or until solid to the touch.
- Lift from pan and peel off paper.
- Cut into squares and serve!

103. Chocolate Mint Fudge Recipe

Serving: 12 | Prep: | Cook: 10mins | Ready in:

Ingredients

- 1 cup milk chocolate chips
- 1 cup semisweet chocolate morsels
- 1 cup green mint flavored chocolate chips
- 14 ounce can sweetened condensed milk

- 1 cup chopped walnuts
- 1 teaspoon vanilla extract

Direction

- Line square baking pan with foil.
- Combine milk chocolate and semisweet morsels and milk in medium heavy duty saucepan.
- Warm over lowest possible heat stirring until smooth.
- Remove from heat then stir in nuts and vanilla extract.
- Put mint chips over warmed mixture and spread evenly.
- Spread evenly into prepared pan the refrigerate 2 hours or until form.
- Lift from pan then remove foil and cut into pieces.

104. Chocolate Mint Truffles Recipe

Serving: 36 | Prep: | Cook: 30mins | Ready in:

Ingredients

- 48 oz (4 bags) Ghirardilli Double chocolate chips
- 1 cup butter softened
- 4 egg yolks
- 1 pint whipping cream
- 1/2 cup mint schnapps (or 2 tsp. mint extract)*
- Sweet cocoa powder
- crushed candy canes (optional)
- cookie sheets
- wax paper
- shortening (optional)

Direction

- Space in the freezer for a cookie sheet.
- In large bowl, beat egg yolks at medium speed until they are a thickened and lemon colored.
- Melt 2 bags of chips in microwave or in a double boiler. Be sure to watch carefully so it doesn't burn. Remove from heat and add butter one table spoon at a time, blend thoroughly. Gradually add chocolate mixture to beaten egg yolk, adding about 1/4 of chocolate at a time.
- Stir in whipping cream and schnapps or mint extract.
- Return to heat and cook about 1 minute stirring constantly.
- Chill, covered, for at least 8 hours or until firm.
- Shape into balls (this is a messy process!) and roll in cocoa powder. Return to freezer.
- (You can stop here if you like or you can continue to the last step.)
- While balls are chilling, melt the remaining chocolate for coating. You may add a little shortening to keep it smooth and make the chocolate shinier.
- Dip balls in chocolate and sprinkle with crushed candy cane.
- Serve at room temperature.
- Store in air tight container. These will l keep for about one month in the refrigerator, or 2 months in the freezer.
- * I have always used the Schnapps.

105. Chocolate Nut Chews Recipe

Serving: 36 | Prep: | Cook: 5mins | Ready in:

Ingredients

- 1 1/2 cups sugar
- 1/4 cup cocoa
- 1/2 cup evaporated milk
- 1/3 cup butter
- 1/3 cup peanut butter
- 1 teaspoon vanilla
- 1 1/2 cups quick rolled oats
- 1/2 cup salted peanuts

Direction

- In a heavy 2-quart saucepan, mix sugar, cocoa, milk and butter.
- Stir over medium heat until mixture bubbles all over top. Boil and stir 2 minutes longer.
- Remove from heat. Stir in the peanut butter until melted; add the vanilla, uncooked quick rolled oats and nuts.
- With 2 teaspoons, drop on waxed paper. Let stand until set.

106. Chocolate Nut Clusters Recipe

Serving: 0 | Prep: | Cook: 10mins | Ready in:

Ingredients

- Plain/dark chocolate
- chocolate chip cookies, crushed
- nuts, dried fruits, coconut, marshmallows
- white chocolate, melted

Direction

- Melt chocolate in a pan over low heat (you can also use a double boiler or microwave).
- Once chocolate has completely melted, add cookies and nuts and mix thoroughly.
- Spoon out (heaping tablespoon amount) onto a baking sheet lined with waxed paper.
- Let cool completely. Refrigerate till set.
- To serve, place in the baking cups/pastry cases and drizzle the melted white chocolate decoratively over the clusters.

107. Chocolate Nut Drops Recipe

Serving: 34 | Prep: | Cook: 10mins | Ready in:

Ingredients

- 1 1/2 pounds Hershey Bars with almonds
- 1/2 cup chunky peanut butter
- 1 cup dry roasted peanuts
- 1 1/2 cup Rice Krispies
- 1 cup mini marshmallows
- 1/2 cup toffee bits
- waxed paper

Direction

- Melt Chocolate in a double boiler with peanut butter until smooth.
- In a large bowl combine the nuts, cereal and toffee.
- Pour chocolate over mixture and mix well.
- Gently fold in marshmallows.
- Drop, by teaspoon, onto waxed paper lined cookie sheets.
- Refrigerate to cool.

108. Chocolate Orange Truffles Recipe

Serving: 0 | Prep: | Cook: 5mins | Ready in:

Ingredients

- 1/3 cup whipping cream
- 2 tablespoons unsalted butter
- 1 1/2 tablespoons orange flavoring
- 8 ounces bittersweet chocolate, broken into chunks
- cocoa powder
- 6 ounces bittersweet chocolate
- 2 tablespoons solid vegetable shortening

Direction

- 1. Heat the whipping cream and butter together just to a simmer, then add chocolate. Remove from heat while chocolate melts. Add flavoring. Stir until glossy and pour into a chilled bowl. Set aside until firm.

- 2. Once firm, use a small melon baller and scoop ganache out. Roll by hand, using cocoa powder to reduce stickiness. Chill until firm.
- 3. Melt 6 ounces bittersweet chocolate with 2 tablespoons solid vegetable shortening in the microwave for about 1 minute. Stir until melted; microwave additional seconds as needed. Drop each ball individually into chocolate, roll with a fork until coated, then use the fork to lift out and place on parchment paper. Chill and keep refrigerated.

109. Chocolate Peanut Butter Fudge Recipe

Serving: 12 | Prep: | Cook: 10mins | Ready in:

Ingredients

- 2 cups semisweet chocolate morsels
- 14 ounce can sweetened condensed milk
- 1 cup peanut butter chips
- 1 cup chopped peanuts
- 1 teaspoon vanilla extract

Direction

- Line square baking pan with foil.
- Combine chocolate morsels and milk in medium heavy duty saucepan.
- Warm over lowest possible heat stirring until smooth.
- Remove from heat then stir in nuts and vanilla extract.
- Spread peanut butter chips over top and spread.
- Spread evenly into prepared pan the refrigerate 2 hours or until form.
- Lift from pan then remove foil and cut into pieces.

110. Chocolate Peanut Butter Rocky Road Clusters Recipe

Serving: 14 | Prep: | Cook: 8mins | Ready in:

Ingredients

- 16 - ounces semisweet baking chocolate, coarsely chopped
- 3- tablespoons creamy peanut butter
- 1 1/2- cups plain corn flakes (not frosted)
- 1 1/2 cups miniature marshmallows
- 1/2- cup peanuts .toasted

Direction

- Line 2 - baking sheets with parchment paper or wax paper.
- Melt the chocolate and peanut butter in the top of a double broiler or in a medium glass bowl in a microwave and stir until smooth.
- Combine the corn flakes, marshmallows, and peanuts in a large bowl.
- Add the melted chocolate, stir gently with a rubber spatula until all the ingredients are thoroughly combined.
- Using 2 heaping tablespoons or 1 - # 20 ice cream scoop, portion 7 clusters, about 1 inch apart, width wise and lengthwise, on each baking sheet.
- Refrigerate the clusters until firm about 30 minutes.
- Makes 14 clusters

111. Chocolate Peanut Butter Squares Recipe

Serving: 16 | Prep: | Cook: 10mins | Ready in:

Ingredients

- 1 cup peanut butter (smooth or chunky)
- 1 cup dry instant non-fat milk powder
- 1/2 cup honey
- 1 cup chocolate chips

Direction

- In a 9 x 9 inch baking dish, mix peanut butter, milk powder, and honey until well blended. It should be a smooth paste, like play dough.
- Press mixture into an even layer in the bottom of the pan.
- Sprinkle chocolate chips over the peanut butter mixture.
- Bake at 350 degrees for 10 minutes. The chocolate chips should be soft.
- Spread the melted chocolate chips evenly over the top of the peanut butter layer.
- Let cool completely.
- Cut into 16 pieces.

112. Chocolate Peanut Popcorn Crunch Recipe

Serving: 1 | Prep: | Cook: 30mins | Ready in:

Ingredients

- 6 cups plain popcorn, popped (about 1/2 regular bag)
- 1-1/4 cup salted peanuts
- 1 cup semi-sweet chocolate chips
- 1/2 cup light corn syrup
- 1/3 cup peanut butter
- 2 tbsp (1 ounce) butter
- 1/2 cup white chocolate candy coating (optional)

Direction

- 1. Prepare a 13x9 pan by spraying it with non-stick cooking spray. Cover a baking sheet with aluminum foil and spray the foil with non-stick cooking spray; set the baking sheet aside for now. Preheat the oven to 300 degrees.
- 2. Place the popcorn and nuts in the 13x9 pan, stir to distribute them evenly.
- 3. In a medium saucepan, combine the butter, corn syrup, chocolate chips, and peanut butter. Cook over medium-high heat, stirring constantly, until the candy reaches a steady boil.
- 4. Remove from the heat, and carefully pour the boiling candy over the popcorn and peanuts. Mix until all pieces are evenly coated.
- 5. Place the pan in the oven and cook for 30 minutes. Stir every 10 minutes so that it cooks evenly. It is done when the candy is bubbling completely and very fragrant.
- 6. Pour the cooked candy on the prepared baking sheet and spread it in a thin layer. Allow it to cool and set at room temperature.
- 7. If desired, melt the white candy coating and add any oil-based candy colors you desire. Using a fork, flick the coating over the popcorn candy to create decorative stripes. Allow the coating to set, then break the candy apart with your hands into small chunks.
- 8. Store the candy in an airtight container at room temperature for up to a week.

113. Chocolate Peanut Sweeties Recipe

Serving: 60 | Prep: | Cook: | Ready in:

Ingredients

- 1 cup peanut butter
- 1/2 cup butter-softened
- 3 cups confectioners' sugar
- 60 miniature pretzels(about 3 cups)
- 1 1/2 cups milk chocolate chips
- 1 tablespoon shortening

Direction

- In a small mixing bowl, beat peanut butter and butter until smooth.
- Beat in confectioners' sugar until combined.
- Shape into 1" balls. Press on each pretzel.
- Place on waxed paper lined baking sheets. Refrigerate until peanut butter is set.

- In a microwave safe bowl or heavy saucepan, melt chocolate chips and shortening, stirring until smooth.
- Dip peanut butter balls into chocolate. Return to baking sheet. Pretzel side down.
- Refrigerate at least 30 minutes before serving.
- Store in an airtight container in the refrigerator.

114. Chocolate Pecan Candy Recipe

Serving: 1 | Prep: | Cook: 5mins | Ready in:

Ingredients

- 4-1/2 cups sugar
- 12 oz. can evaporated milk
- 1 cup butter or margarine
- 3 cups (18 oz) semisweet chocolate chips
- 7 oz. jar marshmallow cream
- 3 cups chopped pecans

Direction

- Bring first 3 ingredients to a boil in a Dutch oven over medium heat, stirring constantly; boil, stirring constantly, 5 minutes.
- Remove from heat; stir in chocolate chips, marshmallow cream and pecans until blended. Pour into a buttered 13X9 pan; let stand at least 2 hours or until firm. Cut into squares.
- Yield: 5 pounds.

115. Chocolate Potato Candy Recipe

Serving: 36 | Prep: | Cook: | Ready in:

Ingredients

- 1 medium baking potato, baked
- 1 teaspoon vanilla extract
- 1/2 teaspoon salt
- 4 cups powdered sugar
- 1/3 cup Hershey's® cocoa
- chocolate Glaze:
- 1 square Hershey's® unsweetened baking chocolate
- 1/2 teaspoon butter

Direction

- Place waxed paper on a cookie sheet, set aside.
- Bake potato and mash; should yield 3/4 cup.
- In a large bowl, combine mashed potato, vanilla and salt.
- Gradually add powdered sugar and cocoa, beating until mixture is stiff enough to be shaped into 1-inch balls.
- Refrigerate balls until cold.
- Dip balls, one at a time into Chocolate Glaze.
- Let excess chocolate drip off balls.
- Place on prepared cookie sheet.
- Refrigerate until chocolate is set.
- Store tightly covered in refrigerator in a tightly covered container.
- Chocolate Glaze:
- In top of a double boiler over hot, not boiling, water, melt chocolate and butter.
- Stir until mixture is smooth.
- Cool slightly.
- Recipe yields 36 candies.

116. Chocolate Pretzel Rings

Serving: 0 | Prep: | Cook: | Ready in:

Ingredients

- 48 to 50 pretzel rings or squares
- 48 to 50 milk chocolate or striped chocolate kisses
- 1/4 cup milk chocolate M&M's

Direction

- Place the pretzels on greased baking sheets; place a chocolate kiss in the center of each pretzel. Bake at 275° until chocolate is softened, for 2-3 minutes. Remove from the oven.
- Place an M&M's candy on each, pressing down slightly so chocolate fills the pretzel holes. Refrigerate until chocolate is firm, 5-10 minutes. Store in an airtight container at room temperature.
- Nutrition Facts
- 2 each: 69 calories, 3g fat (2g saturated fat), 2mg cholesterol, 55mg sodium, 9g carbohydrate (6g sugars, 0 fiber), 1g protein.

117. Chocolate Pretzel Rings Recipe

Serving: 50 | Prep: | Cook: 3mins | Ready in:

Ingredients

- 50 pretzel rings or miniature pretzels
- 50 chocolate kisses
- M&M's (choose M&M color according to holiday or special occasion)

Direction

- Preheat oven to 275.
- Place chocolate on parchment paper lined baking sheet.
- Place a pretzel ring around chocolate kiss.
- Put in oven 2-3 minutes or until chocolate has softened.
- Remove from oven.
- Put an M&M candy on each, pressing down so chocolate fills ring.
- Refrigerate until chocolate firms.

118. Chocolate Raspberry Truffles Recipe

Serving: 12 | Prep: | Cook: 60mins | Ready in:

Ingredients

- 1/2 cup heavy cream
- 12 ounces of semi-sweet chocolate, chopped fine
- 1/4 cup unsalted butter, cut into bits and softened
- 1/2 cup seedless red raspberry jam
- 2 tablespoons Chambord
- pinch of salt
- 1/2 cup sifted unsweetened cocoa powder

Direction

- In a saucepan bring cream just to a boil over medium heat.
- Remove the pan from the heat.
- Add the chocolate.
- Stir the mixture until chocolate is melted completely and mixture is smooth.
- Let the mixture cool slightly and then add butter, bit by bit.
- Stir the mixture until it is smooth.
- Stir in the jam, the Chambord and a pinch of salt.
- Transfer mixture to bowl.
- Chill it, covered, for 4 hours. or until it is firm.
- Make teaspoon sized balls out of the mixture and roll the balls in the cocoa powder.
- Chill the truffles on a baking sheet lined with wax paper for 1 hour or until they are firm.
- Keep them in an airtight container, chilled, for 2 weeks.
- Makes about 40 truffles

119. Chocolate Roses Recipe

Serving: 12 | Prep: | Cook: | Ready in:

Ingredients

- 10 oz chocolate (chopped chunks or chips)
- 1/3 cup light corn syrup

Direction

- The chocolate modelling clay is made by combining melted chocolate and light corn syrup.
- Note: the chocolate can be substituted with almond bark, or colored candy disks to create different colored flowers.
- *Chocolate clay:
- Melt the chocolate in a microwave for 1 minute.
- Stir. If chocolate is not completely melted, return to the microwave for 30 seconds at a time and stir until smooth.
- If you don't have a microwave, place the chocolate in the top of a double boiler over hot water and stir until melted.
- When the chocolate is melted, add the corn syrup and blend.
- Pour the mixture onto a waxed paper sheet.
- Spread the chocolate with your fingers until it's about 1/2 inch thick. Cover loosely with waxed paper and let it stiffen for at least a couple hours or overnight. The chocolate will become very pliable.
- *Making a Chocolate Rose:
- Roll 10 marble-sized balls from the chocolate clay.
- Place the balls on a waxed paper sheet, about 1 inch apart.
- Place another waxed paper sheet on top.
- Use your thumbs to press each marble into a flat disk (about the size of a quarter).
- *To form the rose:
- Remove 1 disk and curl it into a teepee shape, narrow at the top and wider at the bottom.
- Wrap the next disk around the opening of the teepee and the third disk at the back of the teepee.
- This is the rose bud.
- Continue adding disks which will look like petals.
- Continue to layer them to create a rose in bloom.
- *Roses can be used as edible decorations for a cake or to create a basketful of blooms. They will harden after a few days and can be saved by storing in a cool, dry place.

120. Chocolate Truffle Meringues Recipe

Serving: 24 | Prep: | Cook: 210mins | Ready in:

Ingredients

- Meringues
- 2 egg whites
- 1/3 cup granulated sugar
- 1/2 cup powdered sugar
- 2 tablespoons unsweetened baking cocoa
- Filling
- 1/4 cup whipping cream
- 3 oz bittersweet baking chocolate, chopped, or 1/2 cup dark chocolate chips
- 2 tablespoons butter or margarine, cut into small pieces

Direction

- Heat oven to 200°F. Line cookie sheet with cooking parchment paper. In medium bowl, beat egg whites with electric mixer on medium speed until soft peaks form. Gradually add granulated sugar, beating at high speed just until stiff peaks form.
- In small bowl, mix powdered sugar and cocoa. Fold cocoa mixture, 1/3 at a time, into beaten egg whites. Spoon mixture into decorating bag fitted with star tip. Draw 1 1/2-inch diameter circle on white paper; place under parchment paper as a guide for piping rounds. Pipe mixture into twenty-four 1 1/2-inch rounds on parchment lined cookie sheet. With back of teaspoon, make an indentation in each to hold filling. (Or, mixture can be spooned into dollops on parchment paper.)
- Bake 1 to 1 1/4 hours or until crisp. Cool completely, about 10 minutes.

- Meanwhile, in 1-quart heavy saucepan, heat whipping cream just to simmering over medium-low heat. Remove from heat; stir in chocolate with wire whisk until melted. Stir in butter pieces, a few at a time, until melted. Refrigerate until thickened, about 30 minutes.
- Just before serving, spoon or pipe about 1 teaspoon filling into indentation of each meringue.

121. Chocolate Truffles

Serving: 0 | Prep: | Cook: | Ready in:

Ingredients

- 3 cups semisweet chocolate chips
- 1 can (14 ounces) sweetened condensed milk
- 1 tablespoon vanilla extract
- Optional coatings: Chocolate sprinkles, Dutch-processed cocoa, espresso powder and cacao nibs

Direction

- In a microwave, melt chocolate chips and milk; stir until smooth. Stir in vanilla. Refrigerate, covered, 2 hours or until firm enough to roll.
- Shape into 1-in. balls. Roll in coatings as desired.
- Nutrition Facts
- 1 truffle: 77 calories, 4g fat (2g saturated fat), 3mg cholesterol, 12mg sodium, 11g carbohydrate (10g sugars, 1g fiber), 1g protein.

122. Chocolate Truffles Recipe

Serving: 40 | Prep: | Cook: 60mins | Ready in:

Ingredients

- 1 pkg. (12 oz.) semi-sweet chocolate chips, or 12 oz. good quality chocolate
- 1/4 c. butter
- 1/2 c. whipping (heavy) cream or flavored non-dairy creamer (hazelnut is a nice choice)
- flavor oil, such as orange, peppermint, raspberry, coffee - only use flavor oil - I'll tell you why
- cocoa, chopped nuts, or additional chocolate chips, for coating

Direction

- ***Cook time includes chilling time.***
- Heat chocolate chips and butter in heavy 2-quart saucepan over low heat, stirring constantly, until chocolate is melted; remove from heat.
- Stir in whipping cream (or creamer, if using). If you would like to flavor your truffles, add a few drops of flavor oil. The reason to use flavor oils is because adding water- or alcohol-based extracts to chocolate will cause it to 'seize', causing it to become grainy and hard.
- Refrigerate 30 to 40 minutes, stirring frequently, until thick. Using about teaspoon-sized amounts, roll mixture into small balls.
- Roll in cocoa powder or chopped nuts. If you prefer, you may chill the centers; melt additional chocolate chips in glass or metal bowl set over a pan of simmering water. Don't get any water in the chocolate or it will seize! Dip the chilled centers into the chocolate with a fork; gently tap fork against side of bowl to shake off excess chocolate, set on waxed paper. Let set to firm up chocolate coating.
- Store in covered container up to three weeks. I don't suggest freezing these if coated in chocolate. Sometimes the freezing and thawing process can cause the chocolate to 'oxidize', which, while perfectly edible, is not very pretty. It kind of leaves a white film on the outsides of the candies.

123. Chocolate Truffles With Rum And Raisins Recipe

Serving: 24 | Prep: | Cook: 15mins | Ready in:

Ingredients

- 2 dl double cream
- 150 g dark chocolate (70%)
- 50 g milk chocolate
- 150 g nougat
- 40 g icing sugar
- 10 g butter
- 1 dl raisins
- 0.5 dl rum
- white chocolate
- Chopped pistachio nuts

Direction

- Coarsely chop the raisins, place in a bowl and add the Rum, cover with cling-film. Leave for a couple of hours.
- Slowly heat the double cream in a casserole. Add the chopped chocolate. Stop heating when the chocolate has melted.
- Add the nougat and stir until melted.
- Stir in the butter and the icing sugar.
- Add the raisins
- Pour the truffle-mass into a cling-film covered tray. Place in the freezer for a couple of hours.
- Melt the white chocolate, cut the truffle-mass in squares and make small balls. Dip the balls in the melted chocolate. Sprinkle some chopped pistachios on top.

124. Chocolate Turtle Bars Recipe

Serving: 12 | Prep: | Cook: 20mins | Ready in:

Ingredients

- 1 bag of Rollo chocolate caramel candies, unwrapped
- 2 cups of pecan halves
- 1 cup of chopped pecans
- 1 cup of semi-sweet chocolate chips
- 12 caramel squares, unwrapped
- 1 TB butter

Direction

- Preheat oven to 350 degrees
- Cover an 8x8 inch pan with "release" aluminum foil, leaving extra foil on the sides (to remove candy out of the pan after cooling)
- Pour one cup of pecan halves into the pan, spread out evenly.
- Place the Rollo candies over the pecans.
- Place in oven and cook for 10 minutes at 350 degrees.
- Remove pan from the oven and pour 1 more cup of pecans over the now melted Rollo candies.
- Press the pecans into the Rollos. Set the pan to the side and keep the oven on.
- In a microwave-proof bowl, add the caramels and 1 TB of butter.
- Melt on high for one minute, remove and stir to combine.
- Place back in microwave for 30 seconds.
- Stir well and pour caramel directly over the last layer of pecans.
- Sprinkle the chocolate chips over the caramel evenly.
- Place the pan back into the oven and bake for 5 minutes until the chips look shiny and are beginning to melt.
- Remove pan and spread the chocolate across the surface of the caramel.
- Sprinkle the chopped pecans over the melted chips and using your hands, press them firmly over the warm chocolate.
- Let cool in pan until the chocolate is firm.
- Slice into long bars or into small squares and serve.
- These candies look lovely in clear cellophane bags tied with bows and make a nice food gift. You can freeze these in zip lock bags for months! These are also great for bake sales, potlucks and any family event....

125. Chocolate Walnut Toffee Candy Recipe

Serving: 36 | Prep: | Cook: 15mins | Ready in:

Ingredients

- 1 cup butter
- 1 cup granulated sugar
- 2 cups (12-ounce pkg)Nestle Semi-sweet chocolate morsels, divided
- 1 cup finely chopped walnuts

Direction

- Heat butter and sugar in a medium-size, heavy saucepan to boiling over medium heat, stirring constantly.
- Boil for 6 minutes or until golden colored, stirring constantly.
- Pour into buttered 9-inch square baking pan. Let stand for 3 minutes or until top begins to firm.
- Sprinkle with 1 cup morsels over candy. Let stand for 5 minutes or until morsels are shiny; spread chocolate over surface.
- Sprinkle 1/2 cup walnuts over chocolate; press down slightly.
- Chill for 15 minutes or until chocolate is firm.
- Invert candy onto waxed paper-lined tray.
- Microwave remaining cup of morsels in a small microwave-safe bowl on High (100%) power for one minute, stir. Microwave for an additional 10 to 20 second intervals, stirring until smooth.
- Remove any excess moisture from candy surface. Spread chocolate over candy.
- Sprinkle with remaining walnuts; press down slightly. Chill until firm.
- Break into bite-size pieces.
- Store in the refrigerator.

126. Chocolate [Turds] Drops Recipe

Serving: 10 | Prep: | Cook: 10mins | Ready in:

Ingredients

- 3 cups rolled oats
- 1 cup coconut
- 6 Tbsp cocoa
- 1/2 cup butter
- 1/2 cup milk
- 2 cups White sugar
- 1/2 tsp vanilla

Direction

- Aka "Quick Chocolate Drops"
- Mix oats, cocoanut and cocoa. Heat butter, sugar and milk. Pour over dry ingredients and stir well. Drop by teaspoon onto wax or parchment paper and chill.
- Note: Easier to form drops if slightly chilled first
- Another note: Any crumbs can be saved for a crunchy ice cream topping.

127. Chocolate And Butterscotch Fudge Recipe

Serving: 0 | Prep: | Cook: | Ready in:

Ingredients

- 2 cups (12 ounces) semi-sweet chocolate chips
- 1 (14-ounce) can EAGLE BRAND sweetened condensed milk (NOT evaporated milk), divided
- 1/2 cup chopped walnuts (optional)
- 1 teaspoon vanilla extract
- 1 cup butterscotch chips

Direction

- In heavy saucepan, over low heat, melt chocolate chips with 1 cup EAGLE BRAND. Remove from heat; stir in nuts (optional) and vanilla. Spread evenly into wax-paper-lined 8- or 9-inch square pan.
- In clean heavy saucepan, over low heat, melt butterscotch chips and remaining EAGLE BRAND. Spread evenly over chocolate layer
- Chill 3 hours or until firm. Turn fudge onto cutting board; peel off paper and cut into squares. Store leftovers covered in refrigerator

128. Chocolate Butterscotch Pecan Fudge Ala Easy Recipe

Serving: 120 | Prep: | Cook: 5mins | Ready in:

Ingredients

- 1 12-ounce package semi-sweet chocolate chips
- 1 12- ounce package butterscotch chips
- 1 can Eagle Brand milk
- 2 cups chopped pecans (can toast)
- 1/2 stick unsalted butter
- 1 teaspoon vanilla

Direction

- In large bowl, place the chips and Eagle Brand milk.
- Place in microwave to cook.
- Watching closely, stop and stir as needed until melted.
- Remove bowl.
- Stir in butter, stir quickly to mix.
- Add pecans, vanilla.
- Pour into a greased 13x9 dish, or 2-8 inch square dishes.
- Chill until firm, about 2 hours.
- Cut into 1 inch squares, or size of your choice.

129. Chocolate Candy With Dates And Peanuts Recipe

Serving: 5 | Prep: | Cook: | Ready in:

Ingredients

- 5 dates (Mazafati dates)
- 5 peanuts
- 25g of dark chocolate 75% o higher
- 5 short toothpicks
- a pinch of salt

Direction

- Melt the chocolate in a small pan, meanwhile remove the seeds of the dates, preserving the integrity of the dates, and insert in place of it the smashed peanuts, then pierce the dates with a toothpick.
- When the chocolate is melted pour it on dates.
- Let stand in refrigerator at least 15'.

130. Chocolate Popcorn Recipe

Serving: 1 | Prep: | Cook: | Ready in:

Ingredients

- 1 quart popcorn
- Spray (oil)
- 3 tablespoons hot chocolate mix
- 1 teaspoon cinnamon

Direction

- Put popped popcorn into bowl and spray with oil.
- Add the chocolate powder and cinnamon and stir.
- Eat.

131. Chocolate Covered Peanut Butter Crisp Squares Recipe

Serving: 36 | Prep: | Cook: 15mins | Ready in:

Ingredients

- Yield: 36 squares
- 1½ Tablespoons butter
- 5 ounces (or ½ bag) marshmallows
- ½ cup creamy peanut butter
- 3 cups crisped rice cereal
- 2 cups (1 bag) milk chocolate chips
- 2 Tablespoons vegetable shortening
- 1. Grease an 8×8-inch pan. Set aside.

Direction

- In a medium saucepan over medium-low heat, melt the butter. Add in the marshmallow and stir until melted. Add the peanut butter and continue stirring until completely melted. Remove from heat. Stir in the cereal until completely coated.
- 3. With buttered hands, press the mixture into the greased pan and place in refrigerator for at least 1 hour, or until set.
- 4. Remove pan from refrigerator, run a knife around the edges and turn out onto a cutting board. Cut into 36 squares.
- 5. Using either a double boiler or a microwave heating in 30-second intervals, melt the chocolate chips and shortening together until completely melted and smooth.
- 6. Working with one square at a time, drop a square into the chocolate and, using a toothpick, turn it over so it is completely covered in chocolate and then remove it to a baking sheet lined with a sheet of wax paper. Repeat with all squares.
- 7. Refrigerate until chocolate has set. Store in an airtight container in the refrigerator for up to a week.

132. Chocolate Macadamia Caramels Recipe

Serving: 24 | Prep: | Cook: 30mins | Ready in:

Ingredients

- 1 15-oz can sweetened condensed milk
- 1 cup light corn syrup
- 1 tbsp butter
- 2 ounces unsweetened chocolate
- 1 tsp vanilla extract
- 1/4 tsp rum extract
- 2/3 cup chopped macadamia nuts

Direction

- Prepare an 8-inch square baking pan by lining it with aluminum foil and spraying the foil with non-stick cooking spray.
- 2. Mix 1/3 of the sweetened condensed milk and the corn syrup in a medium heavy-bottomed saucepan. Cook over medium heat, stirring constantly, until it reaches 235 degrees.
- 3. Continue stirring as you add in the rest of the sweetened condensed milk. Keep the mixture boiling and gradually stir in the chocolate. Cook until mixture again reaches 235 degrees.
- 4. Remove from heat and stir in the vanilla and rum extracts.
- 5. Scatter half of the macadamia nuts in the bottom of the pan, and pour the chocolate caramel on top. Sprinkle the remaining nuts evenly on the caramel.
- 6. Allow to cool thoroughly before cutting.

133. Chocolate Peanut Butter Truffles Recipe

Serving: 18 | Prep: | Cook: 1mins | Ready in:

Ingredients

- 8 (1 ounce) squares Semi-Sweet baking chocolate
- 1/2 cup peanut butter
- 1 (8 ounce) tub Cool Whip, thawed
- *Suggested coatings, such as powdered sugar, unsweetened cocoa, finely chopped peanuts, multi-colored sprinkles, coconut, finely crushed cookies or Semi-Sweet baking chocolate

Direction

- Microwave chocolate in large microwaveable bowl on HIGH 2 min. or until chocolate is almost melted, stirring every 30 sec. Stir until chocolate is completely melted.
- Add peanut butter; stir until well blended.
- Cool to room temperature. Gently stir in whipped topping. Refrigerate 2 hours.
- Scoop truffle mixture with melon baller or teaspoon, then roll into 1-inch balls.
- Roll in suggested coatings.
- Store in tightly covered container in refrigerator.

134. Chocolate Coconut Candiesmounds Like Recipe

Serving: 5 | Prep: | Cook: 15mins | Ready in:

Ingredients

- (Candy)....
- 3/4C. mashed potatoes (Homemade are the best.. NO spices or milk..
- Just Plain potatoes!!
- 1 Pound flaked coconut
- 1 Pound Confectioners sugar
- 1t. vanilla or almond extract (I'm allergic to almonds that are
- Concentrated in any way)!
- (Coating)....
- 1 16 oz. bag semi-sweet chocolate chips
- 1/8 bar of paraffin (for added glossiness)
- Melted in double boiler....

Direction

- Candy)
- Mix all ingredients together.
- Drop by heaping teaspoons onto waxed paper (refrigerate for an hour if you cannot roll into balls.)
- Roll into balls and refrigerate until firm and can withstand dipping.
- (I usually refrigerate twice before rolling and after rolling. I've even covered and left over night after rolling then dipped the next day.)
- (Coating)
- In a double boiler melt chocolate and paraffin to smooth & glossy.
- Dip, making sure all sides are covered. I use a fork then let set-up. Can put in chill chest at this point. Even overnight. These candies freeze very well and are first sellers at craft shows and bake sales.
- Remember. Warn people that there is Coconut in these!!! Enjoy!!!!

135. Chocolate Coconut Truffles Recipe

Serving: 48 | Prep: | Cook: 10mins | Ready in:

Ingredients

- 1 cup (2 sticks) real butter, softened
- 1 pound confectioner's sugar
- 1/2 can sweetened condensed milk
- 1 11-ounce package shredded coconut
- 1 cup chopped pecans (optional)
- 1/2 teaspoon vanilla extract
- 1/4 bar paraffin wax
- 1 16-ounce package semi-sweet chocolate chips
- waxed paper

Direction

- In large mixing bowl, combine softened butter, confectioner's sugar, sweetened condensed

milk, coconut, and vanilla, and chopped pecans, if desired. Mix until well blended.
- Refrigerate until firm enough to form balls. (Approximately 1 hour)
- Roll into small balls and place on waxed-paper lined baking sheet.
- Chill once again until firm.
- In double-boiler, melt paraffin wax and chocolate chips until melted and smooth.
- Dip coconut balls into chocolate mixture using toothpicks and place on waxed paper to set.
- May sprinkle additional coconut on top as garnish!
- Refrigerate in plastic container with lid.
- We make several layers with waxed paper to prevent sticking together.
- These also freeze well!

136. Chocolate Dipped Peanut Butter Balls Recipe

Serving: 36 | Prep: | Cook: 15mins | Ready in:

Ingredients

- 4 1/4 cups confectioners' sugar
- 2 cups creamy peanut butter
- 1 stick (4 ounces) unsalted butter, at room temperature
- 3 cups crisp puffed rice cereal
- 12 ounces semisweet chocolate, coarsely chopped
- 12 ounces milk chocolate, coarsely chopped
- 2 tablespoons vegetable oil

Direction

- Have ready several large baking sheets lined with parchment paper.
- In a large bowl, using an electric mixer on low speed or by hand, combine the confectioners' sugar, peanut butter and butter until well blended. Add the puffed rice cereal and mix well. Using your hands, form the mixture into walnut-size balls (about 1 generous tablespoon each) and place them on a tray. Cover and refrigerate for about 1 hour, or until firm.
- Melt the chocolates in a bowl set over a saucepan of barely boiling water or in the microwave. Add the oil and stir until smooth. Using a fork and working with 1 chilled peanut butter ball at a time, dip the balls into the melted chocolate mixture, rolling to coat evenly. Shake off any excess chocolate and transfer to the lined baking sheets. Set aside for at least 2 hours to set.
- The peanut butter balls can sit for as long as 8 hours at room temperature before serving. Refrigerate in an airtight container for up to 2 weeks.
- A variation I found that looks yummy as well!
- Ingredients:
- 2 c. crushed graham crackers
- 2 c. powdered sugar
- 2 c. peanut butter (creamy or chunky, your choice)
- 1/4 c. butter (barely melted in the microwave)
- Dipping chocolate
- Mix together the first 4 ingredients as you would a pie crust. Chill in the fridge for at least 1 hour.
- Melt the dipping chocolate. Roll peanut butter mixture into small balls, and dip into the chocolate. Allow to set on wax paper. Chill until served.

137. Christmas Bon Bons Recipe

Serving: 24 | Prep: | Cook: 10mins | Ready in:

Ingredients

- 8 ounces cream cheese softened
- 1/2 cup butter flavored shortening
- 2 cups sifted all purpose flour
- 1-1/2 cups sifted confectioners' sugar
- 20 ounces maraschino cherries drained

Direction

- In a medium bowl stir together shortening and cream cheese until well blended.
- Stir in flour using hands to help form a dough.
- If mixture seems too dry add a couple teaspoons of water.
- Cover and chill several hours or overnight.
- Preheat oven to 375 then lightly grease cookie sheets.
- Before rolling out the dough dust rolling surface heavily with confectioners' sugar.
- Roll dough out to 1/8" thickness then cut into strips.
- Place a cherry on the end of each strip then roll up each strip starting with the cherry.
- Place on prepared cookie sheets and dust with a little of the confectioners' sugar.
- Bake 10 minutes in the preheated oven.
- Cookies should brown slightly then dust again with confectioners' sugar.
- Allow cookies to cool before serving as the cherries will be very hot.

138. Christmas Crack Recipe

Serving: 24 | Prep: | Cook: 20mins | Ready in:

Ingredients

- 2 cups of the following:
- M and Ms
- Square pretzels
- peanuts
- plain Cheerios
- rice or Corn Chex cereal
- 2 bags of white chocolate morsels

Direction

- Mix the dry ingredients together in large bowl.
- Microwave (slowly) the white chocolate morsels. Pour melted morsels over the dry ingredients and mix well. Pour out onto wax paper to about 1 inch thick. Let cool. Break apart. Store in the fridge.

139. Christmas Cracker Candy Recipe

Serving: 4 | Prep: | Cook: 12mins | Ready in:

Ingredients

- 1/4 lb saltine crackers
- 1/2 lb (2 sticks; 1 cup) butter
- 1 cup sugar
- 12 oz white chocolate chips
- 1/2 cup finely chopped pistachio nuts
- Red and green sugar crystals, opt.

Direction

- Preheat oven to 350 degrees. Line a large cookie sheet (with sides) with saltine crackers, having edges touching. In a medium saucepan, melt butter and sugar together. Bring to low boil, and simmer until mixture is white and frothy. Pour butter mixture over saltines, using a spatula to spread and cover all crackers. Bake 10 minutes or until golden brown. Remove from oven and sprinkle chips over crackers. Return baking sheet to oven for 1-2 minutes until chips soften. Remove from oven and spread white chocolate evenly over saltines. Sprinkle with nuts, and if desired, red and green sugar crystals. Refrigerate or freeze until hard. Break into small pieces.

140. Christmas Sweet Treats Recipe

Serving: 24 | Prep: | Cook: 10mins | Ready in:

Ingredients

- 1 package semi-sweet chocolate chips

- 2-3 Tbsp. butter
- 1 egg
- 1-1/2 cups confectioners' sugar
- 1/2 cup coconut or cocoa powder
- 1 cup walnuts, chopped
- 2 cups miniature marshmallows, either plain or colourful

Direction

- Melt butter and chocolate chips over heat in double boiler.
- Remove, cool slightly and blend in egg.
- Stir in powdered sugar, nuts and marshmallows.
- Roll mixture into balls and roll over coconut to cover.
- Spoon onto waxed paper and chill until set.
- Keep refrigerated until ready to serve.

141. Cobblestone Candy Recipe

Serving: 123 | Prep: | Cook: 10mins | Ready in:

Ingredients

- 3-6 ounce packages of semi-sweet chocolate morsel (3 cups)
- 2 cups miniature marshmallows
- 1 cup coarsely chopped nuts; walnut, pecan, peanut, macadamia

Direction

- Melt the semi-sweet morsels in a double boiler.
- Stir until melted and smooth.
- Add marshmallows and nuts.
- Line an 8-inch square pan with aluminum foil.
- Turn chocolate mixture onto the foil-lined pan.
- Let stand until firm.
- Cut into squares.
- Makes 1-2/3 pounds candy.

142. Coconut Bon Bons Recipe

Serving: 4 | Prep: | Cook: | Ready in:

Ingredients

- 15 oz sweetened condensed milk
- 1/2 c butter, or margarine
- 2 c confectioners' sugar
- 12 oz coconut, grated dried
- 24 oz Semi-sweet chocolate
- 4 tb shortening

Direction

- Mix together condensed milk, butter, sugar and coconut.
- Cover with wax paper and chill for 24 hours.
- Melt chocolate with shortening.
- Roll coconut mixture into balls and using a fork dip the balls into the chocolate.
- Drop on wax paper to cool and dry.

143. Coconut Macadamia Truffles Recipe

Serving: 64 | Prep: | Cook: 10mins | Ready in:

Ingredients

- • 8 oz Lindt white chocolate
- • 1 cup salted dry-roasted macadamia nuts (5 oz)
- • 1/4 cup heavy cream
- • 2 tablespoons dark rum
- • 1 1/2 cups finely shredded unsweetened desiccated coconut

Direction

- Finely grind white chocolate in a food processor and transfer to a bowl. Pulse nuts in

food processor until finely ground (be careful not to grind to a paste).
- Bring cream to a simmer in a medium skillet. Remove from heat and stir in rum. Whisk in white chocolate until melted and ganache is smooth. Stir in nuts. Pour ganache into a plastic-wrap–lined 8-inch square baking pan and chill, uncovered, until firm, about 4 hours.
- Invert ganache onto a work surface and remove plastic wrap. Cut ganache into 64 squares and roll each piece between your palms to form a ball. When all balls are formed, roll in coconut to cover completely, then chill truffles, covered, until ready to serve.
- Cooks' note: • Truffles keep, covered and chilled, 1 week.

144. Coconut Mounds Recipe

Serving: 24 | Prep: | Cook: | Ready in:

Ingredients

- 3/4 cup mashed potatoes
- 1 pound powdered sugar
- 1 pound macaroon coconut
- 1/2 teaspoon almond extract

Direction

- Combine all ingredients then roll into balls using powdered sugar to roll.
- Chill in refrigerator for one hour then dip in melted chocolate.

145. Coconut Patties Recipe

Serving: 18 | Prep: | Cook: 10mins | Ready in:

Ingredients

- 1 1/4 C Confectioners sugar
- 1/2 C unsalted butter, cut into small pieces
- 1 egg white
- 1/8 tsp salt
- 1 1/4 C coconut , packed (sweetened or unsweetened)
- 1 1/2 tsp vanilla
- 4 ounce semi-sweet or milk chocolate (I found that 4 wasn't enough & would recommend 8 oz just to be safe)

Direction

- Make the coconut filling: In a medium heatproof bowl set over a pan of simmering water, whisk together the confectioner's sugar, butter, egg white and salt until very liquid and warm to the touch, about 10 minutes.
- Remove from heat and, with a spoon, stir in the coconut and vanilla until well combined. Cover with plastic wrap and refrigerate for 1 to 2 hours, up to overnight.
- When ready to coat the coconut, in a small heatproof bowl set over a pan of simmering water melt the chocolate. When almost melted, turn off the heat and let the chocolate continue to melt completely, stirring occasionally. Keep the bowl over the warm water. If you are using milk chocolate, you will need to add 1 tsp. of vegetable oil while melting.
- Form the balls: Line a small tray with parchment paper. Using a scant ounce of the coconut mixture, roll into a small ball and place on the parchment-paper lined tray. (I used a small scoop to form the balls, to ensure they were uniform in size). Repeat with remaining mixture, forming 18 balls.
- Arrange 18 paper or foil mini-cups on the tray. Gently place one of the balls into the warm melted chocolate and, using two forks, roll the ball in the chocolate until well coated. Life (do not pierce) the coated coconut ball with one of the forks, allowing some of the chocolate to drip back into the bowl, and carefully place in one of the prepared cups. Repeat with the remaining coconut balls and melted chocolate. Refrigerate until the chocolate has hardened and use as desired.

- To Prepare ahead: the rounds can be prepared ahead and will keep for at least 1 week, refrigerated in a covered container.
- I would refrigerate for 1/2 hour or so until they are firm to the touch. The heat from my hands made these soft when I rolled them and it was semi-disastrous when trying to roll them in chocolate. Also, I place just a tad bit of coconut on top, I think it's a little preview of what the eater can expect to find inside. I'm not sure why these are called patties, as they are clearly balls, but I'm sure they would be good too if you gave them a bit of a smush. Or you can make these into a square pan cool and coat in chocolate. To make the real patties.

146. Coconut Almond Candy Bars Recipe

Serving: 0 | Prep: | Cook: 1hours | Ready in:

Ingredients

- 3-1/2 cups sifted powdered sugar
- 1 3-ounce package cream cheese, softened
- 1 teaspoon vanilla
- 1-1/2 cups coconut
- 50 blanched whole almonds (about 1/3 cup)
- 1-1/2 pounds dipping chocolate or confectioner's coating

Direction

- Butter a 12x9-inch piece of foil; set foil aside.
- In a small bowl combine powdered sugar, softened cream cheese, and vanilla.
- Stir in the coconut.
- Turn coconut mixture onto the buttered foil.
- Pat coconut mixture into a 10x5-inch rectangle.
- Cut the mixture into 2x1-inch rectangles.
- Press 2 blanched whole almonds into the top of each rectangle.
- Melt the dipping chocolate or confectioner's coating.
- Carefully dip the rectangles, one at a time, into the melted chocolate.
- Let excess chocolate drip off rectangles.
- Place the dipped rectangles on a baking sheet lined with waxed paper until dry.
- Store tightly covered in a cool, dry place. .

147. Coffee Chocolate Truffles Recipe

Serving: 24 | Prep: | Cook: 5mins | Ready in:

Ingredients

- 12 ounces- (350 g) plain semi-sweet chocolate
- 5- tablespoon (75 ml) heavy cream
- 2 -tablespoon (30 ml) coffee liqueur, such as Tia Maria, Kahula, or Toussaint
- 4- ounces (115 g) good quality white dessert chocolate
- 4- ounces (115 g) good quality milk dessert chocolate

Direction

- Melt 8 ounces of the plain chocolate (semi-sweet) in a bowl set over a pan of barely simmering water.
- Stir in the cream and liqueur, then chill the mixture in the refrigerator for 4 hours, until firm.
- Divide the mixture into 24 equal pieces and quickly roll each into a ball.
- Chill for another 1 hour until they become firm again.
- Melt the remaining plain, white and milk chocolate in separate bowls.
- Using 2 forks carefully dip 8 of the truffles one at a time into the melted milk chocolate.
- Repeat with the white and plain chocolate.
- Place the truffles on a board covered with parchment or foil.
- Leave to set before removing and placing in a serving dish with paper cases.
- Makes 24.

- Variations
- You can changes the flavors by adding one of the following below to the truffle mixture.
- Ginger: stir in 1/4 cup finely chopped crystalized (candied) ginger.
- Candied fruit: stir in 1/3- cup finely chopped candied fruit.
- Pistachio: stir in 1/4- cup chopped skinned pistachio nuts.
- Hazelnut: roll each ball of chilled truffle mixture around a whole skinned hazelnut.
- Raisin: soak 1/4- cup raisins overnight in 1-tablespoon coffee liqueur and stir into the trufle mixture.

148. Cognac Truffles Recipe

Serving: 48 | Prep: | Cook: 10mins | Ready in:

Ingredients

- 3 ounces unsweetened chocolate
- 1-1/4 cup confectioners' sugar
- 1/3 cup butter
- 3 egg yolks
- 2 tablespoons cognac
- Melt chocolate.

Direction

- Combine sugar and butter in bowl then cream together.
- Add egg yolks 1 at a time then stir in melted chocolate and cognac.
- Chill mixture at least one hour then break off pieces and form into balls.
- Roll in coating of your choice and air dry for 1 hour.
- Store in airtight container in very cool place.
- Coatings: ground almonds, cocoa, confectioners' sugar, coconut or chopped pecans.

149. Cool Whip Candy Recipe

Serving: 4 | Prep: | Cook: 2mins | Ready in:

Ingredients

- 3 (8 oz) Hershey Bars
- 2 cartons Cool Whip (medium)
- 1-2 C. vanilla wafer crumbs OR cookie crumbs OR chopped nuts

Direction

- Melt chocolate in microwave. Stir until smooth. Cool slightly. Stir in Cool whip. Drop by teaspoons into crumbs or nuts. Place on waxed paper. Store covered in refrigerator.

150. Copy Cat Chunky Bars Recipe

Serving: 1 | Prep: | Cook: 15mins | Ready in:

Ingredients

- 1 cup semisweet chocolate chips
- 1 can sweetened condensed milk
- 1/8 tsp. salt
- 1 cup nuts (cashews and peanuts)
- 1 cup raisins

Direction

- Melt chocolate in a double boiler
- Add milk and salt and cook until blended and thickened, stirring constantly
- Fold in nuts and raisins
- Drop by tablespoonful onto a cookie sheet lined with parchment paper
- Refrigerate until firm

151. Cranberry Nut Chocolate Bark Recipe

Serving: 12 | Prep: | Cook: 15mins | Ready in:

Ingredients

- 1 cup dried cranberries
- 3/4 cup toasted diced pecans
- 2 2/3 cups chopped semisweet or bittersweet chocolate, melted
- 2 2/3 cups chopped white chocolate, melted

Direction

- Toss the cranberries and pecans together. Set them aside.
- Melt the dark chocolate, and spread it into an 8" x 12" oval on parchment paper.
- Allow the chocolate to set, but not harden completely.
- Melt the white chocolate and mix it with about 3/4 cup of the cranberries and pecans.
- Spread this over the dark chocolate.
- Sprinkle the rest of the nuts and fruit on top, pressing them in gently.
- Allow the candy to cool until hardened, then break it into chunks.

152. Cranberry Orange Almond Bark Recipe

Serving: 24 | Prep: | Cook: 5mins | Ready in:

Ingredients

- 24 ounce package White Bark Coating (Almond Bark)
- 1 1/2 cups toasted slivered almonds
- 1 1/2 cups dried cranberries
- grated zest of one orange

Direction

- Melt bark coating in microwave in a large bowl per package directions, stirring until smooth.
- Stir in remaining ingredients until coated and well mixed.
- Quickly spread candy on 18 inch long sheet of waxed paper into a thin layer. A large, offset icing spatula works well for this.
- Let cool until set, then break up into pieces.
- Store tightly covered.

153. Cranberry Orange White Chocolate Fudge Recipe

Serving: 64 | Prep: | Cook: 11mins | Ready in:

Ingredients

- 2 Tbs   butter
- 2/3 cup   evaporated milk
- 1 2/3 cups   sugar
- 1/2 tsp   salt
- 2 cups   mini marshmallows
- 1 tsp   vanilla
- 1 1/2 cups   good quality white chocolate
- 3/4-1 cup   orange flavored dried cranberries (use plain if that's what you have)
- 1/2 cup   chopped walnuts (optional)
- grated zest of one orange

Direction

- Butter an 8" square pan, or line with parchment.
- In a medium saucepan, combine butter, milk, sugar and salt.
- Bring to a boil over medium heat, stirring constantly for 5 minutes.
- Remove from heat.
- Stir in marshmallows, chocolate chips, cranberries, nuts, vanilla and orange zest.
- Stir quickly for 1 minute until the marshmallows melt and blend.
- Pour into pan, cool, and cut into squares.

154. Cranberry White Chocolate Fudge Recipe

Serving: 12 | Prep: | Cook: 10mins | Ready in:

Ingredients

- 2-1/2 cups powder sugar
- 2/3 cup milk
- 1/4 cup butter
- 12 ounces white chocolate coarsely chopped
- 1/2 teaspoon almond extract
- 3/4 cup dried cranberries
- 3/4 cup toasted almond slices

Direction

- Line square pan with foil then grease foil.
- Mix powder sugar and milk in a heavy saucepan.
- Over medium heat add butter and stir constantly and bring to boil.
- Without stirring boil constantly for 5 minutes.
- Over low heat add chocolate and almond extract.
- Stir then whisk until chocolate melts and mixture is smooth.
- Stir in dried fruit and toasted almonds then pour mixture into prepared pan.
- Refrigerate 2 hours until firm then invert pan and peel off foil then cut into squares.

155. Creamy Chocolate Fudge Recipe

Serving: 12 | Prep: | Cook: | Ready in:

Ingredients

- 1 (7 oz.) jar marshmallow creme
- 1 1/2 c. white sugar
- 2/3 c. evaporated milk
- 1/4 c. butter
- 1/4 t. salt
- 2 c. milk chocolate chips
- 1 c. semi-sweet chocolate chips
- 1/2 cup nuts
- 1 t. vanilla

Direction

- Line an 8 x 8 inch pan with aluminum foil. Set aside.
- In a large saucepan over medium heat, combine marshmallow cream, sugar, evaporated milk, butter and salt. Bring to a full boil and cook for 5 minutes, stirring constantly.
- Remove from heat and pour in semi-sweet chocolate chips and milk chocolate chips. Stir until chocolate is melted and mixture is smooth. Stir in nuts and vanilla. Pour into prepared pan. Chill in refrigerator for 2 hours, or until firm.
- Yummy good! :D

156. Crispy Chocolate Peanut Butter Bars Recipe

Serving: 26 | Prep: | Cook: 8mins | Ready in:

Ingredients

- 1/2 cup lite corn syrup
- 1/4 cup brn sugar (packed)
- 1/4 tsp salt
- 1 cup peanut butter
- 1 tsp vanilla x-tract
- 2 cups rice crispies
- 1 cup corn flakes
- 1 1/4 cup semi-sweet morsels (8 oz)

Direction

- In medium sauce-pan combine 1st 3 ingredients, (corn syrup, brown sugar, salt) bring to full boil over med-hi heat.

- Remove from heat and add the peanut butter and vanilla, stirring until smooth and blended.
- Cool for 5 minutes, while cooling, butter 13x9 inch baking dish.
- Now add the rice krispies, and corn flakes.
- Stir until almost incorporated and add the chocolate morsels.
- They will melt slightly.
- Press mixture into buttered dish, cut into squares.
- Cover with plastic wrap.
- Place in the fridge for 15-20 minutes, or until hard.

157. Crock Pot Candy Recipe

Serving: 2 | Prep: | Cook: 180mins | Ready in:

Ingredients

- 2-lbs of almond bark
- 12-oz. bag of chocolate chips
- 1 4-oz. bar of German chocolate
- 2-lbs of nuts (can use peanuts, mixed, cashews, etc)

Direction

- Put everything in a crock pot. Set to low setting. Cover and do no open for 3 hrs. After 3 hrs. open and stir all together. Drop by spoonfuls on waxed paper. They will harden in a few minutes.
- Makes approximately 200 peanut clusters and they are very, very good.
- Can also add some dried cherries if you would like.

158. Crock Pot Chocolate Fritos Candy Recipe

Serving: 4 | Prep: | Cook: 180mins | Ready in:

Ingredients

- 2 cups Fritos
- 2 cups pretzels
- 1 stick (1/2 cup) butter
- 1/2 cup brown sugar
- 2 tablespoons peanut butter
- 12 ounces chocolate chips
- 1/2 cup peanuts or honey roasted nuts

Direction

- Smash Fritos and pretzels in plastic bag.
- Line a 13 x 9-inch pan with foil or parchment paper.
- Place butter, brown sugar, peanut butter and chocolate chips in crock pot and cook on HIGH for 1 - 2 hours until melted and mixed well.
- Stir in Fritos and pretzels and pour into pan. Sprinkle peanuts on top and refrigerate until set. Break into pieces.

159. Crockpot White Chocolate Candy Recipe

Serving: 4 | Prep: | Cook: 120mins | Ready in:

Ingredients

- 16 oz jar unsalted dry roasted peanuts
- 16 oz jar salted dry-roasted peanuts
- 4 oz German chocolate squares
- 12 oz chocolate chips
- 24 oz bark* white chocolate
- Pam spray

Direction

- Spray Pam in crock pot.
- Put into the crock pot in order as written. Cook on low for 2 hours. Stir mixture and dip out by spoonfuls onto wax paper.
- *Barks are slabs of chocolate used for candy making.

160. Darianas Easy Chocolate Truffles Recipe

Serving: 60 | Prep: | Cook: 120mins | Ready in:

Ingredients

- Two 12 oz. packages semi-sweet chocolate chips
- Three 4 oz. sweet chocolate bars (chopped)
- One 7 oz. jar marshmallow cream
- 4 1/2 cups sugar
- 2 Tablespoons butter
- One 12 oz. can evaporated milk

Direction

- FILLING:
- Place one 12 oz. package of chocolate chips, plus all the chocolate bars and the marshmallow cream into a heat-proof bowl.
- Heat sugar, butter, and evaporated milk in a heavy-bottomed sauce pan until sugar dissolves and mixture comes to a full boil.
- Boil mixture for 5 minutes, stirring constantly.
- Pour hot mixture into the bowl of chocolate and mix well. (The resulting mixture will become firm and cool enough to scoop.)
- Line one cookie sheet with Saran Wrap.
- Using a small scoop, form individual balls and place on cookie sheet.
- Refrigerate until firm and chilled.
- CHOCOLATE COATING:
- In the top part of a double boiler melt the second package of chocolate chips and stir until smooth.
- Using your hands, roll the refrigerated chocolate balls until smooth and then place back in the refrigerator to chill for a few minutes. (Chilling sets the chocolate to make dipping easier.)
- Rest each ball on a fork and dip into the melted chocolate. Then gently place the ball on a clean cookie sheet lined with wax paper.
- Refrigerate the truffles or serve immediately at room temperature.

161. Dark Chocolate ButterCrunch Recipe

Serving: 24 | Prep: | Cook: 20mins | Ready in:

Ingredients

- 1 cup (2 sticks, 1/2 pound) butter*
- 1 1/2 cups (12 ounces) sugar
- 3 tablespoons water
- 1 tablespoon light corn syrup
- 2 cups (8 ounces) diced pecans or slivered almonds, toasted
- 1 pound semisweet or bittersweet chocolate, finely chopped (chocolate chips are an easy solution here; you'll need about 2 2/3 cups)
- *If you use unsalted butter, add 1/2 teaspoon salt.

Direction

- In a large, deep saucepan, melt the butter. Stir in the sugar, water and corn syrup, and bring the mixture to a boil. Boil gently, over medium heat, until the mixture reaches hard-crack stage (300°F on an instant-read or candy thermometer), about 20 minutes. The syrup will seem to take a long time to come to the hard-crack stage, but be patient; all of a sudden it will darken, and at that point you need to take its temperature and see if it's ready. (If you don't have a thermometer, test a dollop in ice water; it should immediately harden to a brittleness sufficient that you'll be able to snap it in two, without any bending or softness). Pay attention; too long on the heat, and the syrup will burn. And what a waste of good butter and sugar that would be!
- While the sugar mixture is gently bubbling, spread half of the nuts, in a fairly closely packed, even single layer, on a lightly greased baking sheet. Top with half the chocolate.

- When the syrup is ready, pour it quickly and evenly over the nuts and chocolate. Immediately top with the remaining chocolate, then the remaining nuts. Wait several minutes, then gently, using the back of a spatula, press down on the chocolate-nut layer to spread the chocolate around evenly.
- While the candy is still slightly warm, use a spatula to loosen it from the baking sheet. When cool, break it into uneven chunks.
- Yield: about 24 big bite-sized pieces, if you want to be scientific about it.

162. Dark Chocolate Cococans Recipe

Serving: 30 | Prep: | Cook: 10mins | Ready in:

Ingredients

- 1 14 ounce bag of sweetened shredded coconut
- 1 bag of dark chocolate chips-you can use semi-sweet
- 6 ounces of sweetened condensed milk
- 1/2 tsp vanilla extract
- 1/2 tsp almond extract
- 2 cups of powdered sugar
- 1 pound of large pecan halves
- 1/4 cup of honey
- 1/4 tsp. salt
- (butter for your hands!)

Direction

- Mix the condensed milk with the sugar
- Add extracts and salt and mix well.
- Press this mixture evenly into a 13x9 pan covered in Release aluminum foil with extra foil on sides for easy removal.
- Place in the freezer for one hour.
- Remove the pan from the freezer and remove the candy from the pan using the foil.
- Cut into small 2 inch squares
- Using buttered hands, roll the candy into small log-shaped pieces, rounding off the edges slightly.
- Dip only the bottom of one pecan half lightly into the honey and press on top of each coconut log or piece. (Honey is the glue!)
- Place all of the candy on wax paper or a silicon mat (or use the foil!)
- Melt the dark chocolate in a glass bowl or large glass measuring cup.
- Using 2 forks, quickly dip each candy and pecan into the chocolate and allow excess to drip off.
- Place dipped candy back on foil or waxed paper to dry and set.

163. Dark Chocolate Fudge With Almonds Recipe

Serving: 16 | Prep: | Cook: 10mins | Ready in:

Ingredients

- 12 ounces dark chocolate
- 8 ounces softened cream cheese
- 3 cups powdered sugar sifted
- 1 tablespoon vanilla extract
- 1/2 cup slivered almonds

Direction

- Melt chocolate as directed on package then beat cream cheese in large bowl with electric mixture until smooth then gradually beat in sugar on low speed until well blended.
- Add melted chocolate and vanilla and mix well.
- Stir in nuts.
- Spread evenly in foiled lined square pan.
- Garnish with additional nuts and refrigerate at least 1 hour.
- Cut into squares and store in refrigerator.

164. Decadent Fudge Recipe

Serving: 8 | Prep: | Cook: 12mins | Ready in:

Ingredients

- chocolate, peanutbutter(Reeses)butterscotch chips. Choose a mix of 11.5 oz measure them out...
- 5 Oz sweet condensed milk per 11.5 ozs.
- 2 Tbls butter per 11.5 ozs of chips.
- 2 ozs nuts of choice per 11.5 ozs chips.
- 1/2 tsp vanilla & 1/2 tsp almond extract per 11.5 oz of chips.
- Some people like minty taste use only some sprinkled on top of fudge Creme De Mint if you like.

Direction

- Add all except nuts to microwavable bowl and heat 1-2 minutes then carefully remove from microwave place on pads.
- Stir and add choice of nuts. Pour into 8" pan that has been sprayed with vegetable oil. Place in refrigerator and allow to cool 1-2 hours.
- You might score before placing in refrigerator. Makes 16 large pieces.
- For a party double everything for 32 pieces and place in (2) 8" pans or (1) 9"X13" pan.

165. Deep Fried Candy Bars Recipe

Serving: 0 | Prep: | Cook: 4mins | Ready in:

Ingredients

- 4 pop sticks
- 3 cups vegetable oil
- 4 candy bars, such as Mars Bars, Snickers, and milky Ways
- powdered sugar
- 1 cup all-purpose flour
- 1 cup milk
- 1/2 tbsp sugar
- 1/4 tsp baking soda
- 1/4 tsp salt

Direction

- Preheat oil in a large, heavy pot over medium-high heat. Line a baking sheet with parchment paper.
- Pierce each candy bar with a pop stick, place on the prepared baking sheet, and refrigerate 30 minutes.
- Whisk all batter ingredients until little to know lumps remain. One at a time, dip chilled candy bars in batter and coat well.
- Once oil reaches 390°F, carefully place candy bars in oil one at a time and fry about 3 to 4 minutes. Drain on a paper towel, sprinkle with powdered sugar if desired, and serve hot.

166. Deep Fried Candy Bars Recipe

Serving: 8 | Prep: | Cook: 4hours | Ready in:

Ingredients

- Deep-Fried Candy Bars
- Ingredients for Deep-Fried Candy Bars
- To make deep-fried candy bars, you will need:
- •Up to 8 full-size candy bars
- •2 quarts of vegetable oil
- •1.5 cups flour
- •1 tsp baking soda
- •1/2 tsp salt
- •1 cup milk
- •2 tbsp white vinegar
- •You will also need a candy/deep fry thermometer
- Freeze Candy Bars
- Before you fry the candy bars you want them really cold, so unwrap them and place them on a baking sheet and freeze them for at least 3 hours.

Direction

- Prepare the Oil for Frying
- When you're ready to fry, get the oil ready. Pour it into a heavy-duty pot over medium-high heat and insert your candy thermometer. You want the oil to come to 375, which takes a while. Keep one eye on the oil while you get the rest of the ingredients ready.
- Mix Ingredients for Batter
- Place ½ cup of the flour on a plate or in a pie tin, and set it aside. Place the remaining cup of flour in a medium bowl, and stir in the baking soda and salt.
- Combine the milk, vinegar, and 1 tablespoon of vegetable oil and mix it together. Add the wet ingredients to the dry and whisk them until it's really smooth and there aren't any lumps.
- Dip Candy Bars
- Once the oil is at 375, it's time to start dipping. If you have a huge pan you can probably do several at once, but it's easiest to just fry one at a time.
- Frying the Candy Bars
- Roll a candy bar in the flour then dip it in the batter, making sure that it's completely covered. Carefully lower it into the hot oil-- you don't want to get too close and burn your fingers, but be carefully not to throw it in and cause oil to splatter. Use a slotted spoon to push down on the candy bar and keep it submerged in the oil so it cooks evenly.
- Once it's a beautiful, golden brown color, remove the candy bar from the oil and place it on a plate covered with paper towel to soak up the excess grease. Repeat the battering and frying process with the remaining candy bars.
- Serving Deep-Fried Candy Bars
- After your candy bars are fried, let them cool slightly, then dust them lightly with powdered sugar and serve while still slightly warm. The outside is crisp but the insides liquefy and become this awesome gooey, chocolaty, caramel heaven. They are outrageous!

167. Delicious Copycat Almond Joy Bars Recipe

Serving: 26 | Prep: | Cook: 10mins | Ready in:

Ingredients

- Copycat almond Joy Bars
- (26 servings)
- 4 c (8 1/2-oz) shredded coconut
- 1/4 c light corn syrup
- 1 pk (11 1/2-oz) milk chocolate pieces
- 1/4 c vegetable shortening
- 26 Whole natural almonds (1-oz)

Direction

- Line two large cookie sheets with waxed paper.
- Set large wire cooling rack on paper; set aside.
- Place coconut in large bowl; set aside.
- Place corn syrup in a 1-cup glass measure. Microwave on high (100%) 1 minute or until syrup boils.
- Immediately pour over coconut. Work warm syrup into coconut using the back of a wooden spoon until coconut is thoroughly coated.
- This takes a little time, there is enough syrup.
- Using 1 level measuring tablespoon of coconut, shape into a ball by squeezing coconut firmly in palm of one hand, then rolling between both palms.
- (HINT: Measure out all of the coconut then roll into balls.)
- Place 2 inches apart on wire racks. Let dry 10 minutes.
- Reroll coconut balls so there are no loose ends of coconut sticking up.
- Place milk chocolate and shortening in a 4-cup glass measure or 1 1/2 quart microwave-safe bowl. Microwave on high 1 to 2 minutes or until mixture can be stirred smooth and is glossy; stirring once or twice.
- Working quickly, spoon 1 level measuring tablespoon of the chocolate over each coconut

- ball, making sure chocolate coats and letting excess chocolate drip down onto waxed paper.
- While chocolate coating is still soft, lightly press whole almond on top of each.
- Let stand to set or place in refrigerator. Store in a single layer in airtight container.
- Keeps best if refrigerated.

168. Delicious Homemade Creme Filled Chocolate Candy Recipe

Serving: 24 | Prep: | Cook: 5mins | Ready in:

Ingredients

- Centers:
- 1 cup of sweetened condensed milk
- 1/4 lb softened margarine
- 2 1/2 lbs powdered sugar
- 1 tsp vanilla (or any extract you'd like! mint or maple are great inside chocolates!)
- 1/2 cup of ground up pecan or walnut halves- optional

Direction

- Blend ingredients, then shape into 1" balls and chill for a few hours or overnight.
- Using a toothpick, dip each ball into the chocolate (recipe below) and cool on waxed paper or tin foil.
- (Cover the toothpick hole with a little teensy bit more of the chocolate, using the toothpick)
- Chocolate:
- 12 oz. of semi-sweet bits
- 6 oz. unsweetened chocolate
- Melt in microwave or in a double boiler to dip the centers (above) in! Keep the chocolate warm while dipping centers.

169. Deviled Egg Candy Recipe

Serving: 24 | Prep: | Cook: 15mins | Ready in:

Ingredients

- 1 pound white confectionery coating
- Yellow powdered candy coloring
- 1-1 1/2 cups (approx.) Rice Krispies cereal, may need more or less
- Red colored sanding sugar

Direction

- Melt chocolate on top of double boiler or in the microwave until completely melted and smooth.
- Fill the cavities of the egg mold and put into fridge or freezer to set up.
- Meanwhile, color remaining chocolate with the yellow powder to achieve an egg yolk shade.
- Mix the rice krispies in until thick enough to be able to mound onto the egg without dripping.
- Unmold the eggs onto waxed paper and immediately dollop a mound of the "yolk" mixture onto each to resemble the filling.
- Sprinkle with the red colored sugar to resemble the "paprika" while still soft.
- Allow to dry completely.
- NOTE: The amount of rice krispies that are used varies depending on the consistency of the chocolate once it is melted, so you may need more than called for. Also, if you have any "yolk" mixture left just make small mounds onto waxed paper, allow to dry and have an instant treat.

170. Diabetic Chocolate Candy Recipe

Serving: 30 | Prep: | Cook: 10mins | Ready in:

Ingredients

- 3 oz. package cream cheese (softened)
- 2 tablespoons skim milk
- 1 1/2 teaspoons white vanilla extract
- 1 cup powdered sugar replacement (Splenda)
- 1 recipe semisweet dipping chocolate (below)
- Beat cream cheese, milk and vanilla until fluffy; stir
- in powdered sugar replacement. Form into 30 balls and
- dip each one in chocolate.
- Yield: 30 creams
- Calories 1 cream: 31
- Exchange 1 cream: 1/4 low fat milk
- Semisweet Dipping chocolate is Below

Direction

- Semisweet Dipping Chocolate
- 1 cup non-fat dry milk powder
- 1/3 cup cocoa
- 2 tablespoons paraffin wax
- 1/2 cup water
- 1 tablespoon liquid shortening
- 1 tablespoon liquid sugar replacement
- Combine milk powder, cocoa and wax in food processor or blender; blend to soft powder.
- Pour into top of double boiler and add water, stirring to blend. Add liquid shortening.
- Place over hot (not boiling) water, and cook and stir until wax pieces are completely dissolved and mixture is thick, smooth and creamy.
- Remove from heat. Stir in sugar replacement and let cool slightly.
- Dip candies according to recipe. Shake off excess chocolate. Place on very lightly greased waxed paper and allow to cool completely. (If candies do not remove easily, slightly warm the waxed paper over electric burner or with clothes iron.)
- Store in a cool place.
- Yield: 1 cup
- Calories full recipe: 427
- Exchange full recipe: 3 low fat milk

171. Dipped Chocolate Graham Sticks Recipe

Serving: 40 | Prep: | Cook: 3mins | Ready in:

Ingredients

- 1 box chocolate Graham Sticks (I use honey Maid)
- 12 ounces white chocolate chips, or any white chocolate candy coating
- holiday cookie decorations, optional

Direction

- Melt the white chocolate in the microwave. I use a 1 cup measuring cup, so that I have a narrow, deep container, making it easier to dip the sticks. I just fill it with the white chocolate chips, melt it, and keep adding more chips and melting it as I need more coating.
- Have a large piece of waxed paper on the counter.
- Dip each graham stick halfway into the melted white chocolate.
- Set it on the waxed paper, and sprinkle with holiday edible decorations (tinted sugars or any of the cute decorations that are now available for sprinkling on cookies, etc.).
- Once the melted white coating has hardened back up, the sticks will peel right off the waxed paper and you can store them in a container.

172. Dressed Up Chocolate Bark Recipe

Serving: 12 | Prep: | Cook: 10mins | Ready in:

Ingredients

- chocolate (milk or semi-sweet)

- Classic Toppings: dried fruits such as apricots, raisins, candied orange peel, cranberries, and cherries. toasted nuts including hazelnuts, pecans, almonds, and pistachios.
- Contemporary Toppings: caramelized cocoa nibs (see recipe), cereal, candied ginger, and dried fruits such as pineapple, blueberries, and strawberries. toasted pumpkin seeds and pine nuts.

Direction

- Line a chilled baking sheet with parchment paper. Pour warm (not hot), melted chocolate into the prepared pan.
- Spread the chocolate evenly to about 1/8 inch thick using a small offset spatula. Sprinkle toppings on the chocolate and place in the freezer to set, approximately 20 minutes.
- For even-sized pieces, cut up bark before it sets completely. If you like a more rustic look, allow the bark to harden completely before breaking it up into pieces. Store in a cool, dry place.

173. EASY CHOCOLATE CLUSTERS Recipe

Serving: 54 | Prep: | Cook: 15mins | Ready in:

Ingredients

- one 8 ounce package (8 squares) white almond bark
- one 12 ounce package semi-sweet chocolate chips
- one 16 ounce jar salted, roasted peanuts

Direction

- In a large saucepan, start melting almond bark over VERY low heat. When it's almost completely melted, add chocolate chips and melt together, stirring until smooth (the almond bark melts much slower than the chocolate chips, so it's a good idea to let it melt most of the way before adding the chips so the chips don't overcook). Remove from heat and stir in peanuts. Cool slightly. Drop by teaspoon onto wax paper. Let sit until firm. Store in airtight container.
- Note: These make nice gifts presented in decorative candy papers and arranged on a nice plate or in a fancy tin. I get about 9 dozen medium sized pieces of candy. If each person eats only two pieces (just try to!) that makes 54 servings.

174. Eagle Brands Rocky Road Candy Recipe Recipe

Serving: 36 | Prep: | Cook: 2mins | Ready in:

Ingredients

- 2 cups of semi-sweet chocolate chips
- 2 cups of peanuts
- 1 10 ounce bag of mini marshmallows
- 2 TB. butter
- 1 14 ounce can of Eagle Brand sweetened condensed milk
- (from Eaglebrand.com)

Direction

- Place the chocolate, condensed milk and butter in a microwave-proof glass bowl.
- Microwave on High for 3 minutes.
- Remove from microwave and stir until smooth.
- Let this cool for five minutes.
- Line a 13 x 9 pan with wax paper or release aluminum foil.
- After five minutes, fold the peanuts and marshmallows into the chocolate and press down into the pan.
- Cover and refrigerate for 2 hours.
- Cut and serve!
- OR

- Line 13×9-inch baking pan with wax paper. In heavy saucepan, over low heat, melt chocolate chips and butter with EAGLE BRAND®; remove from heat.
- In large bowl, combine peanuts and marshmallows; stir in chocolate mixture. Spread in prepared pan. Chill 2 hours or until firm.
- Remove candy from pan; peel off paper and cut into squares. Store loosely covered at room temperature.
- *****This is great with walnuts instead of peanuts.

175. Earl Grey Tea Chocolate Recipe

Serving: 16 | Prep: | Cook: 48hours | Ready in:

Ingredients

- Loose-Leaf Earl Grey tea
- Dark Chocolate Bar broken into individual squares (Cadbury is excellent)

Direction

- Place chocolate squares -unwrapped of course- in an airtight container (Tupperware or Rubbermaid works well).
- Cover with loose leaf tea; be generous with tea amount!
- Remember that you can drink the tea when you are done flavoring the chocolate! Seal container and let sit undisturbed for 48 hours.
- Taste chocolate for flavor intensity.
- If pleasing, remove from tea and wrap individually in foil. If not flavored enough, let sit longer.
- **
- Other tea flavors would probably work as well; raspberry or orange black teas sound good. Herbal teas don't work!

176. Easiest Chocolate Candy Recipe

Serving: 12 | Prep: | Cook: 4mins | Ready in:

Ingredients

- wax paper
- 1 package butterscotch chips
- 1/2 package chocolate chips
- 1 can Spanish peanuts (or whatever kind you prefer)

Direction

- Heat the bowl in the microwave for 1 minute on high before you put in the chips.
- Add one package butterscotch chips and one half of the package of chocolate chips.
- Microwave on high about 2-4 minutes depending on your microwave, until melt enough to mix.
- Add as many Spanish peanuts as you like and stir.
- Using a tablespoon, spoon mixture onto wax paper (I usually put the wax paper on a cookie sheet).
- Put in refrigerator or freezer until solid enough to eat (like about 15 minutes).
- Enjoy!!!

177. Easiest Chocolate Candy With Flavors Recipe

Serving: 12 | Prep: | Cook: 5mins | Ready in:

Ingredients

- 1 1/2 large (8 oz) chocolate bar with almonds
- 9 oz tub Cool Whip
- 1/2 tsp peppermint flavoring Or favorite flavoring, like cherry, pineapple, orange, almond, rum.. so many flavors to use)

- crushed nuts. (I use almonds)

Direction

- Melt chocolate bars in top of double boiler, remove from heat and stir. Add Cool Whip and peppermint to melted chocolate and beat until well blended. Refrigerate 45 minutes, remove and form spoonfuls of mixture into balls and roll balls in crushed nuts.
- Return balls to refrigerator for at least one hour before serving.

178. Easy Bark Cookies Recipe

Serving: 20 | Prep: | Cook: | Ready in:

Ingredients

- 1 pkg. almond bark
- 1 c chunky peanut butter
- 2 c miniature marshmallows
- 3 c Rice Krispies

Direction

- Melt almond bark in 200 degree oven.
- Stir in peanut butter.
- Add rest of ingredients and mix well.
- Drop by spoonfuls on waxed paper.

179. Easy Breezy Fudge Recipe

Serving: 8 | Prep: | Cook: 3mins | Ready in:

Ingredients

- 1 pound box of powdered sugar
- 3 eggs (beat with sugar)
- ½ teaspoon vanilla
- Mix together with mixer

- 1 Large package (12oz.) real chocolate chips
- 1 cube of real butter

Direction

- Melt together (butter and chips) over low heat (do not over heat).
- Mix together with sugar mixture.
- Add nuts as many as desired, pour into an 8x8 pan and refrigerate.
- Note: I have doubled this recipe and it makes a 9x13 pan very nicely.

180. Easy Chocolate Cashew Clusters Recipe

Serving: 18 | Prep: | Cook: | Ready in:

Ingredients

- 2 cups semisweet or milk chocolate chips
- 1 tablespoon shortening-optional
- 2 cups unsalted or lightly salted cashews- whole or very roughly chopped.

Direction

- In a small saucepan over medium low heat, combine chocolate chips and shortening.
- Stir constantly until melted.
- Remove from heat immediately and let stand for 5 minutes.
- Add cashews and stir until well coated.
- Drop in tablespoons onto wax paper lined cookie sheet.
- Chill until set.
- If using microwave to melt chocolate, shortening may be omitted.
- Keep refrigerated.

181. Easy Chocolate Dipped Coconut Creams Recipe

Serving: 96 | Prep: | Cook: 10mins | Ready in:

Ingredients

- 1 (14-ounce) can sweetened condensed milk
- 1/4 cup butter, melted
- 1 TBSP. lemon juice
- 8 cups sifted powdered sugar
- 1 (7-ounce) can flaked coconut
- 1/2 cup toasted almonds, finely chopped
- 16 ounces chocolate-flavored candy coating

Direction

- Combine the condensed milk, butter, and the lemon juice. Stir well.
- Gradually stir in the powdered sugar. Mix well.
- Add coconut and the almonds. Mix well.
- Shape into 3/4-inch balls.
- Cover and freeze 4 hours or until firm.
- Put candy coating in top of a double boiler. Bring water to a boil.
- Reduce heat to low. Cook until the coating melts.
- Remove from the heat but leave the coating over the water.
- Using 2 forks dip frozen candy balls in melted coating.
- Allow the excess to drip off.
- Cool on wax paper.
- Store in the refrigerator.
- ....
- To make a nice presentation but the candies in paper candy cups.
- Yields 8 dozen

182. Easy Chocolate Mint Covered Pretzils Recipe

Serving: 1100 | Prep: | Cook: 5mins | Ready in:

Ingredients

- 1 oz bakers unsweetened chocolate (if desired)
- 1 bag (12 oz) semisweet chocolate chips
- 1/2 bag mint chips
- 1 1/2 tsp. shortening
- salted pretzils (I just used the little ones)

Direction

- Put a pan inside a pan of water (double boiler).
- Melt on medium heat, unsweetened chocolate, semisweet chocolate chips and 1 tsp. shortening in the pan that does not have water in it.
- Place pretzels into melt goodness, remove with tongs and place about 1/2 inch apart on aluminum foil or a cookie sheet.
- Place coated pretzels in the refrigerator for about 20 minutes until coating is hard.
- Meanwhile, melt mint chips and 1/2 tsp. shortening in another double boiler as above.
- Remove pretzels from fridge and drizzle mint over top of them.
- Place back in fridge to cool.
- Remove from foil. Walla!

183. Easy Chocolate Mint Truffles Recipe

Serving: 10 | Prep: | Cook: 3mins | Ready in:

Ingredients

- * 1/3 cup semisweet mint-chocolate morsels or plain or Raspberry flavor.
- * 4 ounce cream cheese
- * 1-16 ounce package powdered sugar, sifted
- * 1/4 cup unsweetened cocoa
- * 1/4 cup additional powdered sugar

Direction

- PREPARATION:

- Place 1/3 cup morsels in a medium glass bowl and microwave at high 1 minute or until morsels are almost melted, stirring until smooth. Let cool. Add the softened cream cheese to melted morsels, beat at medium speed of mixer until smooth.
- Add powdered sugar and beat until well blended. Press mixture into a 6 inch square on heavy duty plastic wrap, cover and chill at least one hour.
- Cut mixture into 48 squares. Roll each square into a ball and place on wax paper. Roll half in unsweetened cocoa and half in powdered sugar. Melt 2T mint chips and drizzle each ball. Serve at room temperature. Can be frozen.

184. Easy Chocolate Truffles Recipe

Serving: 60 | Prep: | Cook: 2mins | Ready in:

Ingredients

- 1 1/2 pk chocolate;semi sweet; 12 squares
- 1 8 ounces Pkg Cream Cheese; softened
- 3 c powdered sugar
- 1 TB coffee liqueur
- 1 TB orange liqueur
- 1 TB almond liqueur
- Nuts; chopped
- unsweetened cocoa
- flake coconut
- Sprinkles; colored

Direction

- Cook chocolate in large microwave-safe bowl on HIGH for 2 minutes, stirring halfway through heating time. Stir until chocolate is melted.
- Beat cream cheese in large bowl with electric mixer on medium speed until smooth. Gradually beat in sugar until well blended. Stir in chocolate until blended. Divide mixture into thirds, add 1 flavor liqueur to each third; mix well. Refrigerate about 3 hours or until firm. Shape into 1-inch balls. Roll in nuts, cocoa, coconut or sprinkles. Keep in refrigerator. Makes 5 dozen

185. Easy White Chocolate Popcorn Recipe

Serving: 6 | Prep: | Cook: 10mins | Ready in:

Ingredients

- 2 bags (regular butter) microwave popcorn
- 1/2 bag of white chocolate morsels (about 5.5oz)
- 1/2 med bag of peanut M&M's (about 5.5oz)

Direction

- Pop both bags of popcorn according to directions on box and place in large mixing bowl, try to keep the unpopped kernels out.
- Melt morsels in micro for about 1 1/2min (cooking times vary by micros, but watch closely as not to burn).
- Pour melted chocolate over popcorn, careful it's hot. Mix well with a spatula and add candies (I use peanut M&M's). Stir well.
- Place in fridge to allow popcorn to "set" for about 15min. It's ready to go. It doesn't have to stay in the fridge at all after that, it just helps the chocolate cool quickly. I will also zip lock baggy a batch, fits in a gallon bag, and refill my bowl if I am having company :) Super Simple, *don't tell the guests it's chocolate, let them think it's regular popcorn and watch the looks on their faces!!

186. Edible Chocolate Body Paint For Romantics Recipe

Serving: 30 | Prep: | Cook: 5mins | Ready in:

Ingredients

- 1/3 cup granulated sugar
- 1 pinch kosher salt
- 3 tbl water
- 2 tbl butter
- 1/4 cup cocoa powder
- 1/2 teaspoon vanilla extract
- 1/2 teaspoon (or more) your favorite alcohol, or to taste
- Heating pad
- Fine soft brush for painting
- You can also add flavorings like raspberry, etc. Experiment.

Direction

- Put sugar, salt and water in a small saucepan over medium heat.
- Don't stir but wait for the mixture to come to a boil then reduce heat to a simmer and watch closely until all of the sugar granules have dissolved. Don't touch it or sugar crystals will form and crack the sugar! And don't walk away from it.
- Remove from heat.
- Add butter and stir with a wire whisk until well incorporated.
- Add cocoa powder, vanilla and your choice of alcohol. Whisk until well incorporated.
- Pour into a small crock, mug or other deep container.
- Use the paint as soon as it is cooled enough to be comfortable. The warmer the sauce the easier it is to paint with but you don't want to burn your canvas.
- To keep pliable place on a heating pad on low next to you.
- If the sauce becomes hard because you are pre-occupied, warm it in the microwave for 20 seconds. Stir and test the temperature again before using.
- Stores for a few days in the fridge.

187. English Toffee Recipe

Serving: 16 | Prep: | Cook: 10mins | Ready in:

Ingredients

- 1 cup broken blanched almonds
- 1 cup butter
- 1 cup light brown sugar packed
- 1/2 cup chocolate chips
- 2 tablespoons finely chopped walnuts

Direction

- Toast almonds in a 300 degree oven until lightly browned.
- In a heavy saucepan melt butter slowly then add sugar and mix well.
- Cook slowly stirring constantly until mixture reaches 290 on a candy thermometer.
- Remove from heat and stir in almonds.
- Pour immediately into a buttered cookie tin and spread thin.
- Sprinkle chocolate chips over candy while hot.
- When chips are melted spread out with spatula and sprinkle with finely chopped walnuts.
- Let cool and then break into pieces when chocolate is set.

188. Erins Mini Squares Recipe

Serving: 4 | Prep: | Cook: 1mins | Ready in:

Ingredients

- 1 Hershey chocolate bar (she is firm on the brand!!!)
- 12 mini marshmallows
- 6 whole graham crackers

Direction

- Break the Hershey bar into 12 pieces.
- Break the crackers into 24 squares.
- Place a chocolate piece and marshmallow on 12 cracker squares.
- Top with cracker square.
- Arrange on a microwave safe dish and microwave for 30 seconds to one minute.
- Be careful not to let the marshmallows explode, because then you need to pry the dish off the turntable, pry the turntable out of the microwave, and work for hours to get all the marshmallow off. While mom stands over you not looking too happy. Oh yeah, remember to ask her first, then maybe she'll look a little happier.

189.   Fairy Or Sponge Candy Recipe

Serving: 36 | Prep: | Cook: 30mins | Ready in:

Ingredients

- 2 cups White sugar
- 2 cups dark corn syrup
- 2 tablespoons vinegar (cider is best)
- 2 tablespoons vanilla extract
- 2 tablespoons baking soda

Direction

- Cook sugar, corn syrup, vinegar together in a heavy candy pan covered until it comes to a boil
- Remove cover and cook to 290 degrees on a candy thermometer, then add vanilla, and cook to 300 degrees. DO not stir while boiling.
- Gradually reduce heat to as mixture thickens to prevent scorching.
- Remove from heat and quickly stir in sifted soda. Pour into buttered large cookie sheet as it forms. Do not spread, it will spread itself.
- When cool break into small pieces. Dip into melted chocolate.
- Melt Chocolate (milk or semisweet) in double boiler with 1/2 cake of paraffin wax.

190.   Famous Chocolate Bourbon Balls Recipe

Serving: 12 | Prep: | Cook: 10mins | Ready in:

Ingredients

- chocolate bourbon Balls
- 6 ounces semi-sweet chocolate morsels
- 3 T. corn syrup
- 1/2 cup bourbon
- 2 1/2 cups vanilla wafer crumbs
- 1/2 cup sifted confectioners' sugar
- 1 cup nuts, finely chopped
- Granulated sugar

Direction

- Melt chocolate morsels over simmering water.
- Remove from heat. Add corn syrup and bourbon; set aside.
- In large bowl, combine vanilla wafer crumbs, confectioners' sugar and nuts.
- Add chocolate mixture; mix well. Let stand 30 minutes.
- Form into 1-inch balls. Roll in granulated sugar. Let season in covered container for several days.

191.   Fancy Coffee Cup Truffles Recipe

Serving: 18 | Prep: | Cook: 10mins | Ready in:

Ingredients

- Use the best chocolate you can find!

- 9 oz. bittersweet or semisweet chocolate broken into pieces
- 2/3 c. heavy cream
- 1/3 vanilla bean
- 2 tbsp. unsalted butter
- Pinch of cinnamon
- 3 tbsp. unsweetened cocoa powder
- Sm. pinch of salt
- 1 c. confectioners' sugar, sifted

Direction

- Line the inside of 8 x 4 inch loaf pan with wax paper.
- In top of double boiler over gently simmering water, melt chocolate, stir occasionally. Remove from heat, stir until smooth. Set aside.
- STIR CHOCOLATE SMOOTHE...DO NOT BURN!!
- (Alternatively, microwave chocolate in medium glass or plastic bowl at medium power for 60 seconds, stirring between heating well, until chocolate can be stirred smooth.)
- In small pan warm cream with the vanilla bean over low heat.
- First place cream in a glass measuring cup, then split vanilla bean, scrape it and add bean scrapings to cream.
- Microwave full power 60 seconds. Remove from heat and remove vanilla bean. Gradually stir in cream into the melted chocolate until smooth. Add butter, cinnamon, cocoa and salt. Stir until well mixed. Scrape mixture into prepared pan and smooth top. Cover - refrigerate. (Truffles can be prepared up to 3 days ahead.)
- To unmold run a thin knife around edges. Cut chocolate crosswise into 3/4 inch strips. DO NOT draw knife out by pulling toward you, pull straight up after making cut, holding down chocolate.
- Cut into cubes, place on baking sheet lined with waxed paper. (Can be frozen up to 1 week at this point.)
- Place confectioners' sugar in a bag. Add frozen chocolate cubes to bag in batches, shake. Place on small decorative plate or sugar bowl. Serve with fresh coffee and pitcher of warm milk.

192. Flat Truffles Recipe

Serving: 0 | Prep: | Cook: |Ready in:

Ingredients

- 1/2 cup margarine
- 1/3 cup cocoa
- 3/4 cup icing sugar
- Crushed nuts, for coating

Direction

- Cream margarine until soft.
- Sift in cocoa and blend well.
- Sift in icing sugar. Mix well adding more icing sugar if too soft to roll.
- Shape into a roll.
- Roll in nuts.
- Wrap in plastic and chill for several hours.
- Serve in slices.
- NOTE
- I think it would be nice rolled in toasted coconut, crushed candy canes or any number of things besides nuts. This sounds like a very versatile recipe so let your imagination run wild!

193. Fluted Kisses Cups With Peanut Butter Filling Recipe

Serving: 24 | Prep: | Cook: 1mins |Ready in:

Ingredients

- 72 - hersheys kisses milk chocolate divided ....now here a job the kids can do is take off all the foils lol.......
- 1- cup reeses creamy peanut butter
- 1- cup powdered sugar

- 1- tablespoon butter, softened

Direction

- Line small baking cups (1 3/4 inches in diameter) with small paper bake cups.
- Remove all wrappers from kisses.
- Place 48 kisses in small microwave - safe bowl.
- Microwave on high 100% for 1 minute or until the chocolate is melted and smooth when stirred.
- Using small brush coat inside of paper cups with melted chocolate.
- Refrigerate 20 minutes and then reapply melted chocolate to any thin spots.
- Refrigerate again until firm or overnight.
- Gently peel paper from chocolate cups.
- Beat peanut butter, powdered sugar, and butter with mixer on medium speed in a small bowl until smooth.
- Spoon into chocolate cups.
- Before serving top each cup with a Hershey's kiss on top.
- Makes 2 dozen pieces.

194. Frozen Peppermint Patties Recipe

Serving: 15 | Prep: | Cook: 15mins | Ready in:

Ingredients

- 1 pkg unflavored gelatine
- 1 T boiling water
- 1 cup heavy cream
- 3 drops peppermint flavor
- 1 ounce cream cheese
- 1 ounce unsweetened chocolate, melted
- 1/2 tsp vanilla extract
- 2 T sugar(10 packs of splenda)

Direction

- Soften gelatine in boiling water.
- Add all ingredients into a blender and blend well.
- Chill for 10 minutes.
- Spoon onto parchment paper. Freeze till solid.
- Pack in an airtight container.

195. Fruit And Nut Chocolate Chunk Candy Recipe

Serving: 36 | Prep: | Cook: 5mins | Ready in:

Ingredients

- • 1 1/4 lb fine-quality bittersweet chocolate (not unsweetened), broken into small pieces
- • vegetable oil for greasing pan
- • 2/3 cup dried cranberries
- • 2/3 cup raisins
- • 2/3 cup salted roasted shelled pistachios (3 oz)
- • 2/3 cup salted roasted cashews (3 oz)

Direction

- Melt chocolate in top of a double boiler or metal bowl set over a saucepan of barely simmering water, stirring occasionally until smooth.
- While chocolate is melting, line bottom and sides of an 8-inch square baking pan with foil, leaving a 2-inch overhang, then lightly oil foil.
- Remove chocolate from heat and stir in fruit and nuts, then spread evenly in baking pan. Freeze until firm, about 20 minutes. Lift candy in foil from pan using overhang and transfer to a cutting board. Peel off foil and cut candy with a long heavy knife into 36 pieces.
- Cooks' notes: • If you have more time, chill the candy in the refrigerator (instead of in the freezer) until firm, about 1 hour. • Candy keeps, wrapped well in foil and chilled, 2 weeks.

196. Ganache Recipe

Serving: 12 | Prep: | Cook: 3mins | Ready in:

Ingredients

- Semi-sweet chips or bittersweet chips
- Fresh heavy whipping cream only
- Flavored extracts of your choice

Direction

- I'm just going to post the basic steps for making a ganache which is the ultimate formula for making truffles, some frostings and glazes and or chocolate mousses that do not require eggs as part of the ingredients.
- ...Truffles
- 1/2 cup cream
- 1 cup chocolate chips or chopped chocolate.
- (Never use milk chocolate)
- Put chocolate in a glass bowl with the cream.
- Using a 1000 watt microwave, melt for one minute and stir.
- If the chocolate has melted completely, stir until you have satiny "sauce" adding a teaspoon of whichever flavored extract you wish to use at this point.
- Let the mixture cool for an hour or more depending on the temp of your kitchen. When cooled enough to be solid yet soft enough to make balls, remove teaspoonfuls of ganache and roll into balls, setting on wax paper or foil while continuing to make more. You can eat them this way or roll the ganache in chopped nuts, chocolate, powdered cocoa, coconut, chopped candies or anything else that your heart desires. Try some of those flavored coffee powders sold in all of the markets.
- ...Glazes
- 1/3 cup cream
- 1 cup chocolate
- Melt for one minute in microwave until mixture is blended and let cool until your cakes or cookies have cooled completely. Pour the glaze over your baked products once it too, has cooled.
- ...Mousses
- 1 cup cream
- 1 cup chocolate
- Mix with whipped toppings such as Cool Whip and use in parfait glasses with layers of puddings or more whipped cream. This is also great as a sauce for ice cream.
- As far as the extracts go, you can flavor the ganache with many of them with great success.
- Peppermint extract will give you wonderful mint truffles or a lovely mint sauce if used with the glaze. Use sparingly as the mint extract is very strong and a little goes a long way in a truffle. Use a 1/4 of a teaspoon first and taste it. I once used a full teaspoon and ended up with something that tasted like chocolate toothpaste. So start with small amounts and taste it all before adding more.
- Orange extract makes really lovely flavored truffles and a chocolate sauce as well.
- Lemon extract is fabulous!
- You can also add a tablespoon of flavored liqueurs such as coffee flavored and almond flavored liqueurs. There are fruit flavored liquors as well that are worth trying. Rum, cognac and champagne also make flavorful truffles.
- For a treat, make brownies and place a scoop of ice cream over the brownie and add some of the ganache with some whipped cream on top of that. YUM!
- Now that I'm in a chocolate mood, here's one last suggestion for a great treat. If you do make brownies, add a layer of the truffle recipe over the warm brownies and let the whole pan cool. Do not refrigerate this. Just let it cool for a few hours. This is my version of Death by Chocolate! (This can also be used on top of plain cheesecakes (and it's so good on top of a lemon cheesecake. omg!)
- *I am using a pic I found on the web! I confess!

197. Georgia Cookie Candy Recipe

Serving: 2 | Prep: | Cook: 1mins | Ready in:

Ingredients

- 1 cup (2 sticks) butter or margarine, softened
- 1 cup crunchy peanut butter
- 3 cups confectioners' sugar, sifted
- 1 1/2 cups graham cracker crumbs
- 1 1/2 cups semisweet chocolate chips
- Line a 13 by 9 by 2-inch pan with foil.

Direction

- Combine the butter, peanut butter, sugar, and graham cracker crumbs in a food processor. Process until the mixture forms a ball. Press into the foil-lined pan using your hands or a spatula.
- Melt the chocolate chips in a double boiler over simmering water or in a microwave-safe glass dish in the microwave for 1 minute on high (100%). Stir. If the chocolate has not completely melted, microwave for 10 seconds more, then stir. Spread evenly over the cookie layer with a spatula. Chill for several hours.
- When ready to serve, allow the candy to come to room temperature before cutting into pieces. Store in an airtight container in the refrigerator.

198. Ghost Candies Recipe

Serving: 12 | Prep: | Cook: 45mins | Ready in:

Ingredients

- 1 roll fruit by the foot fruit snack, or any flexible fruit roll -any flavor
- small pretzel sticks (2-3 inch size)
- 2/3 cup white chocolate chips
- 1 small bag mini chocolate chips (milk or semisweet-your choice)

Direction

- Line cookie sheet with wax paper.
- Unroll & unwrap fruit roll.
- With Kitchen shears cut 3/4 inch fringe along one side of the roll and then cut into 2 inch sections. If using a normal fruit roll, 1st cut into 1X2 inch rectangles & then cut fringe along the bottom 2 inch side.
- Wrap each pretzel stick along one end with a 2 inch section of the fringe and press edge to seal. This will be the broomstick.
- Place each broomstick on wax paper about 4 inches apart.
- Melt white chocolate chips in microwave or in a double boiler.
- After white chocolate is melted drop about a teaspoon crossways onto middle of pretzel stick. Use tip of spoon to shape into a ghostly form sitting on the broomstick.
- Press 3 mini chocolate chips into each ghost to form eyes & mouth.
- Let stand at room temp for about 45 minutes or place in freezer until set (about 5-10 mins).
- Peel candies from wax paper and serve.

199. Gold Brick Candy Recipe

Serving: 4 | Prep: | Cook: 10mins | Ready in:

Ingredients

- 4 1/2 cup sugar 1 large can pet milk
- 1 large jar marshmallow creme 1/2 pound butter or margarine
- 1 tbsp vanilla extract 1 cup or more of nuts
- 3 packages chocolate chips

Direction

- Combine sugar and milk in a heavy bottomed pot. Bring to a rolling boil for nine minutes. Remove from fire; add the 3 packages of chocolate chips, the marshmallow crème and butter. Beat together; add the chopped nuts and the vanilla. Pour in a buttered pan and place in the freezer for one hour. Cut in squares and return to freezer.

200. Goo Goo Bars Recipe

Serving: 12 | Prep: | Cook: 4mins | Ready in:

Ingredients

- 1 Can condensed milk
- 1 sm. bag real chocolate chips (Hersey's is good)
- 2 cups mixed nuts
- 1 bag sm. marshmallows
- 2 tes. butter for pan

Direction

- Melt chips and condensed milk together until chips are totally melted (about 3 or 4 minutes in Microwave).
- Still in nuts and marshmallows until well mixed together.
- Pour into buttered 9x13 pan and refrigerate about an hour.
- Cut into squares.

201. Goo Goo Clusters Recipe

Serving: 12 | Prep: | Cook: 10mins | Ready in:

Ingredients

- 1 large bag miniature marshmallows
- 12 oz Bag of milk chocolate chips (I use Ghiradelli)
- 2 cups dry roasted peanuts (Planters)
- 1 can Eagle Brand milk
- 2 tsp. butter

Direction

- Melt chocolate chips in pan with Eagle Brand milk, on low heat. Keep your eye on this! Stir until melted.
- While this is heating, mix marshmallows and peanuts in a large bowl.
- Pour melted mixture over nuts and marshmallows.
- Mix together. Pour in buttered pan. Chill 2 hours and cut.
- Done and delicious!

202. Graham Break Aways Recipe

Serving: 24 | Prep: | Cook: 25mins | Ready in:

Ingredients

- 12 honey graham crackers broken in half (24 pieces)
- 1/2 c. butter
- 3/4 c. packed brown sugar
- 1 c. semi-sweet chocolate chips
- 1/2 c. finely chopped pecans or other nuts (optional)

Direction

- Preheat oven to 350. Arrange graham crackers in a single layer on a cookie sheet.
- In a medium sauce pan, bring butter and sugar to a boil over medium heat, cook 2 minutes.
- Pour over grahams and spread quickly to cover all the crackers.
- Bake 6-8 minutes or until sugar mixture is slightly browned and bubbly.
- Remove and sprinkle with chocolate chips
- Bake another 1-2 minutes until chocolate is melted.
- Remove from oven and spread chocolate, add nuts if desired.
- Cool completely and break into squares.
- Enjoy!

203. Grand Marnier And Chocolate Truffles Recipe

Serving: 20 | Prep: | Cook: 10mins | Ready in:

Ingredients

- 1/2 cup double cream
- 6 oz dark chocolate, broken into pieces
- 4 tbsp Grand Marnier
- Zest of 1/2 orange
- 1 1/2 cup dark chocolate to dip, or sifted cocoa powder to roll

Direction

- Line a baking sheet with non-stick paper.
- Put the cream into a pan and bring to boil. Remove the pan from the heat and add the chocolate pieces, the Grand Marnier and the orange zest. Stir until really well mixed. Cool and chill for 15 min.
- Beat the mixture for around 5 min until it gets a consistency like fudge. Shape into small balls and place them on the baking sheet. Freeze for 1 hour.
- Melt a cup of the dipping chocolate in a bowl in bain-marie. Lift the bowl off the pan and add the remaining chocolate and stir until melted.
- Using a fork, dip the truffles into the chocolate, then place on the lined baking sheet.
- Alternatively you can roll the truffles in sifted cocoa powder or grounded nuts.
- Use your imagination! :)

204. Grownup Smores Recipe

Serving: 8 | Prep: | Cook: 1mins | Ready in:

Ingredients

- 8 Jules Destrooper Crisp butter Wafers (from a 6.1-oz box)
- 1 bar (3.5 oz) Ghirardelli Intense Dark Citrus Sunset chocolate
- 8 marshmallows
- Different takes :
- Substitute a bar of Ghirardelli espresso Escape chocolate for the
- citrus bar.
- Sprinkle English toffee bits on the chocolate before adding marshmallows.
- Coarsely chop cooled s'mores and stir into your favorite ice cream.

Direction

- For each s'more, top 1 wafer with 2 squares of chocolate and 2 marshmallows.
- Microwave on high 10 to 12 seconds or just until marshmallows start to puff up.
- Top with another wafer. Enjoy warm.

205. HAYSTACKS Recipe

Serving: 24 | Prep: | Cook: 20mins | Ready in:

Ingredients

- 12 OZ PACKAGE chips (chocolate, butterSCOTCH,peanut butter OR mint, OR ANY COMBINATION)
- 1/2 (5 1/2 OZ) CAN CHINESE CHOP SUEY noodles
- 1/2 CUP walnuts
- 1/2 CUP coconut

Direction

- DO NOT TRY AMD MAKE TOO MUCH AT ONE TIME.
- MELT CHIPS IN THE TOP OF A DOUBLE BOILRT.
- STIR IN NOODLES, NUTS AND COCONUT.
- DROP BY SPOONFULS ONTO WAX PAPER AND COOL.

- EAT THEM ALL UP.

206. Harvest Moon Lollipops Recipe

Serving: 12 | Prep: | Cook: 1mins | Ready in:

Ingredients

- Materials:
- 12 (10- to 12-inch-long) lollipop sticks
- 1 (24-ounce) package chocolate Flavor MoonPies
- 1 (14-ounce) package orange candy melts
- 1 zip-top plastic bag
- Scissors
- wax paper
- Halloween candies
- Halloween sugar cake decorations
- Decorator icing
- Ribbon (optional)

Direction

- Step 1: Insert 1 lollipop stick 2 to 3 inches into marshmallow center of Moon Pie.
- Step 2: Microwave candy melts in a glass bowl at MEDIUM (50% power) 1 minute or until melted, stirring once; spoon into plastic bag, and seal.
- Step 3: Snip a small hole in 1 corner of the bag; pipe melted candy around where stick meets Moon Pie to secure. Lay flat on wax paper, and let stand until firm.
- Step 4: Pipe fun border of melted candy around edges. Attach candies and/or cake decorations with decorator icing. Tie ribbons around tops of sticks, if desired.

207. Hazelnut Truffles Recipe

Serving: 120 | Prep: | Cook: 10mins | Ready in:

Ingredients

- 1 14-ounce can sweetened condensed milk
- 1 13-ounce jar (about 1-1/4 cups) chocolate-hazelnut spread
- 4 ounces unsweetened chocolate, chopped
- 1 tablespoon irish cream liqueur or vanilla
- 2/3 cup halved hazelnuts (filberts), toasted*
- Finely or coarsely chopped toasted hazelnuts (filberts)
- unsweetened cocoa powder

Direction

- 1. In a heavy medium saucepan combine sweetened condensed milk, chocolate-hazelnut spread, and unsweetened chocolate. Cook over low heat until chocolate melts, stirring constantly. Remove saucepan from heat. Cool slightly. Stir in liqueur or vanilla until smooth. Transfer to a mixing bowl; cover and chill about 3 hours or until firm.
- 2. Line a baking sheet with waxed paper. For each truffle, form about 1 teaspoon of the chocolate mixture around 1 toasted hazelnut half to make a 3/4-inch ball. Roll in chopped toasted nuts or cocoa powder.
- 3. Store in a tightly covered container in the refrigerator for several weeks or freezer up to 3 months.
- Makes 120 candies.
- To Toast Hazelnuts
- Place nuts in a skillet. Cook over medium-low heat, stirring or shaking skillet often for 7 to 10 minutes or until skins begin to flake and nuts are light golden brown. Watch carefully to avoid overbrowning. Remove nuts from skillet and place on a clean kitchen towel. When hazelnuts are cool enough to handle, rub the nuts together in the towel, removing as much of the brown skin as possible.

208. Hob Nobs Recipe

Serving: 24 | Prep: | Cook: 5mins | Ready in:

Ingredients

- 2 C. sugar
- 3 Tbs. cocoa
- 1/2 C. milk or evaporated milk
- 1 stick butter
- 1/2 C. peanut buttr
- 1 tsp. vanilla
- 2 3/4 C. quick cooking oats

Direction

- Combine in a medium size heavy sauce pan the sugar, milk, and cocoa. Bring to a boil over medium heat, stirring constantly and let boil for 3 minutes.
- Remove from heat and add peanut butter and vanilla and stir until peanut butter is melted.
- Add oats and stir until well coated.
- Drop by teaspoon onto waxed paper.
- Makes about 3 1/2 dozen

209. Homade Peanut Butter Cups Recipe

Serving: 30 | Prep: | Cook: 10mins | Ready in:

Ingredients

- 12 oz milk chocolate chips
- 2 tbsp. of vegetable shortening
- 1/2 cup of butter
- 1/2 cup of peanut butter
- 1 cup of powdered sugar
- 2/3 cups graham crackers crumbs
- supplies -
- mini paper cups
- pastry brush
- 2 sauce pans
- a spoon
- thank you for looking at this recipe my friends taught me how to make this and passed it on to me

Direction

- Melt chocolate chips and the shortening together in a sauce pan on low heat.
- Stir occasionally until it looks completely melted.
- Use pastry brush to paint the sides of the cups until you paint all 30 cups.
- Note-you will have choco. left over save for later to use keep warm.
- Put cups on cookie sheet and chill in fridge till firm.
- In the meantime combine peanut butter and butter in a sauce pan.
- Stir occasionally then stir in the powdered sugar and graham cracker crumbs.
- Use a small spoon fill paper cups with peanut butter almost all the way to the top.
- Put a thin layer of chocolate over the top of the peanut butter cups.
- After applying the remaining chocolate put in freezer until they are firm.

210. Home Made "mozart Kugel" Recipe

Serving: 0 | Prep: | Cook: 60mins | Ready in:

Ingredients

- 150 g marzipan
- 200 g marzipan
- 40 g pistachio nut, not salted (grounded)
- 1 teaspoon maraschino (wild cherry brandy)
- 50 g hazelnut
- 50 g sugar (white)
- 300 g chocolate
- 40 g butter

Direction

- Ground pistachio in a coffee blender and add into first 150 g marzipan and add one teaspoon of maraschino. Mix well to get green paste. Make small balls.
- Cover the green balls with 200g marzipan to make a little bigger ball.

- Melt sugar in a pan (Teflon) until brown. Roast the hazelnut. Add roasted hazelnut into still warm sugar and let it cool.
- When cooled put sugar with hazelnut into blender and make rough mixture of sugar and hazelnut.
- Now cover the marzipan balls with hazelnut/sugar mixture. If it won't stuck, you may use some kind of hazelnut cream (I use Nutella) and then roll the balls into hazelnut/sugar.
- When done, melt chocolate (with some butter) on steam and using toothpick dip the balls into chocolate. Keep them in cool place, but not refrigerator.

211. Homemade "ferrero Rocher" Recipe

Serving: 0 | Prep: | Cook: 2hours | Ready in:

Ingredients

- 100g nut wafers
- 150g hazelnuts
- 200g nutella
- 150g dark chocolate
- 1 tbsp scentless oil

Direction

- Preheat the oven to 180C [356F] and toast the nuts for ~10 minutes.
- Clean the skin off with kitchen towel or with fingers when they cool.
- Set ~30-40 minutes aside [depends on how much you are going to make].
- Chop the remaining nuts. [Not too small pieces]
- Crush wafers with a fork, add chopped nuts, Nutella, and mix well.
- Form balls and add one whole nut into the centre of each ball. It is easier to form them when your hands are a little wet.
- When they all ready, put in a fridge for ~1 hour so that they can stiffen.
- Melt the chocolate on a low heat with oil until it is solid.
- Take one candy and dip into melted chocolate, put on a sheet of baking paper and let the chocolate cool. It will cool faster in a fridge.
- I would suggest to taste them the next day and keep them in a fridge.

212. Homemade Butterfinger Bars Recipe

Serving: 8 | Prep: | Cook: 2hours | Ready in:

Ingredients

- 1 ½ cups candy corn
- ½ cup creamy nut (or seed) butter (use crunchy peanut for traditional flavour)
- 1/3 cup crushed "crunchy" cereal
- 7 oz chopped semisweet or bittersweet chocolate, melted

Direction

- Line a loaf pan with parchment, making sure to cover all sides.
- In a microwave safe dish, melt candy corn, checking and stirring frequently.
- Immediately stir in the nut butter and cereal until fully combined.
- Press mixture firmly into the bottom of the prepared pan and cool completely, about 1 hour.
- Remove from pan and cut into bars.
- Dip bars in the chocolate to evenly coat.

213. Homemade Melt In Your Mouth Dark Paleo Chocolate Recipe

Serving: 8 | Prep: | Cook: 10mins | Ready in:

Ingredients

- 1/2 cup coconut oil
- 1/2 cup cocoa powder
- 3 Tbs. maple syrup
- 1/2 tsp. vanilla extract
- pinch of sea salt

Direction

- 1. Gently melt coconut oil in a saucepan over medium-low heat. Stir cocoa powder, maple syrup, vanilla extract, and salt into melted oil until well blended. Pour mixture into a candy mold or pliable tray.
- 2. If adding add-ins sprinkle on top of liquid chocolate or mix in once other ingredients are combined and before pouring into mold.
- 3. Refrigerate until set and well chilled, about 1 hour (depending how deep your tray is).
- Keep refrigerated.
- Be creative and add orange zest, peanut butter, dried coconut, chopped nuts, cinnamon, cayenne pepper, etc. to taste and amount desired.

214. Homemade Peanut Butter Cups Recipe

Serving: 36 | Prep: | Cook: | Ready in:

Ingredients

- 1 cup creamy peanut butter, divided
- 4-1/2 teaspoons butter, softened
- 1/2 cup confectioners' sugar
- 1/2 teaspoon salt
- 2 cups (12 ounces) semisweet chocolate chips
- 4 milk chocolate candy bars (1.55 ounces each), coarsely chopped
- colored sprinkles, optional

Direction

- In a small bowl, combine 1/2 cup peanut butter, butter, confectioners' sugar and salt until smooth; set aside.
- In a small microwave-safe bowl, melt the chocolate chips, candy bars and remaining peanut butter; stir until smooth.
- Drop teaspoonfuls of chocolate mixture into paper-lined miniature muffin cups. Top each with a scant teaspoonful of peanut butter mixture; top with another teaspoonful of chocolate mixture. Decorate with sprinkles if desired. Refrigerate until set. Store in an airtight container.
- Yield: 3 dozen.

215. Homemade Snickers Bars Recipe

Serving: 24 | Prep: | Cook: 90mins | Ready in:

Ingredients

- INGREDIENTS IN () ARE FOR MAKING HALF A RECIPE.
- peanut caramel
- 2 cups heavy whipping cream (1 cup)
- 1 1/2 cups light corn syrup (3/4 cup)
- 1 1/2 cups sifted sugar (3/4 cup)
- 1/2 cup packed light brown sugar (1/4 cup)
- 2 tablespoons unsalted butter, cut into 1/2" cubes (1 tablespoon)
- 1 tablespoon vanilla (1½ teaspoons)
- 3 1/2 cups salted, roasted peanuts (1 3/4 cups)
- peanut butter NOUGAT
- 2 cups light corn syrup (1 cup)
- 2 cups sifted sugar (1 cup)
- 1 cup packed light brown sugar (1/2 cup)
- 1/4 cup water (1/8 cup)

- 2 large egg whites, at room temperature (1 egg white)
- pinch of cream of tartar
- 2 1/2 cups chunk-style peanut butter (1 1/4 cups)
- 3/4 cup finely chopped, salted, roasted peanuts (3/8 cup)
- 1 tablespoon vanilla (1 1/2 teaspoons)
- chocolate COATING
- 3½ pounds chocolate couverture, tempered (1¾ pounds)
- If you don't want to temper the chocolate (and who does), get some chocolate "bark" coating chocolate in the baking section of your favorite major grocery store or at a store carrying candy making supplies, e.g. Wilton.

Direction

- INSTRUCTIONS IN ARE FOR MAKING HALF A RECIPE.
- MAKE THE PEANUT CARAMEL
- Line the bottom and sides of a 15½ x 10½ (9 x 9) jelly roll pan with heavy duty aluminum foil, leaving a 2" overhang on the short ends. Fold the overhang underneath the pan. Butter the bottom of the blade of an offset metal cake spatula.
- Lightly butter the sides of a heavy 3 ½ or 4 quart saucepan.
- Add the cream, corn syrup, sugars, butter and salt.
- Stir constantly with a wooden spoon, cook mixture over medium-low heat for 5 to 10 minutes, until the sugar crystals are completely dissolved. Wash down the sides of the pan occasionally.
- Raise the heat to medium and bring the mixture to a boil. Insert a candy thermometer and cook 30 to 40 minutes, stirring frequently until the thermometer registers 246°.
- Remove the pan from the heat and stir in the vanilla and peanuts.
- Pour the mixture into the prepared pan and spread with the buttered spatula.
- Set the pan of caramel on a wire rack for 2 to 3 hours or overnight to cool completely.
- MAKE THE PEANUT BUTTER NOUGAT
- Butter the bottom of the blade of an offset metal cake spatula.
- In a heavy 3 ½ to 4 quart saucepan, combine corn syrup, sugars, and water.
- Stir constantly over medium-low heat for 5 to 10 minutes. Wash down the sides of the pan occasionally.
- Raise the heat to medium and bring the mixture to a boil. Insert a candy thermometer and cook 18 to 22 minutes until the thermometer registers 246°. Do NOT stir during cooking process.
- When the syrup reaches 242° start beating the egg whites.
- Beat the egg whites until frothy. Add the cream of tartar. Increase the speed and continue beating until stiff shiny peaks form.
- Transfer the syrup from the pan into a heat resistant measuring cup.
- At low speed, pour the syrup down the side of the egg whites.
- Continue beating for 3 to 5 minutes until mixture forms a thick shiny ribbon.
- Remove the wire whip and replace with the paddle attachment.
- At low speed, beat in the peanut butter, peanuts and vanilla.
- Quickly scrape the nougat over the cooled caramel.
- Cover the surface with plastic wrap that has been lightly sprayed with canola or other vegetable oil and refrigerate for 2 to 3 hours, until the nougat is firm.
- Remove the pan of peanut caramel nougat from the refrigerator and leave at room temperature overnight.
- COAT THE CANDY BARS
- Remove plastic wrap from the surface of the nougat. Invert onto a cutting board. Re-invert so that the peanut butter nougat side is facing upwards. Cut the candy into serving pieces. Dip into couverture. Set onto a chilled parchment covered cookie sheet to set.

216. Homemade Snickers Recipe

Serving: 32 | Prep: | Cook: 3hours | Ready in:

Ingredients

- For the Bottom chocolate Layer:
- 1¼ cups Guittard milk chocolate chips
- ¼ cup organic creamy peanut butter w/sea salt
- ~
- For the Nougat Layer:
- 4 tablespoons organic unsalted butter
- 1 cup fine granulated sugar
- ¼ cup milk
- 1½ cups marshmallow fluff
- ¼ cup organic creamy peanut butter w/sea salt
- 1½ cups roasted salted (50%) peanuts, roughly chopped
- 1 teaspoon bourbon vanilla extract
- ~
- For the caramel Layer:
- 14 ounces Fleur de sel caramels, unwrapped
- ¼ cup organic heavy cream
- ~
- For the Top chocolate Layer:
- 1¼ cups Guittard milk chocolate chips
- ¼ cup organic creamy peanut butter w/sea salt

Direction

- 1. Grease a 9x13-inch baking pan. Line with parchment paper, then grease the parchment paper; set aside.
- 2. Make the Bottom Chocolate Layer: Melt together the chocolate chips and peanut butter over a water bath, until completely smooth and melted, stirring every 30 seconds. Pour into the prepared baking dish and, using a spatula, smooth into an even layer. Refrigerate until completely cool and hard, about 30 minutes.
- 3. Make the Nougat Layer: Melt the butter in a medium saucepan over medium heat. Add the sugar and milk, stirring until dissolved, and bring to a boil. Reduce the heat to low and cook for 5 minutes, stirring occasionally. Remove the pan from heat and add the marshmallow fluff, peanut butter, and vanilla extract, stirring until completely smooth. Fold in the peanuts, then pour over the bottom chocolate layer. Again, refrigerate until completely cool, about 30 minutes.
- 4. Make the Caramel Layer: Combine the caramels and the heavy cream in a small saucepan over low heat. Melt, stirring occasionally, until smooth. Once completely melted, cook for an additional 4 minutes, stirring frequently. Pour the caramel over the nougat layer. Refrigerate until completely cool, about 30 minutes.
- 5. Make the Top Chocolate Layer: Melt together the chocolate chips and peanut butter over a water bath until completely smooth and melted, stirring every 30 seconds. Pour over the caramel layer and, using a spatula, smooth into an even layer. Refrigerate until completely cool and set, 30 to 60 minutes.
- 6. Run a small sharp knife along the edges of the pan to be sure the sides don't stick. Slam the pan upside on to a piece of parchment paper (should pop right out). Peel away the parchment liner and cut into 32 pieces (I run a long serrated knife under hot water, dry it then cut - repeat). Store the bars in the refrigerator and take out 15 minutes before serving (the caramel layer can get a little overly melt if left out too long).

217. Homemade Tootsie Rolls Recipe

Serving: 6 | Prep: | Cook: | Ready in:

Ingredients

- 2 tablespoons margarine, softened
- 1/2 cup unsweetened cocoa powder
- 3 cups confectioners' sugar

- 1 teaspoon vanilla extract
- 3/4 cup instant powdered milk
- 1/2 cup white corn syrup

Direction

- Mix all ingredients together.
- Knead like you would for bread.
- Roll into rope shapes and cut into desired lengths.
- You can roll into candy wrappers from candy supply store or wax paper cut into small squares, roll and twist ends.

218. Indoor S'more Bites Recipe

Serving: 24 | Prep: | Cook: 15mins | Ready in:

Ingredients

- 2 bags quality milk chocolate chips
- 1/4 cup shortening
- 16oz bag miniature marshmallow
- about 10-12oz box regular teddy graham or other bite sized graham crackers

Direction

- Using large glass bowl, melt chocolate chips and shortening over double broiler OR in microwave by heating on high for 1 minute, then stirring for 30 seconds. Repeat at 30 second intervals, stirring for 30 seconds between, until melted. This shouldn't take longer than 2 minutes. DO NOT LET CHOCOLATE COOK
- Add marshmallows and graham crackers and stir well to coat with chocolate.
- Spray regular sized ice cream scoop with no stick spray and "dip" out mounds of the mixture onto a lightly sprayed Silpat, or similar, or wax paper.
- Let cool until set, at least 2 hours.

219. Italian Chocolate Almond Truffles Recipe

Serving: 60 | Prep: | Cook: 25mins | Ready in:

Ingredients

- Ingredients:
- dark chocolate - 625 gms
- almond extract - 2 tsp
- butter - 1/2 cup
- Castor sugar - 50gms
- ground almonds - 50 gms (I run them in the coffee grinder with the skins)
- Sprinkles, grated chocolate, cocoa powder & white chocolate to decorate.Candy cases.

Direction

- Method:
- Melt the chocolate with the extract in a double boiler, or over a pan of simmering water. Stir well to ensure melted right through.
- Add the butter and stir until melted.
- Take off heat, mix in the almonds & sugar.
- Leave for a while to cool down.
- Roll into small bite sized truffles, roll in sprinkles/grated chocolate etc. This is the bit I really enjoy!
- THAT'S IT!! They are so simple to make!!
- Makes approximately 5 dozen truffles.

220. Itsa Chocolate Pizza Recipe

Serving: 24 | Prep: | Cook: 10mins | Ready in:

Ingredients

- 1 -pkg (12 ounces) milk chocolate chips
- 1- pound white almond bark
- 2- cups miniature marshmallows
- 1 - cup Rice Krispies

- 1 - cup peanuts
- 1 - jar -(6 ounces) maraschino cherries cut in half
- 4 - tablespoons green maraschino cherries cut in quarters
- 1/3 -cup -flaked coconut
- 1 - teaspoon oil

Direction

- Melt chocolate chips with 14 ounces of the almond bark in a large saucepan over low heat, stirring until smooth.
- Remove from heat and stir in marshmallows, rice krispies, and peanuts.
- Pour onto greased 12 inch pizza pan and arrange on top with the cherries.
- Sprinkle with the coconut.
- Melt remaining 2 ounces of white bark with the oil over low heat, stirring until smooth.
- Drizzle over coconut and chill until firm. Cut into pizza slices.
- Serves 16 to 24 depending on slices.

221. Kahlua Balls Recipe

Serving: 48 | Prep: | Cook: | Ready in:

Ingredients

- 2 1/2 cups finely crushed Oreo cookies
- 1 cup finely chopped walnuts
- 1 cup confectioners' sugar
- 1/3 cup Kahlua liquor or any coffee flavored liquor would work
- 2 tablespoons dark corn syrup
- Assorted items for rolling the balls into (ie: cocoa powder, fine colored sugar, sprinkles, finely crushed walnuts or oreo crumbs)

Direction

- Combine cookie crumbs, walnuts and confectioners' sugar in a large bowl.
- Add Kahlua and corn syrup; mix well.
- Shape into balls and roll into desired toppings.
- Chill overnight. Store in air tight container in the refrigerator.

222. Kamikazes Recipe

Serving: 12 | Prep: | Cook: 5mins | Ready in:

Ingredients

- 2 Cups chocolate chips
- 2 Cups butterscotch chips
- 1 Cup Chinese Noodles; (sm. can)
- 1 Cup Whole Almonds; (sm. can)

Direction

- Melt chips. (I melt in microwave--1 min. on HIGH).
- Add almonds and noodles.
- Drop by teaspoonfuls onto waxed paper covered cookie sheets.
- Refrigerate 3-5 minutes.
- Store in freezer.

223. Kids Chews Chocolate Recipe

Serving: 12 | Prep: | Cook: 8hours20mins | Ready in:

Ingredients

- 1 cup whole almonds
- ¼ cup whole peanuts
- ¼ cup cocoa powder
- ½ tsp sea salt
- 1 tbsp vanilla
- ¼ cup honey
- 1/3 cup rolled oats

Direction

- In a food processor, finely chop (but do not grind) almonds and peanuts.
- Pulse in cocoa and salt, then pour in honey and vanilla and pulse in.
- Add oats and run until a doughy mix forms.
- With your hands, make small balls or shapes out of the "dough" and place on parchment-paper lined trays.
- Chill a few hours (best if overnight) before enjoying.
- Variation:
- To add extra protein to the mixture, add 2 tbsp. of whey isolate protein powder or (for dairy-free) soy protein isolate to the cocoa mixture.

224. Krafts Chocolate Peanut Butter Snowballs Recipe

Serving: 13 | Prep: | Cook: 80mins | Ready in:

Ingredients

- 1 pkg. (8 squares) BAKER'S Semi-sweet chocolate
- 1/2 cup KRAFT smooth peanut butter
- 2 cups thawed Cool Whip whipped topping
- 1/4 cup icing sugar

Direction

- MICROWAVE chocolate in large microwaveable bowl on MEDIUM 2 min. or until chocolate is almost melted, stirring after 1 min. Stir until chocolate is completely melted.
- STIR in peanut butter until well blended. Cool to room temperature. Gently stir in whipped topping. Refrigerate 1 hour.
- SCOOP peanut butter mixture with melon baller or teaspoon, then shape into 1-inch balls. Roll balls in icing sugar. Store in refrigerator.

225. LONG STEMMED Chocolate Covered CHERRIES SUPREME Recipe

Serving: 0 | Prep: | Cook: 10mins | Ready in:

Ingredients

- 10 oz Jar maraschino cherries with - stems, drained
- 2 tb rum or your choice of liquor
- FONDANT--------------------------
- 1/3 c sweetened condensed milk -(not evaporated)
- 2 ts light corn syrup
- 2 1/2 c powdered sugar
- COATING-------------------------
- 1 c semi-sweet chocolate chips
- 1/4 c light corn syrup
- 1 tb water

Direction

- In small bowl, combine cherries and rum. Let soak 2 hours; drain on paper towels
- In medium bowl, combine condensed milk and corn syrup; blend well. Add powdered sugar gradually, stirring until mixture forms a still smooth dough. (If all powdered sugar can't be stirred in, knead mixture and sugar on counter until smooth dough forms). Wrap small amounts of the fondant around each cherry to cover completely. Refrigerate about 20 minutes or until fondant is firm.
- Line cookie sheet with waxed paper
- Prepare dipping chocolate by cooking ingredients over low heat until melted, stirring occasionally. Holding by stem, dip chilled cherries into chocolate, making sure to cover completely. Place on waxed paper-lined cookie sheet; refrigerate until chocolate sets, about 10 minutes. Dip chilled candies into melted chocolate again, making sure to coat completely. Place on lined cookie sheet then cover lightly with waxed paper. Let stand several days in cool place to allow fondant to

liquefy. (Do not refrigerate). Store in airtight container in refrigerator.
- Makes about 2 1/2 dozen candies.

226. Light Cranberry Fudge Recipe

Serving: 81 | Prep: | Cook: 5mins | Ready in:

Ingredients

- 2 cups (12 ounces) semisweet chocolate chips
- 1/4 cup light corn syrup
- 1/2 cup confectioners' sugar
- 1/4 cup reduced-fat evaporated milk
- 1 teaspoon vanilla extract
- 1 package (6 ounces) dried cranberries
- 1/3 cup chopped walnuts

Direction

- Line a 9-in. square pan with foil. Coat the foil with cooking spray; set aside.
- In a heavy saucepan, combine chocolate chips and corn syrup. Cook and stir over low heat until melted. Remove from the heat. Stir in the confectioners' sugar, milk and vanilla. Beat with a wooden spoon until thickened and glossy, about 5 minutes. Stir in cranberries and walnuts.
- Spread into prepared pan; refrigerate until firm.
- Using foil, lift fudge out of pan; discard foil. Cut fudge into 1-in. squares. Store in an airtight container in the refrigerator.
- Yield: 1-1/3 pounds (81 pieces).
- Nutrition Facts
- One serving: 1 piece Calories: 36 Fat: 2 g Saturated Fat: 1 g
- Cholesterol: 0 mg Sodium: 3 mg Carbohydrate: 6 g Fiber: 0 g Protein: 0 g

227. Low Fat Truffles Recipe

Serving: 24 | Prep: | Cook: 5mins | Ready in:

Ingredients

- 200g good-quality dark chocolate (70% cocoa solids is good)
- 6 tablespoons strong, black coffee (such as espresso)
- 2 tablespoons clear honey, such as acacia (nothing with too strong a flavour)
- cocoa powder, to dust

Direction

- Melt your chocolate gently in a large bowl over a pan of simmering water before removing it and setting aside. At this stage, it should appear like a liquid pool of chocolate.
- Gently (it's always best to be gentle with this most delicate friend) pour in the coffee and, using a spatula, give it a slow turn of the bowl until the consistency thickens. The texture of the chocolate will start to seize and thicken almost instantly.
- Add the honey, a tablespoon at a time, slowly waltzing the chocolate around the bowl until you get a highly glossy lick of chocolate. The whole process will not take more than a couple of minutes.
- Chill the bowl in the fridge for 30 minutes or until the truffle mixture has returned to a nearly solid form.
- Prepare a clean surface on which to roll out the truffles and sieve three generous tablespoons cocoa powder onto it.
- Scrape out a teaspoonful of the mixture into the palm of your hand and roll into a marble-sized ball, then roll this through the cocoa powder until fully coated and pop into a bowl or jar.
- Repeat the process until all the mixture is used up and store the little marbles of wonder in the fridge.

228. MARSHMALLOW PUFFS Recipe

Serving: 36 | Prep: | Cook: 20mins | Ready in:

Ingredients

- Ingredients:
- 36 Large marshmallows
- 1 ½ cups semisweet chocolate chips
- ½ cup chunky peanut butter
- 2 Tbs. butter or margarine

Direction

- Line a 9-inch square pan with foil; butter the foil. Arrange marshmallows in pan. In a double boiler or microwave-safe bowl, melt chocolate chips, peanut butter, and butter. Pour over the marshmallows. Chill completely. Cut between marshmallows.

229. Make Your Own Chocolate Kiss Recipe

Serving: 1 | Prep: | Cook: 3mins | Ready in:

Ingredients

- Hershey Bars without nuts. The amount depends on how bif of a kiss you want to make.
- Chopped nuts of your choice, chopped candies of your choice, caramel, toffee bits, rice crispy cereal, chopped Oreos, dried fruits, sunflower seeds, colored sugar, coconut, chocolate mints, marshmallows, fudge bits, peppermints, etc..
- I'd like to add that some great foil to wrap your candy in can be found at Beauty Supply stores or at a hair salon. The foils used to highlight hair are ultra thin and come in various colors. They cover the chocolate very well and are great to use for other chocolate recipes such as truffles or molded chocolates. They're not expensive and come in large squares which means less foil cutting for you! Ho! Ho! Ho!

Direction

- Make A Homemade Giant Hershey Kiss:
- 1. Select a plastic funnel the size of the kiss you wish to make.
- 2. Decide if you want it plain or with nuts, peanut butter, caramel, white chocolate, Rice Krispies, etc.
- 3. Melt enough Hershey's chocolate bars to make your kiss in a double boiler being careful not to scorch it.
- 4. Plug end of funnel with a mini marshmallow and rest it in a sturdy cup (coffee cup is great).
- 5. Add fillers, if desired, to melted chocolate and pour into funnel. Tap the funnel gently to make sure no air is trapped.
- 6. Cool at room temperature for several hours. Tap funnel and the kiss will slide out. Wrap in aluminum foil and tie with ribbon.
- MY FAVORITE WAY TO MAKE A KISS!
- Melt one cup of semi-sweet chocolate in 1/2 cup of heavy cream in a microwave for 2 minutes. This is a ganache. Let this cool until it is firm which takes about 2 hours.
- When you're pouring your "Hershey" chocolate into your funnel, stop before you have 1/3 of your whole amount of chocolate into the funnel. Add a layer of your ganache filling to fill another 1/3 and then finish filling the funnel with the "Hershey" chocolate. This gives you a truffle filling and a very unique Kiss. You can also pour in enough of the "Hershey" chocolate and swirl that chocolate around the sides of the funnel and fill with the ganache filling then fill the rest to the top of your funnel with the "Hershey chocolate, giving you a truffle filling. I would definitely refrigerate the chocolate filled funnel to allow the softer center harden before wrapping.

230. Mandies Candies Recipe

Serving: 50 | Prep: | Cook: 12mins | Ready in:

Ingredients

- 24 plain graham crackers
- 1 1/2 cups unsalted butter, cut into pieces
- 1 cup packed light brown sugar
- 1/4 teaspoon salt
- 11.5 oz bittersweet chocolate (I used Ghirardelli)*
- 12 oz of semi-sweet chocolate (I used Guittard)*
- 1 cup hazelnuts, chopped (or any nut or no nuts!)
- 3/4 cup of unsweetened coconut (optional)
- * You can use white chocolate and dark chocolate combinations for color contrast. Be creative! I wouldn't recommend using milk chocolate because it's just too sweet with the caramel, but if that's what you like go for it!

Direction

- Preheat oven to 350F. Line a 25 x 17 x full sheet pan with foil, leaving a 2-inch overhang at each end.
- In a separate, smaller pan (a brownie pan works great), spread the coconut out in an even, single layer. Bake, stirring after 5 minutes or so, until the coconut becomes an even golden brown. Remove from the oven and set aside. Increase the oven's temperature to 375F.
- Line bottom of pan with graham crackers (it will be a tight fit and you'll need to break a few in half. Set aside.
- Melt butter in a 3-4 quart heavy saucepan over moderately low heat, then add brown sugar and salt and cook, whisking, until mixture is smooth and combined well, about 2 minutes. Pour over crackers, spreading evenly, and bake in middle of oven until golden brown and bubbling, about 10 minutes.
- Scatter chocolate chips evenly over crackers and bake in oven until chocolate is soft, about 1 minute. Remove pan from oven and gently spread chocolate evenly over crackers with offset spatula. Sprinkle nuts evenly over chocolate and cool crackers in pan on a rack 30 minutes.
- Refrigerate overnight or freeze for 15 minutes.
- Carefully lift crackers from pan by grasping both ends of foil, then peel foil from crackers. Break crackers into serving pieces.
- Note: Crackers keep, chilled and layered between sheets of wax paper in an airtight container, 2 weeks.

231. Marshmallow Butterscotch Chocolate Fudge Recipe

Serving: 12 | Prep: | Cook: 20mins | Ready in:

Ingredients

- 2 cups packed brown sugar
- 1 cup granulated sugar
- 1 cup evaporated milk
- 1/2 cup butter or margarine
- 1 jar marshmallow crème
- 6 ounce package butterscotch morsels
- 6 ounce package chocolate morsels
- 1 cup walnuts
- 1 teaspoon vanilla

Direction

- Combine first 4 ingredients in saucepan.
- Boil 15 minutes at moderate heat stirring occasionally.
- Remove from heat and add next 3 ingredients.
- Stir until morsels are melted and mixture is smooth then add walnuts and vanilla.
- Pour into a greased 9" square pan.

232. Marshmallow Chocolate Cookie Lollipops Recipe

Serving: 1 | Prep: | Cook: | Ready in:

Ingredients

- Round cookies
- marshmallows
- Long narrow, rounded sticks
- chocolate, melted
- Sweets (candy) for decoration
- Sprinkles or anything else for decoration

Direction

- Cover a knife in cornflour.
- Cut a marshmallow in two with the knife.
- Put one half of a marshmallow on one cookie.
- Microwave for about a minute or until the marshmallow is doubled up in size and puffed.
- Put another round cookie on top.
- Press lightly down.
- Push the stick through the marshmallow centre.
- Spread some melted chocolate on one cookie.
- Press the decoration down in the chocolate.
- Refrigerate.
- Eat!!!

233. Martha Washington Balls Recipe

Serving: 20 | Prep: | Cook: 5mins | Ready in:

Ingredients

- 2 cups coconut
- 2 cups chopped pecans
- 1 can condensed milk
- 2 1/2 cups powdered sugar
- 1 teaspoon vanilla
- 1 6oz package chocolate chips
- 1/2 bar parafin

Direction

- Mix all ingredients together. Let chill for about an hour.
- Then roll mixture into balls about the size of between nickels and quarters, not to small but not too big. Rechill.
- Dipping sauce:
- Melt chocolate chips and paraffin in double boiler.
- Dip each round ball into chocolate and set on wax paper to harden.
- Take a toothpick and stick in balls to dip. This makes it easier.

234. Mels Valentine Truffles Recipe

Serving: 12 | Prep: | Cook: 15mins | Ready in:

Ingredients

- 6 oz. semi-sweet chocolate chips
- 1/4 c. margarine (I use Parkay)
- 4 Tbs. International Foods Creme caramel coffee
- 4 Tbs. hot water
- toasted hazelnuts, chopped

Direction

- Melt chocolate and margarine in microwave on med. for 1 min., stir, and put back in if needed--until chocolate is smooth.
- Heat water until it starts to boil; stir in coffee.
- Add coffee mixture to chocolate.
- Refrigerate 1 hour.
- Form chocolate into walnut-sized balls and roll in the chopped hazelnuts.

235. Mendiants Recipe

Serving: 25 | Prep: | Cook: | Ready in:

Ingredients

- 4 ounces best-quality dark chocolate
- 1 tablespoon green pistachio nuts
- 1/4 cup golden raisins
- 1/4 cup blanched almonds
- 2-ounce strips of candied orange peel

Direction

- Place a sheet of acetate or waxed paper on a marble slab or other smooth, cold surface. Melt chocolate in a microwave oven or in a bowl over hot water.
- Place a scant teaspoonful of melted chocolate on the sheet, and shape into a disk using the back of a spoon. Make several at a time so that the chocolate does not become too cool.
- Place a pistachio, raisin, almond, and halved strip of orange peel on each disk, and leave to cool completely. The mendiants are ready when they come off the acetate or waxed paper with ease.

236. Mile High Chocolate Marshmallow Squares Recipe

Serving: 48 | Prep: | Cook: | Ready in:

Ingredients

- 1 12oz bag semisweet chocolate chips
- 1 11oz bag butterscotch chips
- 1/2 cup peanut butter-creamy or chunky
- 1 16oz bag miniature marshmallows
- 1 cup dry roasted peanuts

Direction

- Grease a 9" x 13" x 2" baking pan or line with foil. Set aside.
- Microwave chocolate chips, butterscotch chips, and peanut butter on high for 2 minutes in 30-second intervals or until melted. Stir until smooth. Cool 1 minute.
- Stir in marshmallows and peanuts.
- Spread into prepared pan. Chill until firm.
- Cut into squares.

237. Milky Way Delights Recipe

Serving: 8 | Prep: | Cook: 11mins | Ready in:

Ingredients

- 1 roll crescent rolls
- 3 milky way candy bars

Direction

- Slice candy bars into 8 pieces then unfold crescents and place a piece of candy in center of each crescent then fold crescent around candy being sure to cover all. Pinch seams closed them place on ungreased cookie sheet and bake at 375 for 11 minutes. Serve warm.

238. Million Dollar Fudge Recipe

Serving: 10 | Prep: | Cook: 10mins | Ready in:

Ingredients

- 4 1/2 cups sugar
- 1 can evaporated milk
- 1/4 lb butter
- 18 oz. hershey's bars
- 1 lg package chocolate chips (semi sweet)
- 1 pint marshmallow cream
- 2 c. chopped nuts
- 2 tsp vanilla

Direction

- Boil together first 3 ingredients for 10 minutes stirring constantly.
- Mix chocolate chips and broken up chocolate bars in large bowl
- Pour boiled mixture over chocolate and beat well.
- Add last 3 ingredients and beat until cool, about 5 min.
- Spread in a 9x12x2 buttered pan.
- Cool completely and cut into 1" squares.

239. Mint Chocolate Snacks Recipe

Serving: 8 | Prep: | Cook: 10mins | Ready in:

Ingredients

- fresh mint leaves, washed
- chocolate (your choice: semi-sweet, dark, white, etc.)

Direction

- Lay a sheet of wax paper out on the counter.
- Melt the chocolate in either a double boiler or in the microwave.
- Use tongs or a very clean pair of eyebrow tweezers to dip the mint leaves in the hot melted chocolate.
- Lay flat on the wax paper.
- If you'd like to make the leaves curved, cover a rolling pin with wax paper and lay the leaves across.
- Put in the freezer until firm.
- Serve with hot tea.

240. Mint Cookie Candies Recipe

Serving: 448 | Prep: | Cook: | Ready in:

Ingredients

- 12 ounces white candy coating, coarsely chopped
- 6 tsps. shortening, divided
- 1/4 tsp. green food coloring
- 4 mint cream filled chocolate sandwich cookies, crushed
- 2 pkgs. andes mint candies

Direction

- Melt candy coating in microwave with 4 tsps. shortening. Stir until smooth. Stir in food coloring.
- Pour evenly into miniature muffin cup liners.
- Sprinkle with cookie crumbs.
- Melt mint candies in microwave with remaining shortening. Stir until smooth.
- Pour over cookie crumbs.
- Let stand until set.

241. Mint Meltaways Recipe

Serving: 64 | Prep: | Cook: 100mins | Ready in:

Ingredients

- 16 squares (16 oz.) semisweet chocolate, chopped or 2 2/3 c. semisweet chocolate chips
- 2 TBSP. vegetable shortening
- 1/2 c. heavy whipping cream
- 1 TBSP. peppermint extract
- 2 TBSP. unsweetened cocoa
- mint baking chips, for decorating, optional

Direction

- ***Cook time includes chilling time.***
- Line bottom of 8-inch square baking pan with waxed paper.

- In heavy 3-quart saucepan, melt chocolate and shortening over low heat, stirring frequently, until smooth. Remove from heat.
- Meanwhile, in small saucepan, heat cream to simmering over medium heat. Immediately add hot cream and peppermint extract to chocolate mixture; with wire whisk, mix until blended and smooth.
- Pour mixture into prepared pan, tilting pan to spread mixture evenly. Refrigerate until firm, about 1 1/2 hours.
- With small metal spatula, loosen chocolate mixture from sides of pan. Lightly dust cutting board with cocoa; invert pan onto board. Remove pan and discard waxed paper. Let candy stand 10 minutes at room temperature to soften slightly. With sharp knife, cut chocolate mixture into 8 strips, then cut each strip crosswise into 8 pieces.
- If using, place a mint baking chip on top of each piece for decoration, pressing the chip lightly onto each piece to adhere.
- To store, layer between waxed paper in airtight container. Refrigerate up to two weeks.

242. Mint Thins Recipe

Serving: 12 | Prep: | Cook: | Ready in:

Ingredients

- 1 pkg. (8 squares) BAKER'S Semi-Sweet baking chocolate
- 1/4 tsp. peppermint extract
- 1 sleeve Ritz crackers (36 crackers)
- 1 peppermint candy cane (6 inch), crushed

Direction

- MICROWAVE chocolate in small microwaveable bowl as directed on package. Stir until completely melted. Blend in extract.
- DIP crackers in melted chocolate, completely coating crackers with chocolate. Carefully scrape off excess chocolate. Place on waxed paper-covered baking sheets; sprinkle with crushed candy.
- REFRIGERATE 30 min. or until chocolate is firm.
- ***Chocolate-Peanut Butter Cookies
- Omit peppermint extract and candy cane. Spread each cracker with a thin layer of peanut butter before dipping into the melted chocolate.
- 3 doz. or 12 servings, three coated crackers each

243. Mint Chocolate Almond Fudge Recipe

Serving: 10 | Prep: | Cook: 8mins | Ready in:

Ingredients

- 2 cups of mint chocolate chips
- 1 cup of sliced almonds
- 1 2/3 cups of packed brown sugar
- 2 cups of mini marshmellows
- 2/3 cup of evaporated milk
- 1 tsp. vanilla
- Plastic wrap for pan

Direction

- Put milk and sugar in a med. pot and heat to boiling.
- Reduce heat to med and boil for 5 minutes should start to look curdled.
- Remove from heat and add marshmallows stir until melted.
- Mix in almonds, vanilla, and chips.
- Blend really well should look creamy and be somewhat thick.
- Place plastic wrap inside an 8x8 or 9x9 pan make sure to leave at least 2 inches of wrap hanging over each side for removing the fudge later.
- Pour fudge into pan on top of plastic wrap.
- Put into fridge to cool do not cover.

- After cools cut into small squares and serve.

244. Mock Ferrero Rochers Recipe

Serving: 60 | Prep: | Cook: | Ready in:

Ingredients

- 350 g hazelnut wafer biscuits, crushed
- 100 g ground hazelnuts
- 75 g ground almonds
- 50 g rice flour
- 500 g (about 1 2/3 cups) nutella
- 60 whole hazelnuts
- 500 g dark chocolate, melted
- 2 tbsp Frangelico, optional

Direction

- Combine the crushed wafers, ground nuts, rice flour and Nutella in a large bowl. Mix well.
- Form a small ball of this dough mixture around each whole hazelnut. Place on a lined cookie sheet.
- Freeze 1 hour.
- Melt chocolate in a bowl set over barely simmering water. Stir in Frangelico.
- Dip frozen balls into melted chocolate and allow to harden on wax paper-lined sheets.

245. My Favorite Fudge Recipe

Serving: 50 | Prep: | Cook: 4mins | Ready in:

Ingredients

- 6 cps sugar
- 3 sticks butter (do not use margarine)
- 1 1/2 cp half and half
- 3 8 oz bags dove dark chocolate promises
- 1 large jar marshmallow cream
- 1 1/2 cp chopped pecans
- 1 tbs vanilla
- 1/4 tsp salt

Direction

- Prepare 9x13 pan by lining with aluminum foil, bringing it up the sides of the pan.
- Unwrap dove pieces.
- Place sugar, butter, half and half and salt in large heavy pan.
- On medium heat gently bring to a hard boil stirring all the time.
- Boil for 4 minutes stirring all the time to prevent scorching.
- Turn off heat and add chocolate and marshmallow cream.
- Let stand five minutes to melt the chocolate.
- Add vanilla and stir till completely blended.
- Add pecans and stir in.
- Pour into prepared pan.
- Cool completely.
- Remove from pan and cut into one inch squares.
- Makes about 5 lbs. fudge.
- I wrap mine individually in waxed paper and store in a jar with a lid. Keeps for a long time if someone doesn't eat them all.
- Enjoy and everyone have a Merry Christmas or whatever you celebrate.

246. My First Chocolate Fudge Recipe

Serving: 24 | Prep: | Cook: 20mins | Ready in:

Ingredients

- 4-1/2. cups granulate sugar
- 12 oz. can evaporated milk
- 1/4 lb. butter
- 1 jar marshmallow creme
- 12 oz. semi-sweet chocolate chips

- 12 oz. milk chocolate bar
- 2 cups Chopped pecans or walnuts
- Note: I have added 1 cup miniature marshmallows and 1/2 cup pecans/walnuts to this recipe and it's great!
- 2 tsp. vanilla

Direction

- Cook sugar, milk, and butter to soft ball stage - 234 degrees on candy thermometer, stirring constantly.
- Remove from heat and add the remaining ingredients.
- Stir quickly and thoroughly to blend.
- Pour into a large lightly buttered baking pan or dish
- Cool then cut into squares and store in the refrigerator.

247. No Bake Peanut Butter Bars Recipe

Serving: 24 | Prep: | Cook: | Ready in:

Ingredients

- 1/2 cup butter, softened
- 2 cups creamy peanut butter
- 2 cups powdered sugar
- 3 cups crispy rice cereal
- 1 cup semisweet chocolate chips

Direction

- Butter a 9x13-inch baking dish. In a medium bowl, stir together the butter, peanut butter and confectioners' sugar until well blended. Mix in the rice cereal so that it is evenly distributed. Press the mixture into the prepared pan.
- In the microwave or over a double boiler, melt chocolate chips, stirring occasionally until smooth. Spread the melted chocolate evenly over the peanut butter bars. Refrigerate until set before cutting into bars.

248. No Bake Peanut Butter Cups Recipe

Serving: 6 | Prep: | Cook: 15mins | Ready in:

Ingredients

- 1lb confectioners sugar
- 1c margarine melted
- 1c peanut butter
- 2 pkgs. graham cracker crumbs,ground
- 1/2 lg.pkg. chocolate chips(11/2cups)
- 1/4lb. margarine,melted

Direction

- Mix sugar and crumbs together, add peanut butter and melted margarine. Mix well and press in 13x9 pan. Melt 1/4lb margarine with chips, pour over crumb mixture and refrigerate. Cut into small squares.

249. No Bake Marshmallow Chip Clusters Recipe

Serving: 20 | Prep: | Cook: 10mins | Ready in:

Ingredients

- 3 Tablespoons unsalted butter
- 4 1/4 cup mini marshmallows
- 3/4 cup chopped peanuts (have used cashews , very good)
- 1/2 raisins (i substitute craisins and it was even better)
- 1 1/2 cup broken up pretzel sticks
- 1 cup semi sweet chocolate chips
- 1 tsp. vanilla

Direction

- Melt butter in saucepan.
- Stir in 3 1/4 cups marshmallows to melt.
- Turn off heat and add vanilla.
- Cool slightly.
- Mix peanuts, raisins and pretzels in a bowl.
- Add marshmallow mixture.
- Stir in remaining marshmallows and chocolate chips until coated.
- Roll heaping Tablespoons of mixture with hands into haystack clusters.
- Place on wax paper lined cookie sheet.
- Refrigerate 20 min.
- Store remaining candy in refrigerator.

250. Noir Chocolate Spread Recipe

Serving: 4 | Prep: | Cook: | Ready in:

Ingredients

- 2 Tbsp cocoa
- 2 Tbsp raw agave syrup
- 2 Tbsp unrefined flax oil
- 1/2 tsp vanilla extract
- dash of sea salt

Direction

- Use organic ingredients if you can.
- Mix everything together till smooth and glossy.
- Store covered in the fridge (it will solidify a bit).
- I double this recipe and keep it in a little glass jar in the fridge.
- Enjoy!

251. Nut Goodie Bars Recipe

Serving: 50 | Prep: | Cook: 20mins | Ready in:

Ingredients

- 12 oz. chocolate chips
- 12 oz. butterscotch chips
- 1 18 oz. jar peanut butter
- 1 cup butter
- 1 5 oz. can evaporated milk
- 1/4 cup cook & serve vanilla pudding
- 2 lbs. powdered sugar
- 1 lb roasted salted peanuts

Direction

- Melt first three ingredients over low heat. Spread 1/2 of the chocolate mixture onto a 10x15 metal sheet pan. Then put the pan in the freezer. Set the other half of chocolate mixture aside.
- Put butter, evaporated milk and 1/4 cup of dry pudding mixture into a medium pan. Bring to a boil. Then boil two minutes. Remove from heat. Beat in powdered sugar. Then spread over frozen chocolate layer.
- Warm the second half of chocolate mixture if needed and stir in peanuts. Carefully spread on top of white layer.
- Chill overnight.

252. Nut Goody Candy Bars Recipe

Serving: 24 | Prep: | Cook: | Ready in:

Ingredients

- Candy Bar Topping:
- 1½ pounds sweet chocolate (I use three 8 ounce Hershey Bars) - divided
- ¾ pound Spanish peanuts (not cocktail peanuts)
- Fondant Filling:

- 2½ cups powdered sugar
- ½ cup sweetened condensed milk
- ½ teaspoon maple extract

Direction

- For the topping, melt 16 ounces of chocolate in the microwave. If you've never melted chocolate in the microwave, you must be very careful. Overheating it will turn it into a grainy mess. In a glass microwavable bowl, break up chocolate into small pieces; microwave on High for 45 seconds to start; stir, and then keep heating for 20 to 30 seconds at a time, stirring after each time. When it gets to the point where it only has a few lumps of chocolate left, heat for 10 seconds at a time.
- Once chocolate is completely melted, stir in the Spanish peanuts.
- For fondant, mix together the ingredients. It will be thick and stiff.
- Spray a large piece of waxed paper with cooking spray and use a paper towel to wipe off any excess.
- Roll the fondant into little balls, about 1" in diameter.
- Place the balls about 3" apart on the waxed paper, then flatten each ball with the heel of your hand. The flattened balls should be a circle about the size of a silver dollar, and NOT paper thin.
- Cover the flattened balls with the melted chocolate/nut mixture, letting it cover the top of the fondant and flow slightly over the edges.
- Let the candies cool completely, allowing the chocolate to harden again, then flip each one over (use a spatula for best results - they should come away from the waxed paper easily once the chocolate has cooled and hardened).
- To cover the bottom of the fondant with melted chocolate, melt the remaining 8 ounce chocolate bar in a separate bowl and use a spoon to spread the melted chocolate over the exposed fondant.
- Let the chocolate set and harden completely before storing the candies in a container with waxed paper between the layers. If it's hot outside, I would suggest you keep them in the refrigerator until serving.

253. Nutchos Recipe

Serving: 6 | Prep: | Cook: 20mins | Ready in:

Ingredients

- 1 bag chocolate chips,1bag peanut butter chips,2 cups crushed ruffels potato chips,1 can salted peanuts

Direction

- Melt chocolate and peanut butter chips in a double boiler.
- Add potato chips and peanuts.
- Mix all together drop by teaspoon on baking sheet.
- Press with fork cool in fridge about 10 minutes.
- I dip teaspoon in cold water when mixture starts sticking to spoon, dip fork in cold water as well.
- Bon Appetite!!!

254. Nutty Buddies Recipe

Serving: 4 | Prep: | Cook: 3mins | Ready in:

Ingredients

- buttery crackers, I use Ritz
- creamy peanut butter
- almond Bark chocolate
- wax paper
- Variation, White almond Bark plus 1 Tbsp. peanut butter for every 3 chunks of bark

Direction

- Spread half the crackers with peanut butter.
- Place the other half of the crackers on top to make a sandwich.
- Melt the almond bark in the microwave in a shallow bowl.
- If you're using the white bark, stir in the peanut butter after you've melted the white bark.
- Set one cracker sandwich in the bowl and using a fork, turn it over to coat the other side.
- Slide the fork under the cracker and lift up and let the chocolate drip back into the bowl before setting it on the wax paper.
- Let the cookies cool completely before eating.
- Store in airtight container.

255. Nutty Chocolate Mint Fudge Recipe

Serving: 16 | Prep: | Cook: 5mins | Ready in:

Ingredients

- One 7-ounce jar marshmallow cream
- 1 1/2 cups sugar
- 2/3 cup evaporated milk
- 1/4 cup butter
- 1/4 tsp salt
- One 10-ounce pkg (1 1/2 cups) mint-chocolate morsels (Nestle Toll House)
- 1/2 cup chopped nuts
- 1 tsp vanilla extract

Direction

- In heavy saucepan, combine marshmallow cream, sugar, evaporated milk, butter, and salt. Bring to full rolling boil over medium heat. Add mint-chocolate morsels; stir until morsels are melted and mixture is smooth. Stir in nuts and vanilla extract. Pour into foil-lined 8-inch square pan. Chill until firm (about 2 hours). Cut into 1-inch squares.

256. Nutty Chocolate Rum Truffles Recipe

Serving: 0 | Prep: | Cook: 10mins | Ready in:

Ingredients

- 1/3 cup whipping cream
- 6 tablespoons unsalted butter
- 1 tablespoon rum or brandy flavoring
- 8 ounces bittersweet chocolate, broken into chunks
- 6 ounces bittersweet chocolate
- 2 tablespoons solid vegetable shortening
- 6 ounces almonds, finely ground

Direction

- 1. Heat the whipping cream and butter together just to a simmer, then add chocolate. Remove from heat while chocolate melts. Add flavoring. Stir until glossy and pour into a chilled bowl. Set aside until firm.
- 2. Once firm, use a small melon baller and scoop ganache out. Roll by hand and set aside.
- 3. Melt 6 ounces bittersweet chocolate with 2 tablespoons solid vegetable shortening in the microwave for about 1 minute. Stir until melted; microwave additional seconds as needed. Drop each ball individually into chocolate, roll with a fork until coated, then use the fork to lift out and place into a bowl with the finely ground almonds. Roll around until coated, then lift out and place on parchment. Chill and keep refrigerated.

257. Ohio Buckeyes Balls Recipe

Serving: 12 | Prep: | Cook: | Ready in:

Ingredients

- 1 POUND creamy peanut butter
- 1 1/2 POUNDS powdered sugar
- 1 CUP margarine
- 1 - OF chocolate BARK= (OR MAY USE 12 OUNCES chocolate chips AND 1/2 STICK paraffin wax)
- *** YOU CAN DOUBLE THIS IF NEEDED

Direction

- MIX PEANUT BUTTER AND POWDERED SUGAR TOGETHER LIKE PIE DOUGH, THEN ADD MARGARINE.
- CHILL DOUGH BRIEFY IT MAKES IT EASIER TO ROLL INTO BALLS
- ROLL INTO BALLS AND CHILL FOR 30 MINUTES- 1 HOUR.
- MELT CHOCOLATE BARK ***** OR CHOCOLATES CHIPS AND PARAFFIN....... DIP BALLS INTO CHOCOLATE AND LEAVE A PORTION OPEN ON ONE END FOR BUCKEYES OR COVER ENTIRE BALL IF NOT WANTING THE BUCKEYE LOOK.
- PLACE ON WAX PAPER UNTIL SET
- STORE IN CONTAINER I NORMALLY PUT MINE IN REFRIGERATOR. BUT YOU CAN LEAVE OUT IN A TIGHT CONTAINER OR ZIP LOCK BAG

258. Ohio Buckeye Bars Recipe

Serving: 5 | Prep: | Cook: | Ready in:

Ingredients

- 1 CUP margarine
- 1 -1/2 CUP CREAMY PEANUT BUTTER------ DIVIDED
- 16 OUNCE PACKAGE powdered sugar
- 8 OUNCE PACKAGE milk chocolate CANDY BAR BROKEN UP
- SUCH AS HERSHEYS PLAIN.ETC......

Direction

- MELT TOGETHER MARGARINE AND 1 CUP OF THE PEANUT BUTTER IN A MICROWAVE- SAFE BOWL ON HIGH SETTING FOR ABOUT 1 -1.2 MINUTES.
- MIX WELL, STIR IN POWDERED SUGAR; PAT INTO A GREASED 13 X 9 BAKING PAN.
- MELT TOGETHER CHOCOLATE AND REMAINING PEATNUT BUTTER IN A MICROWAVE SAFE BOWL ON HIGH SETTING FOR ABOUT 1 - 1/2 MINUTES; STIR UNTIL WELL BLENDED.
- POUR THE CHOCOLATE MIXTURE OVER THE PEANUT BUTTER MIXTURE ALREADY IN PAN.
- CHILL IN REFRIGERATOR UNTIL FIRM.
- CUT INTO SQUARES.
- MAKES ABOUT 5 DOZEN....DEPENDING ON HOW YOU CUT THEM.

259. Orange Cappuccino Creams Recipe

Serving: 0 | Prep: | Cook: 40mins | Ready in:

Ingredients

- 1 ½ lbs. white chocolate, chopped
- 3/4 cup whipping cream, divided
- 1 tablespoon finely shredded orange peel
- 1 tablespoon orange liqueur or orange juice
- 1 teaspoon orange extract
- ½ cup finely chopped walnuts
- 72(approx.) foil candy cups (1 ¼ to 1 ½ -inch size)
- 4 teaspoons instant espresso coffee powder or instant
- coffee crystals
- 8 oz. semi-sweet chocolate

Direction

- In a large saucepan, combine white chocolate, ½ cup whipping cream, orange peel, orange liqueur or juice and orange extract.
- Stir over low heat until white chocolate is just melted.
- Remove from heat and stir in walnuts. Cool slightly.
- Place mixture in a disposable heavy plastic bag, making a small opening at the bottom corner.
- Squeeze mixture through hole in bag to fill foil candy cups.
- Chill in refrigerator for 20 minutes.
- In a medium saucepan, heat ¼ cup whipping cream and espresso coffee powder or coffee crystals over low heat until dissolved.
- Add semi-sweet chocolate, stirring over low heat 3 to 4 minutes or until chocolate melts.
- Spoon ½ teaspoon of semisweet chocolate mixture onto each white chocolate cream.
- Store in refrigerator, serve at room temperature.
- Makes approx. 72 creams.
- Of course I am guessing on the cook and prep times!

260. Oreo Balls Recipe

Serving: 8 | Prep: | Cook: |Ready in:

Ingredients

- 1 package Oreo cookies
- 1 block softened cream cheese
- 1 package white baking chocolate squares

Direction

- Crumble entire package of Oreos until smooth.
- Add cream cheese to crumbled Oreos (works GREAT in a food processor).
- Form Oreo mixture into balls and place on cookie sheet covered in wax paper and place in fridge or freezer.
- When balls are stiff, melt the white chocolate in microwave.
- Using a toothpick, dip balls into melted chocolate, place back on cookie sheet.
- When all are covered, place in fridge and chocolate will harden.

261. Oreo Truffle Balls Recipe

Serving: 50 | Prep: | Cook: 1mins |Ready in:

Ingredients

- 1 (1 pound, 2 ounce) package Oreo cookies
- 1 (8 ounce) package cream cheese, room temperature
- 2 (8 ounces) packages semi-sweet chocolate chips
- 8 ounces white chocolate, optional

Direction

- * Use a good-quality chocolate. The taste and quality of these truffles are dependent on the quality of chocolate you start with.
- Line two large baking or cookie sheets with wax paper or a Silpat; set aside.
- In a food processor or blender, process and crush all of the Oreo cookies into fine crumbs. Add cream cheese and process until thoroughly mixed (there should be no white traces of cream cheese).
- Using your hands, roll into walnut-size balls, approximately 3/4-inch diameter. If the mixture becomes too soft to work, place the remaining mixture back into the refrigerator to slightly harden.
- Place Oreo Balls on the lined baking sheet and refrigerate or at least 45 to 60 minutes.
- TIPS:
- The Oreo Balls may be stored in the freezer for up to 1 week.

- If you put the Oreo balls in the freezer for a short time before dipping in chocolate, this helps keep the balls cold longer. I also put the cookie sheets in the freezer first so they are really cold when I place the chocolate covered Oregon Truffle Balls onto the cookie sheet.
- Using one of the below methods, melt the chocolate chips:
- Double Boiler:
- In the top of a double boiler over hot water, not boiling water (don't let the bottom of the bowl touch the water, melt chocolate; stirring until smooth. Be careful boiling water may cause steam droplets to get into chocolate which can result in "seizing," when the chocolate becomes stiff and grainy. NOTE: If you don't have a double boiler you can improvise one by placing a glass or stainless steel bowl over a pot of simmering water. Remove from heat. Let the chocolate cool slightly, but it should not set.
- Microwave Melting Chocolate:
- In a microwave-safe bowl, melt chocolate chips using either the defrost setting or 10-percent power in the microwave. Microwave for 1 minute, then check and stir. If you need more time, do it in 10 to 20 seconds intervals and check and stir after each addition of microwave time. Remove the container from the microwave and stir the chocolate until completely melted. Baking chips and baking chocolate may appear formed and un-melted after heating but will become fluid after stirring. Blend in cream, brandy, liqueur, or coffee
- When ready to coat with chocolate, remove the chilled Oreo Balls from the refrigerator. Replace wax paper on baking sheets if they are not clean. NOTE: A small fork, toothpicks, or chopsticks are great to use as dipping tool. Dip each Oreo Ball into the melted chocolate, allowing the excess to drip back into the pot. Place the Oreo Truffle Balls onto the wax paper. NOTE: If the chocolate gets too hard to dip well, reheat it over the double boiler or in the microwave.
- Optional: In a separate bowl either melt the white chocolate in a double boiler or the microwave. When melted, using a fork, drizzle white chocolate over the hardened chocolate balls to decorate.
- Let Oreo Truffle Balls harden and then store in an airtight container in the refrigerator.
- Makes 40 to 50 candy balls, depending on the size balls your roll.

262. Oven Off Chocolate Chip Divinity Cookies Recipe

Serving: 3 | Prep: | Cook: 2mins | Ready in:

Ingredients

- 1/2 teas. vanilla
- 6 oz. pkg. chocolate chips
- 2 egg whites
- 3/4 cup sugar

Direction

- Set oven to 400 degrees
- Cover a cookie sheet with foil.
- Beat egg whites until stiff.
- Add sugar 1/8th at a time.
- Beat until crystals disappear, don't over beat.
- Add Vanilla and mix for 2 minutes.
- Stir in chocolate chips.
- Drop by teaspoon onto foil lined cookie sheet.
- TURN OVEN OFF!
- Leave cookies in oven for 2 hours.
- Makes 3 dozen.
- Remove from foil and enjoy.

263. PERFECT CHOCOLATE TRUFFLES Recipe

Serving: 24 | Prep: | Cook: 10mins | Ready in:

Ingredients

- Ganache
- 9 ounces semisweet chocolate or bittersweet chocolate, chopped coarse
- 1/2 cup heavy whipping cream
- 2 tablespoons unsalted butter
- 1 tablespoon light corn syrup
- 2 tablespoons cognac, dark rum, Grand Marnier, Framboise, kirsch, Frangelico, Amaretto, Kahlua, or port
- chocolate and cocoa Coating
- 8 ounces semisweet chocolate or bittersweet chocolate
- 2 cups Dutch-processed cocoa powder, sifted

Direction

- Note: These truffles are meant to look like the real thing — small, irregular mounds instead of perfectly spherical balls. If you decide to omit the liquor flavoring, reduce chocolate from 9 to 8 ounces. For microwave-oriented cooks, you can melt the chocolate at 50% power for about 3 minutes. The ganache mixture is quite forgiving. If it cools too much in step 1, place the bowl in a larger pan of warm water and stir the mixture until it has softened and warmed up. If this overwarms the mixture, cool it again as directed. The same flexibility applies if you over whip the ganache by mistake. Simply warm it over the hot water, cool it, and whip it again. One person alone can dip and coat the truffles, but the process is simpler with a second person to roll coated truffles in cocoa and lift them onto a clean pan.
- 1. For the ganache: Melt chocolate in medium heatproof bowl set over pan of almost simmering water, stirring once or twice, until smooth. Set bowl aside. Bring cream, butter, and corn syrup to strong simmer (about 160 degrees) in non-reactive pan over low heat. Remove pan from heat, cool for 5 minutes, then whisk into chocolate. Whisk in liquor. Refrigerate mixture until it cools to 80 degrees, 15 to 20 minutes.
- 2. Either in bowl of electric mixer fitted with whisk attachment or with handheld electric mixer, whip mixture at medium speed until slightly lightened and thickened to a texture like store-bought canned chocolate frosting, 25 to 30 seconds. Spoon ganache into large pastry bag fitted with 1/2-inch plain tube. Following illustration 1, hold bag perpendicular to pan and with tip about 3/4 inch above work surface, and pipe 3/4-inch mounds (pulling tube away to the side to avoid leaving points) onto parchment or wax paper-covered baking sheet. Alternatively, scoop mounds with tiny (less than 1 tablespoon) ice cream scoop or melon baller. Refrigerate mounds until hardened, at least an hour.
- 3. For coating: Following directions in step 1, melt coating chocolate, then cool to 90 degrees, making certain that no water comes into contact with chocolate. Arrange chilled truffle mounds, bowl of melted chocolate, and cocoa-filled high-sided roasting pan on work surface. Working one mound at a time, dip palm of one hand about 1/4-inch deep into melted chocolate, pass one truffle mound with other hand to chocolate-covered hand and close hand around mound to coat, re-dipping hand into chocolate every third or fourth mound (see illustration 3). Drop coated truffle into cocoa; roll to coat using fork held in now empty clean hand, leaving truffles in cocoa until chocolate coating has set, about 1 minute. Repeat process until all mounds are in pan of cocoa. Following illustration 4, gently roll 5 to 6 truffles at a time in medium strainer to remove excess cocoa, then transfer to serving plate or tightly covered container. (Can be refrigerated for up to one week.)
- Note: The Perfect Chocolate Truffle
- 1. Forming truffles: Using a pastry bag fitted with 1/2-inch plain tube, pipe 3/4-inch spheres onto a pan covered with parchment or

wax paper. They do not form perfect balls and will drop slightly.
- 2. Use mini ice cream scooper/cookie scooper to form truffles.
- 3. Use one hand to coat the truffles in the chocolate glaze. Drop the coated truffles into a roasting pan filled with cocoa, nuts, or coconut (depending on variation). Toss in the cocoa, nut, or coconut mix with hands or with fork.
- 4. Gently toss finished truffles in strainer (in batches) to remove excess cocoa, nuts, or coconut.

264. Peanut Butter Pretzel Bites Recipe

Serving: 50 | Prep: | Cook: 5mins | Ready in:

Ingredients

- 1- package (14 ounces) caramels unwrapped
- 1/4 - cup butter cubed
- 2- tablespoons water
- 5 - cups miniature pretzels
- 1- jar (18 ounces) chunky peanut butter
- 26 ounces of milk chocolate candy coating ....(or you can use the candy bark)

Direction

- In a microwave- safe bowl, melt caramels with butter and water stir until smooth.
- Spread one side of each pretzel with 1 teaspoon of peanut butter t and top with 1/2 teaspoon caramel mixture.
- Place on waxed paper- lined baking sheets.
- Refrigerate until set.
- In a microwave, melt chocolate candy coating. Stir until smooth (do not overcook it or it will burn and be lumpy.)
- Using a small fork dip each pretzel into coating until all is covered shake excess off.
- Place on waxed paper.
- Let stand until set.
- Store in airtight container in cool dry place.

- Yields 8 1/2 dozen.

265. Peanut Butter Balls 1 Recipe

Serving: 10 | Prep: | Cook: 5mins | Ready in:

Ingredients

- peanut butter Balls
- 12 ounces peanut butter (smooth or crunchy)
- 1 cup butter (real)
- 1 box confectioners' sugar
- 1 teaspoon vanilla
- 1 package chocolate chips or Chocolate brick (for dipping balls)

Direction

- Mix peanut butter, butter, sugar and vanilla. Roll into balls and place on cookie sheet, place in freezer for an hour. Melt chocolate in a double boiler. Dip balls into mixture. Cool.

266. Peanut Butter Bon Bons Recipe

Serving: 20 | Prep: | Cook: | Ready in:

Ingredients

- 1-1/2 cups graham cracker crumbs
- 1 cup creamy peanut butter
- 1 cup melted butter
- 1 pound powdered sugar
- 12 ounce package milk chocolate chips
- 1/2 bar paraffin

Direction

- Form crumbs, peanut butter, butter and sugar into balls and freeze.

- Melt chips and paraffin in double boiler then dip balls into chocolate mixture.
- Place on plate or cookie sheet and refrigerate for at least 1 hour to allow chocolate to harden.

267. Peanut Butter Bonbons Recipe

Serving: 0 | Prep: | Cook: 30mins | Ready in:

Ingredients

- 1 cup icing sugar
- 1/2 cup smooth peanut butter (I prefer Kraft)
- 3 tbsp. margarine
- 1/2 cup flaked sweetened coconut
- 5 squares Semi-sweet Baker's chocolate

Direction

- Combine the icing sugar, peanut butter, margarine and coconut with a fork and roll into balls a bit smaller than a ping pong ball. Chill 'til hard. In the meantime, melt chocolate squares in a double boiler.
- Dip cold peanut butter balls in melted chocolate and transfer to a waxed paper lined cookie sheet. I sometimes use a combination of a teaspoon and a wooden skewer to roll the balls around in the melted chocolate. If you have any bare spots on the bonbons once you're done you can just paint them with any extra melted chocolate from the pan.
- Return chocolate covered bonbons to the freezer so the chocolate can set. If you can resist eating them straight away, they do keep nicely in the freezer. Store in little gift boxes. I prefer to serve mine straight from the freezer.

268. Peanut Butter Chocolate Balls Recipe

Serving: 12 | Prep: | Cook: 10mins | Ready in:

Ingredients

- 8 ounces of cream cheese
- 1 1/2 pounds of smooth peanut butter
- 3 pounds of chocolate wafers for melting, either dark or milk chocolate OR 3 pounds of Wilbur's chocolate wafers
- 2 1/2 pounds of powdered sugar
- 2 tsp of vanilla extract
- 1 1/4 pounds of margarine

Direction

- Margarine and cream cheese need to be at room temperature.
- Mix together and add peanut butter, then add vanilla.
- Add sugar in small amounts.
- Chill mixture then form into egg shape.
- Rechill.
- Melt chocolate over low heat or on low setting in microwave.
- Dip chilled eggs or balls in melted chocolate and cool on wax paper. Suggestion: Melt 1 lb. Chocolate at a time - use fork for dipping

269. Peanut Butter Chocolate Fudge Easiest Recipe

Serving: 24 | Prep: | Cook: 5mins | Ready in:

Ingredients

- 1 (14-ounce) can sweetened condensed milk
- 1 package (or 2 cups) dark chocolate chips
- 2 cups miniature marshmallows
- 1 cup smooth or chunky peanut butter
- 1 teaspoon vanilla extract

Direction

- Coat an 8-by-8-inch baking dish with butter and set aside.
- Combine milk, chocolate chips, and marshmallows in a medium saucepan over medium heat. Cook, stirring constantly, until mixture is melted and smooth, about 5 minutes.
- Remove from heat and mix in peanut butter and vanilla extract until thoroughly combined.
- Turn into the prepared baking dish, spread out evenly, and let cool to room temperature, about 10 minutes.
- Cover and place in the refrigerator until firm, about 1 hour. Cut into 25 squares and serve.

270. Peanut Butter Chocolates Recipe

Serving: 10 | Prep: | Cook: | Ready in:

Ingredients

- 1 cup creamy peanut butter
- 1 cup flour
- 1 cup powdered sugar
- 3 tablespoon butter, softened
- 1 3/4 cup semisweet chocolate chips
- 1 1/2 teaspoons shortening
- wax paper

Direction

- In an electric mixer bowl, mix together peanut butter, flour, powdered sugar and butter, until it forms a dough and sides of bowl are clean.
- Get a small cookie sheet and line with wax paper. Quickly roll a rounded teaspoon of dough in the palm of your hands and place on cookie sheet. (A melon baller tool is great in keeping the balls a uniform size. A pair of pharmacy grade latex gloves are handy for keeping your hands clean.) Chill in refrigerator 15-25 minutes, until dough balls firm up.
- To melt the chocolate chips
- Use a metal or glass bowl that fits snug over a small pan, but where the bottom of the bowl will not touch the water in the pan.
- Bring one cup of water to a simmer in a small pan, do not let the water boil. You need the low heat to melt the chocolate, not the steam. Put the chocolate chips and shortening in bowl and place over pan. It will take 1-2 minutes to fully melt the chips, so do not walk away.
- When you see the chips starting to melt, get a spatula and gently stir the chocolate. Do not over stir, just move the chips around to help them melt. When you see there's just a few chips left, turn off heat. Go get the peanut butter balls.
- Using the same pan, push all the balls to one side and make room for chocolate dipped balls. With a fork or dipping tool, place one ball in melted chocolate and quickly coat evenly. Lift up ball and gently shake extra chocolate off. Flip coated ball back onto sheet pan. Get another dough ball and repeat steps. Chill in the refrigerator for 5 to 10 minutes, until chocolate coating sets, then they're ready to eat.
- If you're making them ahead of time, up to three days ahead, move to an airtight container after the chocolate coating sets and keep refrigerated until ready to serve.

271. Peanut Butter Coconut Fudge Balls Recipe

Serving: 16 | Prep: | Cook: 10mins | Ready in:

Ingredients

- 2 cups powdered sugar
- 1/2 cup cocoa
- 1 cup sweetened condensed milk
- 1/2 cup creamy peanut butter
- 1 cup coconut

Direction

- Mix sugar and cocoa into milk then add peanut butter and mix well.
- Turn out on waxed paper.
- Knead with hands.
- Roll into small balls about the size of a walnut.
- Roll in coconut.

272. Peanut Butter Cup Squares Recipe

Serving: 24 | Prep: | Cook: 1hours | Ready in:

Ingredients

- COATING:
- 1 12 oz bag of milk chocolate drops, divided
- 2 T shortening, divided
- FILLING:
- 1 c low fat peanut butter
- 1 stick (1/2) c unsalted butter
- 1 c powdered sugar
- 1 c ground graham crackers (one sleeve)
- 1/2 t salt

Direction

- Line an 8x8 pan with parchment paper, bottom and sides. A little fancy folding will get you there with one piece.
- COATING:
- Melt half of the milk chocolate and shortening in a microwave safe dish on 50% power for 2 minutes and stir. Microwave again on 50% power for 1 minute and stir. If needed, microwave on 50% power for 30 seconds. Stir until smooth.
- Pour melted chocolate into pan. Spread on bottom and up the sides of the pan with the back of a spoon.
- Freeze, for a couple of minutes while making filling, to start to harden chocolate.
- FILLING:
- There are two versions of this filling. 1) Use half of the filling ingredients, except use two extra tbsps. butter, for a nicely sized filling. 2) Use all of the filling ingredients for those whom like peanut butter.
- Melt and mix butter, salt, and peanut butter in a small sauce pan over medium heat. Mix in powdered sugar until smooth. Mix in graham cracker crumbs until smooth. Smooth warm filling onto set up chocolate and freeze again for a half hour to harden peanut butter mixture.
- COATING:
- Melt the other half of the chocolate mixture as in the previous directions. Pour and spread melted chocolate onto top of firmed up peanut butter filling. Refrigerate until set.
- Bring up to room temperature.
- Using parchment paper, remove from dish and divide into squares. I use a pizza wheel or a chef's knife for a cutter.
- Refrain from inhaling the entire contents of this recipe.
- This is the closest I've been able to come to that famous store brand of peanut butter cups. Varying brands of chocolate chips will modify the flavor of this delight.
- Technique: Add layer to layer while the previous layer is still not quite firmly set so that the boundaries between the layers will melt just a little and cohesion is better. That way the squares, when cut, will stay stacked together instead of separating.

273. Peanut Butter Cups Recipe

Serving: 6 | Prep: | Cook: 7mins | Ready in:

Ingredients

- 6 oz pkg semi sweet chocolate chips
- 4 Nestles milk chocolate bars
- 1 1/4 cup peanut butter

Direction

- Put chocolate chips, chocolate bars, and 1/4 cup peanut butter in top of double boiler over HOT, not boiling water, stirring till smooth. Use small muffin tin liners, or cut regular cupcake liners down to a 1-inch depth. Spoon HALF of the chocolate mixture equally into the liners. Melt the rest of the peanut butter over hot water, and spoon this equally over the chocolate layer. Top with remaining chocolate. Refrigerate to allow cups to set up before serving.

274. Peanut Butter Date Candy Recipe

Serving: 12 | Prep: | Cook: 5mins | Ready in:

Ingredients

- 2 cups powdered sugar
- 1/2 lb chopped dates
- 1 1/2 cup crunchy peanut butter
- 1/4 c melted butter
- 6 oz chocolate chips

Direction

- Mix first four ingredients together and shape into little logs or balls.
- Chill.
- In a double boiler, melt the chocolate chips.
- Dip the logs into the chocolate. Let dry on waxed paper.
- You can put them in little paper cups to make them nicer. :o)

275. Peanut Butter Easter Eggs Recipe

Serving: 16 | Prep: | Cook: 35mins | Ready in:

Ingredients

- 1/2c butter, softened
- 2 1/3c confectioners sugar
- 1c graham cracker crumbs
- 1/2c creamy peanut butter
- 1/2 tsp. vanilla
- 1 1/2c dark chocolate chips
- 2 Tbs. shortening
- Pastel sprinkles

Direction

- In large bowl, cream butter; gradually add confectioners' sugar, cracker crumbs, peanut butter and vanilla. Shape into 16 eggs; place on waxed paper-lined baking sheets. Refrigerate for 30 mins or till firm.
- In microwave, melt chocolate chips and shortening; stir till smooth. Dip eggs in chocolate; allow excess to drip off. Decorate with sprinkles; return eggs to waxed paper. Chill till set. Store in airtight container in refrigerator.

276. Peanut Butter Nerds Recipe

Serving: 16 | Prep: | Cook: 10mins | Ready in:

Ingredients

- 18 ounce jar creamy peanut butter
- 1 stick butter melted
- 1 pound powdered sugar
- 1-1/4 cups crispy rice cereal
- 12 ounce package semi sweet chocolate chips
- 6 ounce package semi sweet chocolate chips
- 2 tablespoons shortening

Direction

- Put peanut butter in large bowl and add butter and sugar alternately in small amounts at a time.
- Mix well until all sugar disappears then add cereal and continue mixing.

- Form into balls the size of walnuts.
- Melt morsels and shortening in a double boiler then remove from heat.
- Leave water on the stove at medium temperature but do not let water boil.
- Dip balls into chocolate mixture with a large spoon.
- Lift out with two forks rocking back and forth to remove excess chocolate.
- When chocolate gets too thick return to hot water until soft enough to dip again.
- Place dipped balls on wax paper to cool.

277. Peanut Butter Crispy Eggs Recipe

Serving: 24 | Prep: | Cook: |Ready in:

Ingredients

- 1/2 cup butter, softened
- 1 pound powdered sugar
- 28 ounces peanut butter
- 5 1/2 cup crispy rice cereal
- 1 pound chocolate

Direction

- Mix butter and sugar together.
- Add peanut butter and mix well.
- Add cereal. Mix well. You may have to use your hands.
- Form small eggs out of the mixture. Place eggs on cookie sheets lined with waxed paper. Refrigerate eggs until cold and firm.
- Melt chocolate and dip eggs into it.

278. Peanut ButterChocolate Caramel Apples With Honey Peanuts Recipe

Serving: 8 | Prep: | Cook: 20mins |Ready in:

Ingredients

- For the apples:
- -----------------
- 8 large Braeburn apples, at room temperature
- Peanut Butter-Chocolate Ganache, at room temperature
- 8 chopsticks or craft sticks
- --------------
- For the coating:
- ------------
- 2 cups honey roasted peanuts, coarsely chopped
- 2 cups packed light brown sugar
- 1 3/4 cups heavy cream
- 3/4 cup dark corn syrup
- 2 tablespoons unsalted butter (1/4 stick)
- 2 teaspoons kosher salt
- up to 1 day in advance.

Direction

- For the apples:

279. Peanut Buttery Chocolate Balls Recipe

Serving: 70 | Prep: | Cook: 60mins |Ready in:

Ingredients

- 2 sticks of margarine
- 1 box powdered sugar
- 1/2 qt. crunchy peanut butter
- 1/2 cup ground pecans
- 8 oz. chocolate chips
- 1/2 block of parafin wax

Direction

- Mix softened margarine, powdered sugar, peanut butter, and pecans in a large mixing bowl with a spoon (or hands).
- Melt chocolate and paraffin wax in a double broiler until smooth.

- Mold peanut butter mixture into one inch balls, dip into chocolate and wax mixture, being sure to cover all surface.
- Place on wax-covered cookie sheet, and chill in the fridge for at least 1 hour.
- ENJOY!

280. Peanut Clusters Recipe

Serving: 24 | Prep: | Cook: 10mins | Ready in:

Ingredients

- 2 - 6 oz. packages butterscotch chips
- 1 - 6 oz. package semi-sweet chocolate chips
- 2 Tbs. paraffin
- 1 lb. salted dry-roasted peanuts

Direction

- Melt chips and paraffin in top of a double boiler until melted.
- Add peanuts; mix well.
- Drop by teaspoonfuls onto waxed paper.
- Let cool in fridge for several hours.
- Enjoy! :)

281. Peanutty Chocolate Truffles Recipe

Serving: 24 | Prep: | Cook: | Ready in:

Ingredients

- ¾ cup creamy peanut butter
- ¼ cup butter, softened
- 1 teaspoon vanilla extract
- 1/3 cup powdered hot cocoa mix
- 1 cup powdered sugar
- 1 cup finely chopped cocktail peanuts

Direction

- Using a blender or mixer or food processor, mix peanut butter, butter and vanilla extract in a medium bowl until mixture is light and creamy.
- Combine powdered cocoa mix and powdered sugar in another bowl, and then stir it into the peanut butter mixture.
- Place chopped peanuts in a shallow dish.
- Roll peanut butter mixture into 1½" balls, and then roll them in the peanuts to coat evenly.
- Place truffles on wax paper lined baking sheets.
- Refrigerate until firm.
- When chilled, store truffles in air-tight container and keep cool or refrigerate.

282. Pecan Caramel Spiders Recipe

Serving: 30 | Prep: | Cook: 30mins | Ready in:

Ingredients

- 1 1/2 cups toasted pecans
- 1 cup heavy cream
- 1 cup granulated sugar
- 1/2 cup light corn syrup
- 1 teaspoon vanilla extract
- 2 tablespoons unsalted butter, in pieces
- 1/4 teaspoon salt
- 5 ounces thin black licorice strands, cut into 2-inch pieces
- 6 ounces semisweet chocolate, chopped
- 4 ounces milk chocolate, chopped
- chocolate curls or jimmies, optional

Direction

- Line 2 baking sheets with waxed paper and lightly spray with non-stick spray.
- Mound 30 small clusters of pecans, about 3 or 4 pecans each, spaced a couple inches apart on the pan.
- Make caramel: Warm the cream over low heat and keep warm while you cook the sugar.

- Put the sugar and corn syrup and in a deep, heavy-bottomed large saucepan.
- Cook over medium heat, stirring occasionally until the sugar dissolves.
- Stop stirring, raise heat to medium-high, and simmer until the sugar reaches the hard crack stage, or 305 degrees F on a candy thermometer, about 7 minutes.
- Whisk the butter and salt into the sugar mixture.
- Gradually pour in the cream and vanilla taking care since the mixture will bubble up.
- Reduce the heat to medium and continue to cook, stirring occasionally, until the sugar reaches soft ball stage, 240 degrees F on the thermometer, about 5 minutes more.
- Immediately remove from the heat and cool for a minute.
- Ladle a couple tablespoons of warm caramel over some of the nut clusters, to make the spider bodies.
- Then press 6 pieces of licorice into the warm caramel to make the legs.
- Repeat with the remaining caramel and licorice.
- (It's helpful to have an extra hand here, since the caramel can set quickly.
- If caramel hardens, warm over very low heat.)
- Let spiders cool 15 minutes.
- ~
- Meanwhile, put the chocolates in a medium heatproof bowl.
- Bring a saucepan filled with 1-inch or so of water to a very slow simmer; set the bowl over, but not touching, the water.
- Stir the chocolate occasionally until melted and smooth.
- (Alternatively, put the chocolate in a medium microwave-safe bowl. Melt at 50 percent power in the microwave until soft, about 1 minute. Stir, and continue heat until completely melted, 2 to 3 minutes more.)
- ~
- Spoon about 1 tablespoon of melted chocolate on top of each spider.
- Sprinkle with jimmies or chocolate curls, if desired.
- Let cool until firm.
- ~
- Copyright 2007 Television Food Network, G.P. All rights reserved

283. Pecan Clusters Recipe

Serving: 20 | Prep: | Cook: 8mins | Ready in:

Ingredients

- 1 jar marshmellow creme (7 oz)
- 1 1/2 pound milk chocolate kisses
- 5 cups sugar
- 1 can evaporated pet milk (13 oz)
- 2 cups butter
- 6 cups pecan halves

Direction

- Combine sugar, milk, and butter in saucepan; bring to a boil and cook 8 minutes, stirring constantly.
- Pour over marshmallow crème and kisses.
- Stir until well blended.
- Stir in pecans.
- Drop by teaspoonfuls onto wax paper.
- Makes about 12 dozen.

284. Peppermint Patties Recipe

Serving: 28 | Prep: | Cook: | Ready in:

Ingredients

- 3/4 cup sweetened condensed milk
- 1 1/2 teaspoons peppermint extract
- 1 teaspoon vanilla extract
- 3-4 cups confectioners' sugar

- 3 cups semisweet chocolate chips
- 2 tablespoons shortening

Direction

- In a large mixing bowl, combine condensed milk and extracts. Stir well.
- Stir in enough confectioners' sugar to form a stiff dough.
- Knead until no longer sticky.
- Form dough into 1 inch balls and flatten to form patties.
- Chill for 1 hour or until firm.
- In medium saucepan over low heat, melt chocolate with shortening, stirring constantly.
- Remove from heat.
- Dip patties one at a time into chocolate using a fork.
- Place chocolate dipped patties on wax paper and chill until set.
- Keep refrigerated.

285. Peppermint Pattys Peppermint Patties Recipe

Serving: 96 | Prep: | Cook: 5mins | Ready in:

Ingredients

- 1 (14 oz.) can EAGLE BRAND® sweetened condensed milk
- 1 tablespoon peppermint extract
- Green or red food coloring (optional)
- 6 cups powdered sugar, plus additional for kneading filling
- 1 1/2 pounds chocolate-flavored candy coating*, melted
- .

Direction

- IN large bowl, combine EAGLE BRAND® milk, extract and food coloring (optional).
- Add 6 cups confectioners' sugar; beat on low speed until smooth and well blended.
- Turn mixture onto surface sprinkled with confectioners' sugar.
- KNEAD lightly to form smooth ball.
- Shape into 1-inch balls. Place 2 inches apart on wax-paper-lined baking sheets.
- Flatten each ball into a 1-1/2-inch patty.
- LET dry 1 hour or longer; turn over and let dry at least 1 hour.
- With fork, dip each patty into warm candy coating (draw fork lightly across rim of pan to remove excess coating).
- Invert onto wax-paper-lined baking sheets; let stand until firm.
- Store covered at room temperature or in refrigerator

286. Perfect Chocolate Fudge Recipe

Serving: 12 | Prep: | Cook: 30mins | Ready in:

Ingredients

- 20 oz. Hershey's milk chocolate bars - I buy the big ones that are always on sale at Christmas time, but any size will do, just make sure it adds up to 20 oz. If you like darker fudge, substitute some or all of the 20 oz. with the semi-sweet chocolate bars.
- 1 cup butter (not margarine!), softened to room temperature. Also, a little extra butter for your pans.
- 1-12 oz. package of semi-sweet chocolate chips. Use a good brand, as in Nestle's, Hershey's, or Ghiradelli. If you prefer lighter fudge, use milk chocolate chips.
- 4 cups granulated (white) sugar
- 1 and 2/3 cups evaporated milk
- 2 and 1/2 cups mini marshmallows
- 2 teaspoons vanilla, use the real stuff
- 1 pound of nuts, chopped

Direction

- In your large stainless steel bowl, break up the milk chocolate candy bars and the butter into small pieces. Pour in chocolate chips and set aside.
- Grease your pans with butter. You'll need two 9x13 inch flat cake pans, but you can use smaller or larger pans depending on what you have available, and how thick you want your fudge to be. It's best to have a couple of extra smaller pans ready just in case.
- In a large saucepan or pot, combine sugar, evaporated milk and mini marshmallows. Bring to a boil over medium heat, stirring constantly. Tip: Don't scrape the sides of the pot when you are stirring, it tends to make candy taste grainy.
- Cook and stir at a light but steady boil for 7 minutes. You might see some brownish bits floating around as its cooking. This is normal. Remove from heat, pour over butter and chocolate in your bowl.
- With a wooden spoon, stir until melted and well blended. Continue to stir until candy loses some of its shine. (The shine should go from a shiny, high gloss to a matte gloss). Stir in vanilla and nuts, if desired.* Pour into buttered pans. Cool completely before cutting into pieces. Use a knife dipped in hot water for cutting.
- Note: If you don't want nuts in your fudge, this is where you leave them out. If you want to make a pan of fudge without nuts, then first stir in the vanilla, then pour how much you want without nuts into a pan, and then add nuts to the remaining fudge. You'll need to adjust the amount of nuts then. For example, if you're making half of your fudge without nuts and half with, then only use 8 oz. of nuts.

287. Pistachio Truffles Recipe

Serving: 4 | Prep: | Cook: 90mins | Ready in:

Ingredients

- dark chocolate (broken in to pieces) 315g
- butter, chopped 45g
- thickened doubled cream 1/2 cup
- sugar, tablespoons 2
- Galliano liquer, tablespoons 2
- pistachio nuts, chopped 125g

Direction

- Place chocolate, butter, cream and sugar in a heatproof bowl set over a saucepan of simmering water and heat, stirring, until mixture is smooth.
- Add liqueur and half the pistachio nuts and mix well to combine.
- Chill mixture for about 1hour or until firm enough to roll into balls.
- Roll tablespoon of mixture into balls, then roll in remaining pistachio nuts. Chill until required.

288. Potato Chocolate Fudge Recipe

Serving: 12 | Prep: | Cook: 10mins | Ready in:

Ingredients

- 2 unsweetened chocolate squares
- 4 tablespoons butter
- 1/3 cup mashed potatoes
- 1/8 teaspoon salt
- 1 teaspoon vanilla extract
- 1 pound confectioners' sugar

Direction

- Cook and mash a medium potato without using any seasoning, butter or milk.
- Measure 1/3 cup.
- Melt chocolate and butter together.
- Blend into mashed potatoes with the salt and vanilla.
- Mix well.
- Sift sugar.

- Add a small amount at a time blending until no sugar is visible.
- When a spoon is no longer equal to the task of mixing knead in the balance of the sugar with well-buttered hands.
- Turn out onto a board and continue to knead until mixture is smooth, glossy and pliable buttering hands as necessary.
- No crumbs should remain.
- Press into a buttered square pan.

289. ROLLO PRETZELS Recipe

Serving: 50 | Prep: | Cook: 23mins | Ready in:

Ingredients

- 50 small pretzel twists
- 50 pieces rollo candy
- 50 pieces whole pecans or walnuts

Direction

- Place pretzel pieces on a baking sheet.
- Top with one Rollo candy.
- Place in a warm oven (250 degrees) to just let the candy melt on top of the pretzel to hold it in place.
- Remove from oven and place a nut on top.
- Let cool and harden.

290. Raisin Cashew Chocolate Fudge Recipe

Serving: 15 | Prep: | Cook: 20mins | Ready in:

Ingredients

- 1 king size Hershey chocolate Bar.... (7 - 8 oz.)
- 12 oz. bag of Nestle's chocolate Dots --- mini semi sweet chocolate chips
- 1 cup cashews, unsalted, chopped
- 1/2 cup pecans ,chopped
- 1/2 -3/4 cup raisins
- 1 jar (7-8 oz.) marshmallow Fluff
- ....
- 1/3 cup butter
- 1 cup evaporated milk
- 4 1/2 cups superfine sugar
- extra butter

Direction

- In a large heavy bowl that can stand heat.
- Break up Hershey Bar into pieces.
- Add chocolate dots on top.
- Then add the nuts and then the raisins and top with marshmallow fluff.
- Put in a warm spot so the chocolate starts to soften.
- ....
- In a heavy pan, butter the sides and bottom of the pan heavily.
- Put in 1/3 cup of butter and the evaporated milk.
- Heat until warm.
- Slowly add the sugar. Stir after each addition.
- Make sure the dry sugar does not touch the sides of the pan.
- Don't stir too hard. You don't want the sugar mixture all over the sides of the pan.
- Heat slowly until the sugar is dissolved keep stirring.
- DON'T scrap the sides of the pan.
- Then turn the heat up to medium.
- Using a candy thermometer bring temperature to 230 - 232' F.
- Stir mixture to keep from burning.
- Pour hot sugar mixture over chocolate mixture in the bowl.
- DO NOT scrape the pot out.
- Use a new spoon and blend the together as quickly as possible.
- DON"T over mix. There will be some streaks of the fluff that's ok.
- Spread mixture on a well-buttered jelly roll pan. (Large spatula works).

- Work quickly. This fudge sets up very fast.
- Cover tightly with plastic wrap and then foil.
- Put in a cold spot for 4 hours. Cut into pieces.
- ....
- Keep wrapped tightly. This fudge dries out very fast.

291. Raisin Cashew Drops Recipe

Serving: 24 | Prep: | Cook: 180mins | Ready in:

Ingredients

- 2c. semisweet chocolate chips
- 14oz. can sweetened condensed milk
- 1tbs. light corn syrup
- 1tsp. vanilla extract
- 2c. corarsely chopped cashews
- 2c. raisins

Direction

- In a heavy saucepan over low heat, melt the chocolate chips with the milk and corn syrup for 10 minutes, stirring occasionally. Remove from the heat; stir in the vanilla until blended. Stir in cashews and raisins.
- Drop by teaspoonfuls onto waxed paper-lined baking sheets.
- Refrigerate for 3 hours or until firm.
- Store in the refrigerator....

292. Raisin Peanut Clusters Recipe

Serving: 1 | Prep: | Cook: 20mins | Ready in:

Ingredients

- 1 c semisweet chocolate
- 1 cn sweetened condensed milk (14 oz.)
- Ds salt
- 1 c seedless raisins
- 1 c Shelled roasted peanuts

Direction

- Melt chocolate in top part of double boiler over hot water.
- Add condensed milk and salt, cook for 10 minutes or until thickened, stirring constantly.
- Add raisins and peanuts.
- Drop from tablespoon onto wax paper.
- Refrigerate until firm. Makes about 20 clusters.

293. Raspberry Chocolate Chips Recipe

Serving: 10 | Prep: | Cook: 40mins | Ready in:

Ingredients

- 2 oz good quality milk chocolate
- 2 oz good quality semisweet chocolate
- 1 tsp vegetable shortening
- 3-4 DROPS concentrated candy flavouring (i.e. Lorann's)
- 1 tbsp cocoa-powder.html">Raspberry Cocoa Powder (optional, if you don't make the cocoa use a tablespoon of Dutch processed regular cocoa)

Direction

- Melt together chocolates and shortening.
- Stir in candy flavouring and raspberry cocoa until smooth.
- Pipe into chips on a parchment lined sheet and let set.
- Store in the fridge or freezer.
- Serving Size: makes about 2/3 cup (10.6 tbsp.)

294. Raspberry Fudge Balls Recipe

Serving: 24 | Prep: | Cook: 2mins | Ready in:

Ingredients

- 1 cup (6 ounces) semisweet chocolate chips
- 1 package (8 ounces) cream cheese, softened
- 3/4 cup finely crushed vanilla wafers (about 25 wafers)
- 1/4 cup seedless raspberry jam
- 3/4 cup finely chopped almonds

Direction

- In a microwave, melt chocolate chips; stir until smooth. Cool slightly.
- In a small bowl, beat the cream cheese and melted chocolate until smooth and blended. Stir in the wafer crumbs and jam. Refrigerate for 4 hours or until firm. Shape into 1-in. balls; roll in almonds. Store in an airtight container in the refrigerator. Yield: about 2 dozen.

295. Red Velvet Popcorn Recipe

Serving: 15 | Prep: | Cook: 2hours | Ready in:

Ingredients

- ½ cup brown sugar
- ¼ cup sugar
- ¼ cup golden corn syrup
- ¼ cup water
- ¼ cup dairy free margarine
- ¼ cup Dutch processed cocoa
- ½ tsp salt
- 1 tbsp red gel food colouring (or 2 tbsp liquid)
- 1 tbsp vanilla
- ½ cup finely shredded, unsweetened coconut
- 10 cups popped popcorn (ideally plain, no salt/butter)

Direction

- Preheat oven to 250F and line a large rimmed baking sheet with parchment.
- In a large saucepan combine sugars, corn syrup, water, margarine, cocoa and salt.
- Cook over medium heat until well combined and bubbling.
- Remove from heat and stir in the food colouring, vanilla and coconut.
- Allow to cool 3 minutes, then pour over the popcorn in a large bowl and mix thoroughly until evenly coated.
- Pour the popcorn on the cookie sheet and bake for 45-55 minutes, stirring it 3-4 times during cooking.

296. Reese's Peanut Butter Pumpkin Spider Recipe

Serving: 8 | Prep: | Cook: 1hours | Ready in:

Ingredients

- thx to:http://www.hersheys.com/recipes/recipe-details.aspx?id=8758&name=REESE'S-Peanut-Butter-Pumpkin-Spider#share_modal
- there is a photo of the spider there
- REESE'S peanut butter pumpkin Spider
- Ingredients
- REESE'S peanut butter pumpkins(1.2 oz. ea.)
- Large pretzel twists(2-1/2 to 3 in.)
- 1/4 cup HERSHEY'S milk chocolate chips, HERSHEY'S SPECIAL dark chocolate chips or HERSHEY'S Semi-Sweet Chocolate Chips*
- White YORK PIECES candies

Direction

- Directions
- 1 Line tray or cookie sheet with waxed paper. Remove wrappers from desired number of peanut butter pumpkins. For each spider, cut 8 matching curved sections from pretzels which

will form the legs. Set aside remaining pretzels pieces.
- 2 Place milk chocolate chips in small microwave-safe bowl. Microwave at MEDIUM (50%) 30 seconds; stir. If necessary, microwave at MEDIUM an additional 10 seconds at a time, stirring after each heating, until chips are melted and smooth when stirred. Transfer to small heavy duty plastic food storage bag. Cut off one corner of bag about 1/4 inch from the tip.
- 3 For each spider, place peanut butter pumpkin on prepared tray. Attach pretzel legs and white candy "eyes" to spider with melted chocolate; place dot of melted chocolate on each eye. Allow chocolate to set before moving spiders.
- * This amount of chocolate will make about 8 spiders.

297. Reindeer Belly Buttons Recipe

Serving: 4 | Prep: | Cook: 3mins | Ready in:

Ingredients

- 50 pretzel rings
- 1 (8 ounce) package chocolate kisses
- 1/4 cup red and green M&M's

Direction

- Place the pretzels on a greased baking sheet. Place a chocolate kiss in the center of each pretzel. Bake at 275 degrees F for 2-3 minutes or until the chocolate softens. Remove from oven. Place one M&M in the center of the kiss, pressing down slightly, so the chocolate fills the pretzel.
- Refrigerate for 5-10 minutes until firm. These freeze well.
- Makes 4 dozen.

298. Rich Chocolate Pumpkin Truffles Recipe

Serving: 24 | Prep: | Cook: | Ready in:

Ingredients

- 2-1/2 cups vanilla wafers crushed
- 1 cup almonds toasted and ground
- 1/2 cup powdered sugar sifted
- 2 teaspoons ground cinnamon
- 6 ounces semisweet chocolate chips
- 1/2 cup canned pumpkin
- 1/3 cup coffee liqueur
- 1/4 cup powdered sugar sifted

Direction

- Combine vanilla wafer crumbs, almonds, 1/2 cup powdered sugar and cinnamon.
- Blend in chocolate, pumpkin and coffee liqueur then form into 1" balls and chill.
- Dust with remaining powdered sugar just before serving.

299. Rocky Road Balls Recipe

Serving: 30 | Prep: | Cook: 10mins | Ready in:

Ingredients

- 5 oz miniature marshmellows
- 1 1/2 finely chopped pecans
- 5 oz regular raisins
- 1 1/4 cup peanut butter
- 2 tbsp powder sugar
- 1 pkg chocolate almond bark (melting chocolate)
- 1-1 1/2 cup powdered sugar (dusting hands and rolling mixture balls in)

Direction

- Melt almond bark on double boiler. Until all melted.
- In the meantime, in a large bowl, mix marshmallows, pecans, raisins, peanut butter & 2 tbsp. powdered sugar together, thoroughly. Mixture will be stiff but gooey. Make sure all in combined, takes a few minutes but will bind.
- Take 1-1 1/2 cups of powdered sugar place in a shallow bowl. Dust hands with powdered sugar, and grab about 1 1/2- 2 tbsp. of the mixture, it's an eyeball thing, roll in powdered sugar and in hand to make the lumpy balls (excuse the phase, I see how I worded it--sorry) place on a parchment lined cookie sheet, Repeat dusting hands and rolling each lumpy ball until mixture is all gone. Let balls rest for a couple minutes before dipping into melted chocolate.
- Dip each ball quickly in melted chocolate. Shake off excess chocolate as best as you can. Place back on parchment lined pan. You may have extra chocolate, and mixture makes roughly 30 to 40 or so balls. Let balls cool completely until set and chocolate easily releases from the parchment.

300.   Rocky Road Bars Recipe

Serving: 24 | Prep: | Cook: 5mins | Ready in:

Ingredients

- 1(12 oz) pkg. semi sweet chocolate chips
- 1 (14 oz) can sweetened condensed milk
- 2 Tbsp. butter or margarine
- 2 cups unsalted dry roasted peanuts
- 1 (10-/12 oz) pkg. of mini marshmallows (about 5-1/4 cups)

Direction

- In a large bowl combine marshmallows and nuts.
- In top of a double boiler, over boiling water, melt chips with milk and butter, remove from heat.
- Fold chocolate mixture into marshmallow mixture. Spread in a wax paper lined 13x9x2 in baking pan. Chill 2 hours until firm. Remove from pan, peel off paper, cut into 1-1/2 to 2 inch squares.
- Cover and store at room temperature.

301.   Rocky Road Candy Recipe

Serving: 15 | Prep: | Cook: | Ready in:

Ingredients

- 1 12oz bag semi-sweet chocolate chips
- 1 12oz bag butterscotch chips
- 1 cup peanut butter
- 10oz bag of marshmallows
- 1 cup dry roasted peanuts

Direction

- Combine chocolate chips, butterscotch chips, and peanut butter in a glass bowl (or other microwaveable bowl).
- Microwave for 5 minutes on 70%
- Stir until melted.
- Fold in marshmallows and peanuts.
- Pour into greased 9 x 13 pan.
- Refrigerate 2+ hours to harden.

302.   Rocky Road Recipe

Serving: 6 | Prep: | Cook: 5mins | Ready in:

Ingredients

- 2 cups semi-sweet chocolate pieces
- 1 cup peanut butter, creamy or chunky
- 4 cups miniature marshmallows

- chopped peanuts, salted peanuts, chopped walnuts (optional)

Direction

- Grease a 9x9 inch pan. (I use a small cookie sheet lined with parchment paper)
- Melt chocolate chips and peanut butter together in microwave. Make sure all chips are melted.
- Stir in marshmallows and nuts
- Pour into your prepared pan. Cool.
- This can be put into the refrigerator to cool.
- Either cut or break into pieces

---

303. SALTINE CHOCOLATE CRUNCH Recipe

Serving. 10 | Prep: | Cook: 10mins |Ready in:

Ingredients

- 1 sleeve (about 24) saltines
- 3/4 C. brown sugar
- 1 C. butter
- 12 oz. (2 C.) chocolate chips
- 3/4 C. chopped nuts

Direction

- Preheat oven to 400°
- Line a cookie sheet with foil.
- Spray foil very lightly with cooking spray.
- Cover cookie sheet with saltines in one layer.
- Boil sugar and butter for 3 minutes.
- Pour over saltines and spread evenly.
- Bake 5 minutes.
- Remove from oven.
- Sprinkle with chocolate chips.
- Let set one minute, then spread melted chips with spatula.
- Sprinkle with nuts, then press down lightly.
- Cut on diagonal immediately or cool until firm then break up.

- Pieces can be frozen.
- Yields 30 pieces.

---

304. SOFT TORRONE Italian Candy Recipe

Serving: 10 | Prep: | Cook: 45mins |Ready in:

Ingredients

- 450 g (1 lb) orange honey
- 500 g (1 lb 2 oz) almonds, lightly toasted
- 250 g (0.5 lb) sugar
- 80 g (3 oz) powdered sugar
- 3 egg whites
- 20 g (1 Tbsp) pistachios, chopped
- 200 g (7 oz) dark chocolate

Direction

- Whip the egg whites till stiffened.
- Place the honey in top of double boiler over boiling water for 30 minutes. Stir the honey frequently. Add whipped egg whites.
- After 10 minutes add sugar. Cook for 15 more minutes.
- Turn off heat. Stir in almonds and pistachios.
- Pour mixture two inches deep into loaf pans lined with parchment paper. Let cool.
- Remove from pans and cut into 1-inch squares.
- Melt dipping chocolate in top of double boiler. Dip each square into melted chocolate, place on cookie sheet covered with aluminum foil.

---

305. Salted Chocolate Caramels Recipe

Serving: 64 | Prep: | Cook: 30mins |Ready in:

Ingredients

- 2 c. heavy cream
- 10 1/2 oz fine-quality bittersweet chocolate (no more than 60% cacao if marked), finely chopped
- 1 3/4 c. sugar
- 1/2 c. light corn syrup
- 1/4 c. water
- 1/4 tsp. salt
- 3 TBSP. unsalted butter, cut into tablespoon pieces
- 2 tsp. flaky sea salt such as Maldon (this is what the original recipe called for, but I found it to be a bit much, 1 tsp. would probably be plenty)
- vegetable oil for greasing

Direction

- Line bottom and sides of an 8-inch straight-sided square metal baking pan with 2 long sheets of crisscrossed parchment. Lightly oil.
- Bring cream just to a boil in a 1- to 1 1/2-quart heavy saucepan over moderately high heat, then reduce heat to low and add chocolate. Let stand 1 minute, then stir until chocolate is completely melted. Remove from heat.
- Bring sugar, corn syrup, water, and salt to a boil in a 5- to 6-quart heavy pot over moderate heat, stirring until sugar is dissolved. Boil, uncovered, without stirring but gently swirling pan occasionally, until sugar is deep golden, about 10 minutes. Tilt pan and carefully pour in chocolate mixture (mixture will bubble and steam vigorously). Continue to boil over moderate heat, stirring frequently, until mixture registers 243°F on thermometer, about 15 minutes (original recipe said 255, but I find that's a bit high for caramel). Add butter, stirring until completely melted, then immediately pour into lined baking pan (do not scrape any caramel clinging to bottom or side of saucepan). Let caramel stand 10 minutes, then sprinkle evenly with sea salt. Cool completely in pan on a rack, about 2 hours.
- Carefully invert caramel onto a clean, dry cutting board, then peel off parchment. Turn caramel salt side up. Lightly oil blade of a large heavy knife and cut into 1-inch squares.

306. Saltine Candy Recipe

Serving: 8 | Prep: | Cook: 10mins | Ready in:

Ingredients

- 1 sleeve of saltine crackers(approximately)
- 2sticks unsalted butter
- 1 8oz. bag semi-sweet chocolate morsels(more if you want thicker chocolate topping)
- 1c. chopped walnuts(or less)
- 1c. sugar

Direction

- Heat oven to 350. Line cookie sheet with foil and place saltines down in single layer. Melt butter, add sugar to melted butter and cook butter and sugar combo in microwave for a total of 3 mins; stirring every 30 seconds so sugar and butter mixture doesn't burn. Pour butter/sugar over the crackers so all are covered and bake for 5 mins.
- Sprinkle chocolate morsels over the crackers and spread as they melt to cover crackers. Sprinkle with walnuts and freeze for 2 hours.
- Break into pieces (big or small). Enjoy!

307. Salty Chocolate Pecan Candy Recipe

Serving: 134 | Prep: | Cook: 15mins | Ready in:

Ingredients

- 1 cup pecans, coarsely chopped
- 3 (4-oz.) bars bittersweet chocolate baking bars
- 3 (4-oz.) white chocolate baking bars
- 1 teaspoon coarse sea salt*

Direction

- Place pecans in a single layer on a baking sheet.
- Bake at 350° for 8 to 10 minutes or until toasted.
- Line a 17- x 12-inch jelly-roll pan with parchment paper.
- Break each chocolate bar into 8 equal pieces. (You will have 48 pieces total.)
- Arrange in a checkerboard pattern in jelly-roll pan, alternating white and dark chocolate. (Pieces will touch.)
- Bake at 225° for 5 minutes or just until chocolate is melted.
- Remove pan to a wire rack.
- Swirl chocolates into a marble pattern using a wooden pick. Sprinkle evenly with toasted pecans and salt.
- Chill 1 hour or until firm. Break into pieces.
- Store in an airtight container in refrigerator up to 1 month.
- *3/4 tsp. kosher salt may be substituted.
- Note: For testing purposes only, we used Ghirardelli 60% Cacao Bittersweet Chocolate Baking Bars and Ghirardelli White Chocolate Baking Bars.

308. Sea Salted Smoky Almond Chocolate Bark Recipe

Serving: 8 | Prep: | Cook: 5mins | Ready in:

Ingredients

- 1 bar (8 oz.) Nestle Chocolatier 53% Cacao dark chocolate Baking Bar, broken into pieces
- 1/2 cup smoked-flavored almonds, coarsely chopped, divided (but I use more)
- 1/8 teaspoon sea salt (preferably large crystal) (I also use more than this)

Direction

- LINE 8-inch baking pan with parchment or wax paper.
- Microwave the chocolate in uncovered, microwave-safe bowl on high for 1 minute, then stir. The chocolate may keep some of its shape. If necessary, microwave at additional 10- to 15-second intervals, stirring just until smooth.
- Stir in 1/4 cup almonds.
- Pour into the lined pan.
- Sprinkle with remaining almonds.
- Tap pan several times to spread the chocolate and settle the nuts.
- Sprinkle with sea salt. They call for 1/8 tsp., but I give a good sprinkling of the salt, so there's some in every single bite.
- Refrigerate for about 1 hour or until firm.
- Break into pieces.
- Store in air-tight container at room temperature.

309. Sees Candy Recipe

Serving: 15 | Prep: | Cook: 6mins | Ready in:

Ingredients

- 1 12oz can evaporated milk
- 4 1/2 cups sugar
- 3 12 oz packages of semi-sweet chocolate chips
- 2 sticks butter
- 1 7 oz jar marshmellow creme
- 3 cups nuts, chopped
- 5 teaspoons vanilla

Direction

- Bring evaporated milk and sugar to a full boil and cook 6 minutes.
- Pour over other ingredients in another bowl.
- Mix well and pour into a greased 13 x 9 x 2 dish.
- Allow to chill before cutting into squares.
- Yield: 3 dozen squares.

310. Semi Sweet And White Chocolate Peanut Butter Cups Recipe

Serving: 24 | Prep: | Cook: 30mins | Ready in:

Ingredients

- 3/4 cup of smooth peanut butter
- 1 - 6oz pkg Bakers white chocolate squares, chopped
- 3/4 cup of smooth peanut butter
- 1 - 6 oz pkg Bakers semi-sweet chocolate squares, chopped
- 3/4 cup of smooth peanut butter
- 1/4 cup crushed peanuts
- candy foil
- mini muffin or candy pan
- 1 small sandwich bag

Direction

- Line foil in mini muffin or candy pans
- Melt 3/4 c peanut butter and white chocolate squares over low heat.
- Fill foil 1/3 full and refrigerate.
- Put 3/4 cup of peanut butter in a small sandwich bag. Cut tip and pipe on top of each foil cup. Chill.
- Melt 3/4 c peanut butter and semi-sweet chocolates over low heat.
- Spoon on top of each candy cup.
- Top of crushed peanuts and chill again for 20 minutes.

311. Slacker Jacks Recipe

Serving: 6 | Prep: | Cook: 80mins | Ready in:

Ingredients

- 3 ounces popped popcorn, approximately 3 quarts
- 1 cup salted peanuts
- 4 ounces unsalted butter
- 16 ounces dark brown sugar, approximately 2 cups
- 1/4 cup dark corn syrup
- 1/2 teaspoon pure vanilla extract

Direction

- Preheat the oven to 250 degrees F.
- Spray a sheet pan with non-stick spray and line with parchment paper. Spray the parchment paper with non-stick spray as well and set aside.
- Combine the popcorn and peanuts in a large mixing bowl.
- Set aside until ready to use.
- Melt the butter in a medium saucepan over medium heat.
- Add the brown sugar, corn syrup and vanilla and stir until combined.
- Heat the mixture until it reaches 250 degrees F, approximately 10 minutes.
- Pour the syrup over the popcorn and stir to combine.
- You will need to work quickly because the syrup hardens rapidly.
- Spread the mixture onto the prepared sheet pan and bake in the oven for 1 hour.
- Cool completely.
- Break into pieces and serve immediately or store in an airtight container for 2 to 3 days.

312. Snickers Bars Recipe

Serving: 40 | Prep: | Cook: 15mins | Ready in:

Ingredients

- 2 cups milk chocolate chips
- 1/2 cup butterscotch chips
- 3/4 cup creamy peanut butter
- 1 cup granulated sugar
- 1/4 cup plus 4 T. milk
- 1/4 cup butter or margarine

- 1 t. vanilla
- 1 large bag (approximately 40) unwrapped caramels
- 1 jar marshmallow creme (8 ounces)
- 1 1/2 cups chopped dry-roasted peanuts

Direction

- LAYER ONE: Melt together 1 cup milk chocolate chips, 1/4 cup butterscotch chips, and 1/4 cup creamy peanut butter in a small saucepan on low heat, stirring constantly until melted and smooth.
- Spread into an ungreased 9 x 13-inch pan.
- Chill while making next layer.
- LAYER TWO: Combine 1 cup granulated sugar, 1/4 cup milk, and 1/4 cup butter or margarine in medium saucepan on medium heat. Bring to boil and continue boiling for 4-5 minutes while stirring constantly.
- Remove from heat and add 1/4 cup creamy peanut butter, one 8-ounce jar marshmallow crème, and 1 teaspoon vanilla.
- Stir until smooth.
- Mix in 1 1/2 cup chopped dry-roasted peanuts.
- Spread evenly onto layer one.
- LAYER THREE: On low heat in medium saucepan, melt together 1 large bag (approximately 40) unwrapped caramels and 4 tablespoons milk.
- Stir constantly until melted and of smooth consistency.
- Spread evenly over layer two and cool completely in refrigerator.
- LAYER FOUR: Melt together 1/4 cup creamy peanut butter, 1/4 cup butterscotch chips, and 1 cup milk chocolate chips on low heat in small saucepan on low heat, stirring constantly until melted and smooth.
- Spread evenly over caramel layer and cool completely in refrigerator.
- Cut into small squares.

313. Somewhat Sophisticated Chocolate Chews Recipe

Serving: 12 | Prep: | Cook: 8hours20mins | Ready in:

Ingredients

- 3/4 cup whole almonds
- 1/3 cup whole macadamia nuts
- 1/4 cup whole cashews
- 1/3 cup cocoa powder
- 1/2 tsp ground coffee (not instant)
- 1/2 tsp sea salt
- 1 tbsp vanilla
- 1/4 cup honey
- 1/3 cup rolled oats

Direction

- In a food processor, finely chop (but do not grind) almonds, macadamias and cashews
- Pulse in cocoa, coffee and salt, then pour in honey and vanilla and pulse in.
- Add oats and run until a doughy mix forms.
- Press into a parchment-lined 9" square pan.
- Refrigerate overnight before cutting.
- Variation:
- To add extra protein to the mixture, add 2 tbsp. of whey isolate protein powder or (for dairy-free) soy protein isolate.

314. Squidgy Chocolate Bars Recipe

Serving: 10 | Prep: | Cook: 120mins | Ready in:

Ingredients

- 2 bars dark quality/ cooking chocolate
- 2tbl syrup
- half packet of digestive biscuits (graham crackers?)
- 1tbl of butter
- walnuts
- glace cherries

- optional ingredients (add as many or as few as desired.)
- currants raisins sultanas
- marshmellows
- m&m's

Direction

- Break up the biscuits into bite sized pieces.
- Melt the butter and syrup in pan, add the biscuits and mix.
- Break the chocolate into small squares and melt slowly in a glass bowl placed over a pan of simmering water.
- Take the pan off the heat and add the melted chocolate, sliced glace cherries and walnuts (or if preferred add sultanas, marshmallows etc.)
- Line a rectangular loaf tin with plastic wrap/cling film and pour the chocolate mix into the tin.
- Leave to set in the fridge for 2-3 hours. (It doesn't go completely hard so don't worry if it feels a little squidgy. this is normal.)
- Remove the chocolate loaf from the tin decorate with cherries and walnuts and cut into squares/fingers.

315. St Patricks Day Layered Mint Chocolate Fudge Recipe

Serving: 64 | Prep: | Cook: 5mins | Ready in:

Ingredients

- 2 cups (12 oz. pkg.) semi-sweet chocolate chips
- 1 (14 oz.) can Eagle Brand sweetened condensed milk, divided
- 2- tsps. vanilla extract
- 6 -oz. white confectioners' coating* or 1 cup (6 oz.) premium white chocolate chips
- 1 -tbsp. peppermint extract
- Green or red food coloring (optional

Direction

- Line 8- or 9-inch square pan with wax paper.
- Melt chocolate chips with 1 cup sweetened condensed milk in heavy saucepan over low heat; add vanilla.
- Spread half the mixture into prepared pan; chill 10 minutes or until firm.
- Hold remaining chocolate mixture at room temperature.
- Melt white confectioners' coating with remaining sweetened condensed milk in heavy saucepan over low heat (mixture will be thick).
- Add peppermint extract and food coloring, if desired.
- Spread on chilled chocolate layer; chill an additional 10 minutes or until firm.
- Spread reserved chocolate mixture on mint layer.
- Chill 2 hours or until firm.
- Remove from pan by lifting edges of wax paper; peel off paper.
- Cut into squares.
- Yield: About 1 3/4 pounds.

316. Starlight Sugar Cookies Cookie Mix Recipe Recipe

Serving: 20 | Prep: | Cook: 20mins | Ready in:

Ingredients

- Brighten up the holidays with starry sugar cookies made with easy sugar cookie mix.
- Makes about 2 dozen cookies
- 1 pouch (1 pound 1.5 ounces) Betty Crocker® sugar cookie mix
- 1/3 cup butter or margarine, melted
- 2 tablespoons Gold Medal® all-purpose flour
- 1 egg
- 1 container (1 pound) Betty Crocker® Rich & Creamy creamy white frosting
- Betty Crocker® decorating icing (assorted colors)

- Betty Crocker® decorating sprinkles and sugars (assorted colors)

Direction

1. Heat oven to 375 degrees F. In medium bowl, stir cookie mix, melted butter, flour and egg until soft dough forms.
2. On floured surface, roll dough to about 1/4-inch thickness. Cut with about 3-inch cookie cutters. On ungreased cookie sheets, place cut-outs 1 inch apart.
3. Bake 7 to 9 minutes or until edges are light golden brown. Cool 1 minute; remove from cookie sheets. Cool completely, about 15 minutes.
4. Spread frosting on cooled cookies. Decorate as desired with icing, sprinkles and sugars.
- High Altitude (3500-6500 ft.): No change.
- Nutrition Information: 1 Serving: Calories 200 (Calories from Fat 80); Total Fat 9g (Saturated Fat 3 1/2g, Trans Fat 2g); Cholesterol 15mg; Sodium 115mg; Total Carbohydrate 28g (Dietary Fiber 0g, Sugars 20g); Protein 1g
- Percent Daily Value*: Vitamin A 0%; Vitamin C 0%; Calcium 0%; Iron 0%
- Exchanges: 2 Other Carbohydrate; 0 Vegetable; 2 Fat Carbohydrate Choices: 2
- *Percent Daily Values are based on a 2,000 calorie diet.
- Storage
- To keep cookies longer, wrap tightly, label and freeze up to 6 months.

317. Sugar Cookie Chocolate Crunch Fudge Recipe

Serving: 48 | Prep: | Cook: 10mins | Ready in:

Ingredients

- 2 tablespoons light corn syrup
- 2 tablespoons butter or margarine
- 1/4 teaspoon salt
- 1 can (14 oz) sweetened condensed milk (not evaporated)
- 1 roll (16.5 oz) Create 'n Bake refrigerated sugar cookies, cut into small chunks
- 2 bags (12 oz each) semisweet chocolate chips
- 5 teaspoons vanilla
- 6 pecan crunch crunchy granola bars (3 pouches from 8.9-oz box), coarsely crushed (heaping 1 cup)*
- Fresh mint sprigs, if desired

Direction

- In 3-quart heavy saucepan or deep 10-inch non-stick skillet, cook corn syrup, butter, salt and condensed milk over medium heat 2 to 3 minutes, stirring constantly with wooden spoon, until well blended. Reduce heat to medium-low; stir in cookie dough chunks. Cook 3 to 5 minutes, stirring constantly, until mixture is smooth and candy thermometer reads 160°F. Remove from heat.
- Stir in chocolate chips and vanilla until chips are melted and mixture is smooth. Add crushed granola bars; stir until well blended. Cook over low heat 1 to 2 minutes, stirring constantly, until mixture is shiny. Spread in ungreased 12x8-inch or 13x9-inch pan.** Refrigerate uncovered at least 2 hours or until firm.
- Cut into 8 rows by 6 rows. Serve in decorative candy cups or mini paper baking cups on platter garnished with mint sprigs.

318. Sugar Free Chocolate Fudge Recipe

Serving: 16 | Prep: | Cook: 480mins | Ready in:

Ingredients

- Ngredients:
- 2 packages (8-oz each) 1/3 less fat cream cheese

- 2 Squares (1-oz each) unsweetened chocolate, melted and cooled
- 24 packets sugar substitute (equivalent to ½ cup sugar or using stevia (a natural herb sugar substitute), you use less than regular sugar subs ... 2 tbsp is equal in flavor for 1/2 cup.
- stevia is relatively expensive to buy, but it lasts a long time!
- 1 tsp. vanilla extract
- ½ cup chopped pecans

Direction

- In a small mixing bowl, beat the cream cheese, chocolate, sweetener and vanilla until smooth. Stir in pecans. Pour into an 8-inch square baking pan lined with foil. Cover and refrigerate overnight. Cut into 16 squares. Serve chilled.
- Serving size 1 piece
- Nutrition Values: Calories per serving: 147, Sodium: 84mg, Fat: 14gm, Cholesterol: 31mg, Carbohydrate: 5gm, Protein: 3gm
- Diabetic Exchanges: 3 fat
- Note: This recipe is Diabetic Friendly, Gastric Bypass Friendly, and anyone can eat this.

319. Sweet And Savory Munch Mix Recipe

Serving: 10 | Prep: | Cook: 5mins | Ready in:

Ingredients

- 12 oz white chocolate broken into pieces
- 2 cups small pretzels
- 1 1/2 cups dry roasted peanuts
- 1 1/4 cups corn cereal (corn Chex)
- 1 1/4 cups wheat cereal(Wheat Chex)
- 1 1/4 cups rice cereal(rice Chex)
- 1 1/4 cups oat cereal (cheerios)
- 1 cup candy coated chocolate pieces (M&M's)
- 1/4 cup semisweet chocolate chips

Direction

- Lightly oil baking sheet.
- In large bowl combine pretzels, corn, wheat, rice and oat cereals, peanuts, and M&M's.
- Melt white chocolate and stir into the combined ingredients.
- Toss to coat.
- Spread mixture on baking sheet.
- Melt chocolate chips.
- Drizzle over cereal mixture.
- Refrigerate until firm (about 10-15 minutes).
- Break into chunks.
- ENJOY!!!

320. Sweet Cocoa Flax Truffles Recipe

Serving: 25 | Prep: | Cook: 145mins | Ready in:

Ingredients

- 1/3 cup diced dates
- 1 cup water
- 1 tsp honey (or agave nectar)
- 1/2 tsp toasted sesame oil
- 1/4 tsp sea salt
- 1 cup ground flax seeds
- 1/2 cup cocoa powder
- toasted sesame seeds and flax seeds, for rolling

Direction

- Combine dates and water in a small saucepan and place over medium heat.
- Bring to a simmer and cook, stirring often, for 15-20 minutes, until very soft and falling apart.
- Drain, reserving the liquid, and place into a blender with honey, oil and salt. Puree until very smooth (you are looking for a paste consistency).
- Mix together ground flax and cocoa in a small dish and add to the blender. Blend until the mixture is smooth and all one "paste" - add 1-2 tbsp. of the saved date water if necessary, but you need to be able to form the mixture into balls.

- Place sesame and flax seeds in a shallow bowl or plate and roll small balls of the paste in them to coat.
- Place balls on a parchment or foil lined baking sheet and chill 1-2 hours before enjoying.
- Store, covered, in the fridge.

321. Sweet, Salty, Frito Candy Recipe

Serving: 8 | Prep: | Cook: 30mins | Ready in:

Ingredients

- 2 cups pretzels
- 1 cup Fritos
- 8 peanut butter cups (regular sized)
- 1 stick unsalted butter (8 tablespoons)
- 1/2 cup brown sugar
- 1 cup semi-sweet chocolate chips
- 1 cup milk chocolate chips
- Optional: Some peanuts for the top and Reese's Pieces

Direction

- Preheat oven to 350 degrees F and line a 13×9 inch pan with parchment paper or no-stick (Release) foil (I used regular foil with no problem).
- Place pretzels in food processor and pulse to break – don't pulverize Add Fritos, pulse to break (I just crushed the Fritos and pretzels up by hand. Honestly, sometimes it just requires too much effort to drag out the food processor, especially if I don't know where all the parts are :) Dump into pan. Unwrap peanut butter cups (break each into 4 pieces) and throw them in the mix.
- Place butter in a non-stick saucepan and melt over medium heat. When butter is melted, stir in brown sugar. Bring mixture to a full boil and boil for 1 minute, stirring once or twice. Pour over Frito mixture and bake for 8 minutes
- Remove pan from oven and sprinkle chocolate chips over hot candy. Return to oven for 1 minute to soften chips. Spread softened chocolate chips over bars. Sprinkle with peanuts and Reese's Pieces. Cool at room temperature until you feel the pan is cool enough to be transferred to your refrigerator, then transfer to refrigerator to set the chocolate. When chocolate is set, lift from pan and break the candy up as you would toffee. You can eat it cold or let it come back down to room temp. It doesn't have to be refrigerated.

322. THREE CHOCOLATE FUDGE WITH PECANS Recipe

Serving: 48 | Prep: | Cook: 15mins | Ready in:

Ingredients

- Ingredients:
- 3 1/3 cups sugar
- 1 cup butter or margarine
- 1 cup packed dark sugar
- 1 can (12-oz) evaporated milk
- 32 large marshmallows, halved
- 2 cups (12-oz) semisweet chocolate chips
- 2 milk chocolate candy bars (7-oz each) broken
- 2 squares (1-oz each) semisweet baking chocolate, chopped
- 1 tsp. vanilla extract
- 2 cups chopped pecans

Direction

- In a large saucepan, combine first four ingredients. Cook and stir over medium heat until sugar is dissolved. Bring to a rapid boil; boil for 5 minutes, stirring constantly. Remove from the heat; stir in marshmallows until melted. Stir in chocolate chips until melted. Add chocolate bars and baking chocolate; stir until melted. Fold in vanilla and pecans; mix well. Pour into a greased 15-inch x 10-inch x 1-inch baking pan. Chill until firm. Cut into squares.

323. Taras Candy Recipe

Serving: 24 | Prep: | Cook: | Ready in:

Ingredients

- 1 pkg (12 oz.) white chocolate chips
- 48 thin stick pretzels
- 48 cran-cherries
- 24 small muffin papers

Direction

- Using a small size, 24 count muffin pan, line each well with papers.
- Crush pretzels.
- Divide pretzels equally between the 24 papers.
- Melt chocolate.
- Spoon equally into papers.
- Drop 2 cran-cherries into each candy.
- Refrigerate to cool.

324. The Best Darned Peanut Butter Filling For Buckeyes Or Easter Eggs Recipe

Serving: 16 | Prep: | Cook: 60mins | Ready in:

Ingredients

- 1 jar Creamy (or Crunchy) peanut butter (18oz. Jar)
- 1 stick butter Or margarine, Softened
- 1 teaspoon vanilla extract
- 1 box(es) Confectioner's (powdered) sugar (16oz. Box)
- 1 pound milk Or Semi-sweet Confectionary Coating

Direction

- In a bowl, combine peanut butter and butter until totally combined; smooth and creamy. Stir in vanilla; mix well.
- Add powdered sugar a little at a time until dough-like and easy to form into balls. Depending on weather conditions, you may use more or less.
- Roll into balls and place on waxed paper lined cookie sheet. Refrigerate until firm; about 1-2 hours.
- Melt chocolate in microwave or on top of a double boiler until completely melted and smooth.
- Remove balls from fridge and dip bottom half only into the melted chocolate. Return to waxed paper lined sheet to dry. When done dipping all, drizzle remaining chocolate over the tops (I use a spoon). Allow to dry completely. Store in airtight container in the refrigerator.
- For Easter Eggs:
- Shape into egg shapes. Refrigerate about 1-2 hours. Dip into melted chocolate and decorate as desired.
- NOTE: Cooking time is actually the chilling time. This recipe will yield anywhere from 48-60 buckeyes and 20-30 Easter eggs, depending on size.

325. Tias Treats Recipe

Serving: 9 | Prep: | Cook: | Ready in:

Ingredients

- Base
- 2/3 cup rice flour
- 1/4 cup potato flour
- 3 tbsp soy flour
- 1/4 cup tapioca flour
- 7 tbsp arrowroot
- 3 tbsp potato starch
- 1 tbsp cream of brown rice cereal

- ½ tsp salt
- 1/2 tsp guar gum
- 1 tbsp sugar
- ½ tsp baking soda
- 3 oz shortening
- 3/4 cup water
- 1 tsp gluten and corn free vanilla
- Assembly
- 300 g gluten, corn and dairy free bittersweet chocolate
- 2 tsp shortening

Direction

- Base
- Preheat oven to 375F.
- Mix flours, arrowroot, potato starch, salt, sugar and baking soda.
- Cut in shortening until mixture has a consistency of coarse meal.
- Add liquid and stir to form a dough.
- Roll into a very thin sheet.
- Cut into 3 large "base" rectangles (about the size of a large Kit Kat bar) and 12 thinner "sticks" (the length of the large rectangles and a little more than 1/3 as wide), place different sizes on separate un-greased cookie sheets.
- Prick 1-2 times with a fork and make a "seam" of fork pricks down the centre of the larger rectangles (so they can "break" easily after assembly).
- Bake the skinny crackers 6-7 minutes and larger crackers 8-10 minutes, flipping once halfway through. They should be golden - you want them to be crispy!
- Cool on the sheets.
- Assembly
- Melt together chocolate and shortening in a double boiler over simmering water.
- Place one large cracker on a rack placed over a piece of wax paper or foil and brush with a thin layer of chocolate.
- Immediately place two of the thin sticks on top of the large rectangle on either edge.
- Brush entire surface with another layer of chocolate and repeat the layering process with two more thin "sticks".
- Spoon a thicker layer of chocolate overtop of the rectangle and spread gently to enrobe the top and sides. Set aside to set.
- When chocolate has solidified brush the underside of the bar with chocolate and allow to set.
- Repeat process with remaining crackers and chocolate.
- Wrap the completed bars in foil and store in a cool, dry place

326. Tiger Butter Recipe

Serving: 12 | Prep: | Cook: 10mins | Ready in:

Ingredients

- INGREDIENTS
- 1 pound white chocolate
- 1 pound semisweet chocolate, melted
- 1 1/3 cups crunchy peanut butter

Direction

- Line a 10x15 inch pan with parchment. Set aside.
- In the top of a double boiler set over simmering (not boiling) water, heat white chocolate and peanut butter. Stir constantly until white chocolate and peanut butter melts.
- Spread onto prepared pan. Pour melted semi-sweet chocolate over top and swirl through with a knife, to create a marble pattern. Chill until firm. Cut into 1 /2 x 1" pieces.

327. Tiger Stripes Recipe

Serving: 0 | Prep: | Cook: 15mins | Ready in:

Ingredients

- 1 pound white chocolate
- 1 (12 oz) jar chunky peanut butter

- 2 (8 oz) package semi sweet chocolate, melted

Direction

- Combine white chocolate and peanut butter in top of double boiler above water heated to boiling; Reduce heat and stir constantly until mixture is melted and well blended.
- Spread mixture onto a waxed paper lined 10 x 15 inch jelly roll pan.
- Pour semi-sweet chocolate over first layer and swirl with a knife.
- Chill until firm.
- Cut into small squares. Store in refrigerator.
- 6 dozen squares...

328. Toasted Almond Truffles Recipe

Serving: 30 | Prep: | Cook: 3mins | Ready in:

Ingredients

- 1/2 cup evaporated milk
- 1/4 cup sugar
- 1 pkg (11.5 oz) chocolate morsels
- 1/2 to 1 tsp almond extract
- 1 cup finely chopped almonds (that have been toasted)

Direction

- Combine evaporated milk and sugar in a sauce pan.
- Cook over medium heat until mixture comes to a full rolling boil.
- Boil for 3 minutes, stirring constantly.
- Remove from heat.
- Stir in morsels and extract until morsels are melted and mixture is smooth.
- Chill for 45 minutes.
- Shape into 1-inch balls and roll in chopped almonds.
- Chill until ready to serve.

329. Triple Chocolate Sour Cherry Fudge Recipe

Serving: 60 | Prep: | Cook: 10mins | Ready in:

Ingredients

- 1 1/4 cups milk chocolate chips
- 1/2 cup plus 2 tablespoons evaporated milk
- 1/4 cup chocolate hazelnut spread (nutella)
- 1 teaspoon vanilla extract
- 1/4 teaspoon fine salt
- 1 (12-ounce) bag semisweet chocolate chips
- 1 1/2 cups dried sour cherries
- 3/4 cup roughly chopped pecans, toasted

Direction

- Line an 8- x 8-inch glass dish with foil; set aside.
- Put milk chocolate chips, evaporated milk, chocolate hazelnut spread, vanilla, salt and semisweet chocolate chips into a medium pot and cook over medium-low heat, stirring constantly, until smooth, about 5 minutes. Stir in cherries and pecans, then transfer mixture to prepared dish. Shake and tap dish gently on the countertop to remove any air bubbles from the fudge, then smooth out the top with the back of a spoon. Cover and chill until set, about 3 hours.
- Loosen fudge from dish and turn out onto a cutting board; remove and discard foil. Using a serrated knife, cut fudge into pieces and serve.

330. Truffles With Chocolate Raspberry And Hazelnuts Recipe

Serving: 6 | Prep: | Cook: 200mins | Ready in:

Ingredients

- 1 bag semi-sweet chocolate chips
- 1/2 cup water
- 2/3 cup chambord
- 2 sticks butter, unsalted and diced
- 2 large egg yolks
- 1 cup hazelnuts, toasted and finely chopped

Direction

- In metal bowl, put all ingredients except hazelnuts
- Put over double boiler and melt over low heat constantly stirring until all is melted and smooth
- Remove from heat,
- Whisk in egg yolks one at a time, stirring until fully blended together Cool to room temperature
- Cover and refrigerate at least 2 hours
- Scoop with small ice cream scoop or tsp. and roll with hands until round balls
- Roll in hazelnuts

331. Upside Down Peanut Butter Cups Recipe

Serving: 35 | Prep: | Cook: 60mins | Ready in:

Ingredients

- mixing bowl
- spoon
- baking sheet or large plate
- measuring cups
- plastic wrap
- 1 cup peanut butter (I think you'll really need more)
- 1/2 cup honey (again, I think you'd need a little more possibly)
- 1 cup instant nonfat dry milk powder
- 35 Hersey's kisses, peeled

Direction

- Put peanut butter and honey in mixing bowl. Stir together until well mixed.
- Add milk powder and stir.
- Pinch off pieces about the size of a small walnut and roll into balls.
- Stick the point of the Hersey's Kiss into the ball, until you can only see the bottom.
- Place ball on cookie sheet or large plate.
- Use remaining peanut butter mixture and kisses.
- Cover the plate with plastic wrap.
- Refrigerate at least 1 hour.

332. White Chocolate Cherry Fudge Recipe

Serving: 12 | Prep: | Cook: 10mins | Ready in:

Ingredients

- 2-1/2 cups semisweet white chocolate morsels
- 14 ounce can sweetened condensed milk
- 1 teaspoon cherry extract
- 2 teaspoons red food coloring
- 1 cup chopped maraschino cherries
- Combine morsels and milk in medium heavy duty saucepan.
- Warm over lowest possible heat stirring until smooth.
- Remove from heat then stir in extract, food coloring and cherries.
- Spread evenly into prepared pan the refrigerate 2 hours or until form.
- Lift from pan then remove foil and cut into pieces.

Direction

- Combine morsels and milk in medium heavy duty saucepan.
- Warm over lowest possible heat stirring until smooth.
- Remove from heat then stir in extract, food coloring and cherries.

- Spread evenly into prepared pan the refrigerate 2 hours or until form.
- Lift from pan then remove foil and cut into pieces.

333. White Chocolate Cherry Pistachio Bark Recipe

Serving: 0 | Prep: | Cook: 10mins | Ready in:

Ingredients

- 1 1/4 cups dried cherries
- 2 tablespoons water
- 2 (12-ounce) packages white chocolate morsels
- 6 (2-ounce) vanilla candy coating squares
- 1 1/4 cups chopped red or green pistachios

Direction

- Microwave cherries and 2 tablespoons water in a small glass bowl at HIGH 2 minutes; drain.
- Melt chocolate and candy coating in a heavy saucepan over low heat. Remove from heat; stir in cherries and pistachios. Spread into a wax paper-lined 15- x 10-inch jellyroll pan.
- Chill 1 hour or until firm. Cut or break. Store in airtight container.
- Makes 3 & 1/2 pounds

334. White Chocolate Cranberry Bark Recipe

Serving: 10 | Prep: | Cook: 5mins | Ready in:

Ingredients

- 6 oz. white chocolate
- 1/2c dried,sweetened cranberries,coarsely chopped
- 2Tbs. candied orange peel,finely chopped

Direction

- Line a baking sheet with parchment or waxed paper; set aside.
- Melt white chocolate in a small saucepan over low heat, stirring occasionally, until smooth. Remove from heat and stir in 1/4c of the cranberries and 1 Tbs. orange peel.
- Pour chocolate mixture onto lined baking sheet and spread very thinly into roughly 12x10" rectangle. Sprinkle remaining cranberries and orange peel over top. Let set in dry, cool location. Once bark is hard, break into shards.

335. White Chocolate Cranberry Pistachio Bark Recipe

Serving: 0 | Prep: | Cook: 5mins | Ready in:

Ingredients

- 1 c pretzel sticks
- 1/2 c dried cranberries
- 1/2 c shelled pistachios
- 12 oz white chocolate, chopped

Direction

- Line a lightly oiled 23 x 13-cm (9 x 5-inch) loaf pan with plastic wrap, letting the wrap hang over the sides. Distribute the pretzel sticks, cranberries and pistachios evenly in the pan.
- Melt the chocolate in a double boiler until hot to the touch. Pour the chocolate into the pan and mix gently with a knife tip so the chocolate fills the spaces between the other ingredients.
- Refrigerate until the chocolate hardens, about 2 1/2 hours. Grasp the edges of the plastic wrap and lift the confection out of the pan. Peel off the wrap. Using a hot knife, cut into 2.5-cm (1-inch) squares.
- Store at room temperature.

- I made mine on a cookie sheet the 2nd time and then I put it in the freezer till quite hard. I then broke it into pieces....delicious either way!!!

336. White Chocolate Crunch Mix Recipe

Serving: 20 | Prep: | Cook: 5mins | Ready in:

Ingredients

- 1 large box Crispix
- 1 package of White almond Bark
- 1 package of small pretzels
- 1 can of dry roasted peanuts

Direction

- In a large bowl, add all the dry ingredients
- In a microwave safe bowl, in microwave, melt almond bark.
- Pour over dry mixture.
- Stir to coat well.
- Spread the mixture on waxed paper, let dry.
- Break apart in chunks.
- Place in sealed containers or zip lock bags.

337. White Chocolate Fruit And Nut Clusters Recipe

Serving: 10 | Prep: | Cook: 5mins | Ready in:

Ingredients

- White chocolate chips****
- reg and golden raisins
- walnuts coarsely chopped
- peanuts
- ***** can use instead: semi-sweet or milk chocolate chips or
- vanilla chips

Direction

- Put chips into a microwave safe measuring cup and melt.
- Add raisins and the nuts.
- Mix well.
- Fill the paper candy cups.

338. White Chocolate Fudge Recipe

Serving: 12 | Prep: | Cook: 10mins | Ready in:

Ingredients

- 2 6 oz pkgs Nestle's white chocolate chips
- 1 can sweetened condensed milk
- Dash of salt
- 1 tsp vanilla
- 1 small package candied green cherries
- 1 small package candied red cherries
- 1 cup chopped walnuts

Direction

- Melt the chocolate chips with the sweetened condensed milk and a dash of salt in saucepan until chips are melted.
- Add vanilla, cherries and walnuts. Stir. Pour onto a small cookie sheet lined with waxed paper.
- Cool and cut into squares.
- The different variations I've used are to leave the cherries out and add only nuts. I've used peppermint extract and crushed candy canes. Also peanut butter and chopped peanuts. Butterscotch with vanilla extract is good too.
- Folks, I forget from year to year how many packages of chips I use...just a warning. A medium sized saucepan should be about half full of chips.

339. White Chocolate Hazelnut Apricot Truffles Recipe

Serving: 48 | Prep: | Cook: 10mins | Ready in:

Ingredients

- 1-1/4 cup hazelnuts
- 1/4 cup finely chopped dried apricots
- 24 ounces imported white chocolate
- 6 tablespoons heavy cream

Direction

- On a baking sheet spread out hazelnuts and bake at 350 for 10 minutes.
- Remove as much of the skins as possible by rubbing nuts in a terrycloth towel.
- Finely chop nuts in a food processor.
- In large glass container combine 12 ounces of the white chocolate cut up and cream.
- Microwave mixture on medium for 4 minutes stirring twice until chocolate is melted.
- Stir 3/4 cup of the nuts and the dried apricots into the white chocolate.
- Cover mixture and refrigerate 2 hours.
- Form into smooth balls then place on wax paper lined cookie sheet and refrigerate until firm.
- In a small glass dish place another 12 ounces imported white chocolate cut up.
- Microwave on medium for 4 minutes until smooth and warm.
- Using a fork to hold the truffle dip in chocolate and let excess drip off.
- Place on wax paper lined cookie sheet and sprinkle with remaining nuts.
- Store in airtight container in refrigerator up to 2 weeks or in freezer 1 month.

340. White Chocolate Hazelnut Crunch Recipe

Serving: 6 | Prep: | Cook: 10mins | Ready in:

Ingredients

- 1 cup granulated sugar
- 1 cup butter
- 3 tablespoons water
- 1-1/2 cups whole hazelnuts
- 4 ounces white chocolate melted
- 1/2 cup finely chopped hazelnuts

Direction

- Combine sugar, butter and water in a large heavy skillet over high heat.
- Cook stirring constantly about 10 minutes until mixture reaches hard crack stage.
- Stir in nuts and pour mixture onto a buttered slab or baking sheet and form into 1 foot square.
- When almost cool brush with the melted chocolate and sprinkle with the finely chopped nuts.
- Break into pieces when cold.

341. White Chocolate Macadamia Fudge Recipe

Serving: 8 | Prep: | Cook: 15mins | Ready in:

Ingredients

- 3 cups (18 ounces) white chocolate morsels
- 1 1/2 cups mimiature marshmallows
- 1 (14-ounce) can sweetened condensed milk
- 2 teaspoons grated orange rind
- 1 teaspoon vanilla extract
- 1/8 teaspoon salt
- 1 cup chopped macadamia nuts, toasted

Direction

- Line a 9" square pan with aluminum foil; lightly grease foil.
- Cook first 3 ingredients in a heavy saucepan over medium heat, stirring constantly, 10 to 11 minutes or until smooth.
- Remove from heat, and stir in orange rind, vanilla, and salt until blended. Stir in nuts.
- Pour fudge into prepared pan.
- Cover and chill at least 4 hours or until firm.
- Cut fudge into squares, and store in refrigerator.
- Yield: 2 pounds.

342. White Chocolate Marshmallow Drops Recipe

Serving: 48 | Prep: | Cook: 3mins | Ready in:

Ingredients

- 12 oz white chocolate
- 1 Tbsp vegetable oil
- 24 oz marshmallow cream
- 2 Tbsp vanilla sugar

Direction

- Line a baking sheet with wax paper.
- Scoop out 1 Tbsp. portions of marshmallow cream onto wax paper.
- Put in the freezer for 20 minutes.
- After the marshmallow cream has been in the freezer for 15 minutes, begin melting the white chocolate in the microwave at 30 second intervals, stirring between each. (The defrost setting works the best. white chocolate seizes easily, so be careful.)
- After the chocolate is melted, stir in the vegetable oil until completely incorporated.
- Remove marshmallow cream from the freezer and spoon on enough chocolate to the top.
- Sprinkle with vanilla sugar and return to the freezer.
- When the chocolate has set, remove from the freezer and turn each drop.
- Coat the bottom of the drop with chocolate. (You may need to heat the chocolate a little to return to the proper consistency.)
- Sprinkle with vanilla sugar and return to the freezer.
- Remove from the freezer and pull the drops away from the wax paper.
- Store in an airtight container.
- Top you favorite hot chocolate with these drops or eat them as is.
- To make the vanilla sugar, place 1 split vanilla bean in 1 cup of granulated sugar. Leave in an airtight container for at least one week before use.

343. White Chocolate Party Mix Recipe

Serving: 20 | Prep: | Cook: | Ready in:

Ingredients

- 4 cups bite-size pretzels
- 2 1/2 cups Cheerios
- 2 1/2 cups bite-size Corn Chex
- 1 cup salted peanuts
- 1 cup M&M's or Smarties (red and green for Christmas or mixed)
- 2 cups white chocolate baking chips
- 1 tbsp. shortening

Direction

- In a large bowl, combine pretzels, Cheerios, Chex, peanuts, Smarties; set aside.
- In medium microwave-safe bowl, combine white chocolate baking pieces and shortening. Microwave on 100% power (high) for 1 to 2 minutes or until baking pieces are melted, stirring every minute until smooth. Pour over cereal mixture; toss gently to coat.
- Spread on large piece of waxed paper to cool. Break apart large clusters. Store in airtight container at room temperature for up to 1 week.

344. White Chocolate Peppermint Meltaways Recipe

Serving: 48 | Prep: | Cook: 20mins | Ready in:

Ingredients

- 2- 12 oz bags of white chocolate morsels
- 2 -10 oz cans of condensed milk
- 3 tbsp of evaporated milk
- 20 starlight peppermint candies (crushed but not into a powder)

Direction

- In a heavy saucepan over medium heat melt chocolate and milks. Once you have a smooth consistency add in the peppermints.
- Stir the peppermints through and drop by teaspoons onto a wax sheet covered cookie tray.
- Keep them about 2 inches apart.
- Refrigerate for a few hours and enjoy.
- **Note***- There are SO many variations to this recipe. You can add crushed Oreo cookies to this (about 20 does the trick), pecans or almonds are great as well!

345. White Chocolate Truffles Recipe

Serving: 30 | Prep: | Cook: 10mins | Ready in:

Ingredients

- 8 ounces white chocolate
- 48 pecan halves
- 6 tablespoons unsalted butter at room temperature
- 1-1/2 tablespoons water
- 1 large egg yolk

Direction

- Preheat oven to 300.
- Set aside a wax paper lined baking sheet.
- Chop white chocolate into small pieces and set aside.
- Toast nuts on a baking sheet in a single layer for 8 minutes then set them aside.
- In top of a double boiler over hot not boiling water melt chocolate and butter in the water.
- Stir until smooth then pour into a bowl and add the yolk.
- Continue beating until mixture is fluffy and cooled to room temperature.
- Chill for 4 hours then remove from refrigerator and form into 1" balls.
- Sandwich between 2 nut halves then chill until ready to serve.

346. White Chocolate Walnut Decadent Saltines Recipe

Serving: 12 | Prep: | Cook: 10mins | Ready in:

Ingredients

- 24 saltine crackers
- 1 cup light brown sugar
- 1/2 cup unsalted butter
- 6 ounces white chocolate chips
- 1/2 cup chopped walnuts

Direction

- Lay saltines side by side on a cookie sheet.
- Heat brown sugar and butter until dissolved then pour over saltines.
- Bake at 450 for 5 minutes then cover with chocolate chips and spread.
- Sprinkle with almonds and allow to sit at room temperature for at least an hour.

347. White Christmas Jewel Fudge Recipe

Serving: 2 | Prep: | Cook: 30mins | Ready in:

Ingredients

- 3 (6 oz each) pkg white chocolate (18 oz total)
- 1 (14 oz) can sweetened condensed milk
- 1 1/2 tsp vanilla
- 1/8 tsp salt
- 1/2 cup chopped green candied cherries
- 1/2 cup chopped red candied cherries

Direction

- Over low heat, melt chocolate with sweetened condensed milk, vanilla and salt Remove from heat, stir in cherries. Spread into foil-lined 8 - 9" square pan. Chill 2 hours or until firm. Turn fudge out onto cutting board, peel off foil, cut in squares. Store covered in refrigerator.

348. White Trash Recipe

Serving: 20 | Prep: | Cook: 20mins | Ready in:

Ingredients

- 2 Cups M&Ms
- 2 Cups peanut M&Ms
- 3 Cups mixed nuts (Your Choice)
- 3 Cups Rice Chex cereal
- 3 Cups Corn Chex cereal
- 3 Cups Cheerios cereal
- 4 Cups small pretzels
- 1 ½ Pounds white chocolate Morsels

Direction

- Mix the all ingredients except chocolate together in a LARGE bowl.
- Melt the white chocolate in double boiler. Pour melted chocolate over ingredients mixing well. The chocolate must thoroughly cover the mixture. Spread the mix onto waxed paper to cool for about one hour. Try not to sample too much while it's cooling!
- (You may alter the ingredients to suit your particular cravings.)

349. White Or Chocolate Eggnog Fudge Recipe

Serving: 36 | Prep: | Cook: 15mins | Ready in:

Ingredients

- eggnog Fudge
- 1/2 cup sugar
- 3 cups miniature marshmallows
- 2/3 cup purchased eggnog
- 3 tablespoons butter
- 1 tablespoon corn syrup
- 1/8 teaspoon salt
- 1 cup (6 ounces) semisweet white chips or chocolate (your choice)
- 1 cup chopped pecans

Direction

- Butter sides of a heavy 3-quart saucepan. Add sugar, marshmallows, eggnog, butter, corn syrup, and salt to the saucepan; cook over low heat, stirring constantly, until sugar is dissolved. Turn heat up to medium and cook until mixture boils.
- Continue to cook, stirring constantly, to about 232°.
- Add chocolate chips and continue to cook for 5 minutes (should be at soft ball stage*), or until chocolate is melted. Stir in chopped nuts. Pour into a buttered 8-inch square pan. Cool to room temperature, then chill and cut into squares.
- Makes about 3 dozen pieces of eggnog fudge.
- *To Test for Soft Ball Stage
- A small amount of syrup dropped into chilled water forms a ball, but flattens when picked up with fingers (234° to 240°).

350. Candy Haystacks Recipe

Serving: 24 | Prep: | Cook: 10mins | Ready in:

Ingredients

- chow mein noodles
- miniature marshmallows
- walnuts
- chocolate chips

Direction

- 1 can of chow mein noodles
- 1c.miniature marshmallows
- 1/2c.nuts
- 1pkg.chocolate chips
- Melt chocolate chips and then mix all other ingredients into chocolate.
- Drop on waxed paper by the teaspoonfuls and chill.

351. Chocolate Chip Oatmeal Bars Recipe

Serving: 12 | Prep: | Cook: 30mins | Ready in:

Ingredients

- 1/2 cup butter
- 1/3 cup superfine sugar
- 15ml light corn syrup
- 4 cups rolled oats
- 1/2 cup choc chips(of choice)
- 1/3 cup golden raisins

Direction

- Lightly grease a shallow 8 - inch square cake pan.
- Place butter, sugar and syrup in saucepan and cook over low heat, stirring constantly until butter and sugar is melted and the mixture is well combined.
- Remove the pan from heat and add oats with wooden spoon until well coated add choc chips and raisins and mix well.
- Turn into prepared pan and press down well.
- Bake @ 160 for + - 30 mins.
- Cool slightly, then mark into bars when almost cold cut the bars transfer to a wire rack until cold.
- Enjoy with your favourite cuppa.

352. Chocolate Leaves Recipe

Serving: 8 | Prep: | Cook: 30mins | Ready in:

Ingredients

- Attractively -shaped,unblemished leaves washed and dried
- 60 g chocolate
- Paint brush

Direction

- Melt the chocolate.
- With the paint brush paint the chocolate onto the outer surface of the leaf covering it totally.
- Put it to one side to set.
- When all the leaves have been covered, refrigerate them for about one hour.
- When set hard, peel off the leaf from the chocolate.
- Use the chocolate leafs for garnish on cakes.

353. Chocolate Truffles Recipe

Serving: 25 | Prep: | Cook: 20mins | Ready in:

Ingredients

- 800 grams of bittersweet dark chocolate
- 75g of chopped pistachios
- 250mls double cream

Direction

- Chop 500g of the chocolate in to small pieces.
- In a medium pot bring cream to a gentle boil and pour over chocolate and stir gently in a circle from the middle to the edge of the bowl.
- Allow the cream mixture to either in the fridge or in a cool place.
- Once mixture has set to a dough like texture scoop out with either a melon baller or a spoon and form little balls.
- Once all the mixture is used up return the truffles back to the fridge to become a little more firm.
- Temper 2/3 of the chocolate in a large bowl over some simmering water in a medium pot making sure no moisture comes in contact with chocolate over allow heat once melted take off the heat and add the remaining chocolate once that is melted bring back up to temperature.
- Cover the balls in the chocolate and roll in nuts.

354. Ciocolata De Casa Home Chocolate0 Recipe

Serving: 24 | Prep: | Cook: 8mins | Ready in:

Ingredients

- 200 ml water
- 375 gr sugar
- 50 grams cocoa
- 1 stick butter
- 500 gr powder milk

Direction

- Mix water and sugar together.
- Cook for 8 minutes.
- Remove from heat add butter.
- Then add cocoa and stir slightly.
- Add milk mix well.
- Pour into 13"x9" pan and let cool.

355. Easy Chocolate Cranberry Truffles Recipe

Serving: 30 | Prep: | Cook: | Ready in:

Ingredients

- 9 ounces semi-sweet chocolate
- 1/2 cup Ocean Spray® jellied cranberry sauce
- 2 tablespoons heavy cream
- 2 tablespoons cocoa powder
- 1 1/2 tablespoons powdered sugar

Direction

- Place chocolate, cranberry sauce and heavy cream in a medium saucepan. Cook over medium-low heat until sauce is smooth, whisking frequently. Remove from heat and pour into a glass or plastic bowl. Cover with plastic wrap. Let sit at room temperature to thicken.
- Combine cocoa and 1 1/2 tablespoons powdered sugar on a small plate. Scoop out a rounded teaspoonful of chocolate mixture. Roll in cocoa, coating thoroughly. Dust hands with powdered sugar. Roll truffle in hands to form a 1-inch ball. Continue forming truffles with remaining chocolate mixture.
- Makes 30 truffles.

356. Easy Tipsy Turtle Bark Recipe

Serving: 0 | Prep: | Cook: | Ready in:

Ingredients

- 2 cups pecan halves
- 1 cup (about 24) caramel candies, such as Kraft, unwrapped

- 1 tablespoon rum, bourbon, or whisky (see tip, below)
- 1 1/2 teaspoons heavy cream
- 1/4 teaspoon salt
- 1 pound high-quality semisweet chocolate, finely chopped

Direction

- Preheat oven to 350°F. Spread pecans on large shallow baking sheet and toast until golden brown, about 10 minutes. Transfer to plate and let cool. Line baking sheet with parchment or wax paper.
- In small bowl, combine caramels, liquor, cream, and salt. Microwave uncovered at medium power for 2 minutes. Stir with fork. Microwave at medium power for 1 additional minute. Stir until smooth and set aside.
- In medium bowl set over saucepan of simmering water, melt half chocolate, stirring occasionally. Remove from heat, add remaining chocolate, and stir until smooth. Pour half melted chocolate into small bowl and reserve.
- Stir 1 cup nuts into remaining chocolate. Transfer mixture to baking sheet, spreading to 1/4- to 1/2-inch thickness. Spoon caramel over and pat on remaining pecans. Drizzle with reserved chocolate. Let cool at room temperature until set, about 2 hours. Do not chill.
- Chop finished bark into irregular 1 1/2-inch chunks.
- Store airtight at room temperature up to one month.
- Tip: If omitting the alcohol, add an extra tablespoon of heavy cream.

357. Easy Chocolate Fudge Recipe

Serving: 30 | Prep: | Cook: 10mins | Ready in:

Ingredients

- 1 lb 2 ozs dark chocolate
- 1/3 cup sweet butter
- 14 oz can sweetened condensed milk
- 1/2 tsp vaniila essence

Direction

- Lightly grease an 8 inch square cake pan.
- Break choc into pieces and place in a large saucepan with the butter.
- And condensed milk.
- Heat gently stirring until the chocolate and butter melts and the mixture is smooth.
- Do not allow to boil.
- Remove the pan from the heat. Beat in vanilla essence.
- Beat the mixture for a few minutes until thickened.
- Pour into prepared pan level the top.
- Chill in fridge until firm.
- Tip the fudge out onto a cutting board cut into squares & serve.

358. Easy Chocolate Nougat Recipe

Serving: 2435 | Prep: | Cook: 30mins | Ready in:

Ingredients

- 1-12 oz bag semi sweet chocolate chips
- 1- jar marshmallow creme
- 8 squares chocolate almond bark

Direction

- In a large microwaveable bowl, melt chocolate chips, stirring every 30 seconds until chips are melted.
- Remove bowl from microwave and stir in marshmallow crème. Mix until completely blended.

- Divide mixture in half, roll each half into a log and wrap in waxed paper.
- Place rolls into freezer until firm, 15 to 20 minutes.
- Melt chocolate bark in microwave according to directions on package.
- Remove nougat rolls from freezer, and slice then dip in melted bark and set on wax paper to dry.
- Store in covered container at room temperature for up to 2 weeks or freeze until needed.

359. Nutty Chocolate Clusters Recipe

Serving: 30 | Prep: | Cook: 10mins | Ready in:

Ingredients

- 6 ozs white chocolate
- 3 1/2 ozs graham crackers
- 1 cup chopped macadamia nuts / brazil nuts
- 1 oz preserved ginger, chopped (optional)
- 6 ozs dark chocolate

Direction

- Line a cookie sheet with baking parchment.
- Break the white chocolate into pieces and melt in a double boiler.
- Break the crackers into small pieces.
- Stir the crackers together with the chopped nuts and ginger, if using into the melted chocolate.
- Place heaped teaspoons of the mixture onto prepared cookie sheet.
- Chill in fridge until set.
- Carefully remove clusters from parchment.
- Melt dark chocolate and let cool slightly.
- Dip clusters in melted chocolate allowing excess to drip back into bowl.
- Place clusters on parchment.
- Chill in fridge until set.
- Enjoy!!!!!!!!!!!!!!!!!!

360. Pecan Bark Recipe

Serving: 40 | Prep: | Cook: 15mins | Ready in:

Ingredients

- 40 saltines crackers
- 1/2 cup brown sugar
- 2 sticks butter
- 1 cup chopped pecans
- 1 bag chocolate chips
- preheat 350 degrees

Direction

- Line cookie sheet with parchment paper.
- Layer 40 crackers on the paper.
- In microwave melt butter, sugar, until pouring consistency.
- Pour over crackers.
- Bake 12 minutes.
- Immediately put choc chips onto crackers.
- Spread with the back of spoon while melting.
- Sprinkle with crushed pecans.
- Refrigerate for 2 hours.

361. Pistachio Chocolate Apples Recipe

Serving: 6 | Prep: | Cook: 30mins | Ready in:

Ingredients

- *Time varies - kitchen gadgetries lessens the time as modern conveniences.
- 1/2 cup semisweet chocolate chips
- 6 flat wooden popsicle sticks
- 1 1 oz square unsweetened chocolate
- 1 1.4 oz bar chocolate
- toffee candy, chopped coarsely

- 6 medium - size red : eating apples such as Gala, Empire, or Red Delicious
- 3 tablespoons chopped pistachios

Direction

1. In heavy qt. saucepan over low heat or microwave - safe bowl in microwave oven, melt chocolate, stirring until smooth. Set aside.
2. Place apples on a tray or plate. Remove stems if present and insert a stick into each through stem end.
- With teaspoon, spoon melted chocolate over each apple around the stick, letting excess drip down the apple.
3. Sprinkle chocolate with toffee candy and pistachios. Refrigerate apples until chocolate is set.

362. Rocky Road Bites Recipe

Serving: 18 | Prep: | Cook: 10mins | Ready in:

Ingredients

- 4 1/2 ozs milk chocolate
- 2 1/2 ozs mini multicolored marshmallows
- 1/4 cup walnuts
- 1 oz no-need-to-soak dried apricots, chopped

Direction

- Line a cookie sheet with parchment paper and set aside.
- Break the chocolate into small pieces & melt in double boiler.
- Remove chocolate from the heat.
- Stir in the marshmallows, walnuts and apricots and toss in the melted chocolate until coated.
- Place heaped teaspoons of mixture onto prepared sheet.
- Chill the candies in fridge until completely set.
- Once set remove from paper.

- Can be placed in paper candy cases (if kids &grownups allow!)
- Enjoy.

363. True Love Truffles Recipe

Serving: 35 | Prep: | Cook: 2mins | Ready in:

Ingredients

- 1 1/2 cups sugar
- 3/4 cup butter
- 2 pkg 4.67 oz each andes mints
- 1 med jar of marshmallow cream
- 1 tsp vanilla
- 1 can evaporated milk
- 1 and 1/2 pkg white baking chocolate
- just enough to drizzle in top green frosting

Direction

- Combine sugar, butter and milk to a boil, reduce heat stir constantly until candy thermometer reads 236 soft ball stage> remove from heat and stir in mints until melted then add marshmallow cream and vanilla stir until smooth put into a buttered 15x10 inch pan cover and put in refrigerator for one hour roll into balls then dip into melted white baking chocolate and place onto wax paper then drizzle with green frosting!!

364. White Chocolate Cranberry Cashew Truffles Recipe

Serving: 60 | Prep: | Cook: 20mins | Ready in:

Ingredients

- 1 cup lightly salted roasted cashews

- 1/2 cup dried cranberries
- 12 ounces white baking chocolate, chopped
- 1/2 cup whipping cream
- 1 tablespoon butter
- 2 tablespoons brandy or orange juice
- 12 ounces white baking chocolate, chopped
- 2 tablespoons shortening
- flaked coconut and/or snipped dried cranberries (optional)

Direction

- 1. For filling: In a food processor, combine cashews and the 1/2 cup dried cranberries. Cover and process until finely chopped. Transfer to a medium bowl; set aside. Place 12 ounces white chocolate in the food processor. Cover and process until finely chopped. In a small saucepan, combine whipping cream and butter. Cook and stir over medium-low heat until hot but not boiling. Remove from heat.
- 2. With the food processor running, carefully pour hot cream mixture through feed tube into finely chopped white chocolate. Process until smooth, stopping to scrape side of bowl if necessary. Add white chocolate mixture to cranberry mixture. Add brandy; mix well. Cover and chill about 3 hours or until firm. Shape filling into 3/4-inch balls; freeze for 15 minutes.
- 3. Meanwhile, for coating: In a 4-cup glass measuring cup, combine 12 ounces white chocolate and the shortening. Pour very warm tap water (100 degrees F to 110 degrees F) into a large glass bowl to a depth of 2 inches. Place measuring cup containing white chocolate in large bowl. (Water should cover bottom half of measuring cup.) Stir white chocolate constantly with a rubber spatula until melted. (This takes about 20 minutes; don't rush. If water cools, remove measuring cup. Replace cool water with very warm water; return measuring cup to bowl of water.)
- 4. Line a baking sheet with waxed paper. Using a fork, dip frozen balls of filling into coating, allowing excess coating to drip back into measuring cup.
- 5. If desired, sprinkle tops of truffles with coconut and/or snipped dried cranberries. Chill about 10 minutes or until coating is set. Store, tightly covered, in the refrigerator or freezer. Let stand at room temperature for 30 minutes before serving. Makes about 60 truffles.

365. White Chocolate Truffles Recipe

Serving: 20 | Prep: | Cook: 10mins | Ready in:

Ingredients

- 2 TABS sweet butter
- 5 TABS heavy cream
- 8 ounces good quality Swiss white chocolate
- COATING:::
- 3 1/2 ounces white chocolate
- 1 ounce =28 grams

Direction

- Line a Swiss roll pan with parchment paper.
- Place the butter and cream in a small saucepan, and bring slowly to the boil, stirring constantly, boil for 1 minute, remove from the heat.
- Break the chocolate into pieces, add to cream, and stir until melted.
- Pour into prepared pan.
- Place in fridge to chill until firm +-2 HOURS.
- Break off teaspoon size of mixture and roll them into balls.
- Chill again for about 30 minutes.
- Melt the 2nd amount of white chocolate in a double boiler.
- Dip the balls in the melted chocolate.
- Place them on waxed paper, swirl the chocolate with a fork, for an effect.
- Allow to set.
- Drizzle a little melted dark chocolate over the truffles, allow to set.

- Place in tiny gold paper cases to serve to guests, if any left by the time you finish making these.

Index

A

Almond 3,4,5,6,7,11,12,13,21,29,39,68,70,74,76,98,99,107,134,143

Anise 3,30

Apple 3,4,6,7,26,33,44,122,154

Apricot 3,4,7,14,39,43,147

B

Baking 115,134

Blueberry 3,17,18

Bran 5,24,49,50,61,79,90,137

Bread 3,18

Butter 3,4,5,6,7,8,11,19,20,21,26,29,31,32,39,41,46,53,60,61,62,64,68,70,71,73,86,93,94,95,96,100,103,107,109,117,118,119,120,121,122,129,135,141,142,144,146,150

C

Caramel 3,4,6,7,8,25,33,34,35,44,62,97,122,123,132

Cashew 4,5,6,7,41,48,81,127,128,155

Cheese 4,15,42,83

Cherry 3,4,7,27,32,36,37,38,143,144,145

Chilli 73

Chips 6,15,32,128,129

Chocolate 1,3,4,5,6,7,8,10,11,12,13,14,15,18,20,21,24,25,26,27,28,29,30,31,32,33,34,35,36,37,38,39,40,41,42,43,44,45,46,47,48,49,50,51,52,53,54,55,56,57,58,59,60,61,62,63,64,68,70,71,72,73,74,77,78,80,81,82,83,84,85,87,88,91,95,97,98,99,100,102,103,104,105,106,107,108,110,112,115,116,117,118,119,122,123,125,126,127,128,129,130,132,133,134,135,136,137,138,143,144,145,146,147,148,149,150,151,152,153,154,155,156

Coconut 4,5,6,38,63,66,67,68,82,119

Coffee 4,5,68,85

Cognac 4,69

Crackers 3,34,103

Cranberry 4,5,6,7,41,70,71,101,145,152,155

Cream 3,4,5,6,15,24,37,42,71,82,83,86,113,137,141

Crumble 114

D

Date 4,6,61,121

Dried cherries 36

E

Egg 4,5,6,7,40,77,121,122,141,150

F

Fat 6,50,101,138,139

Fleur de sel 97

Fruit 3,4,5,7,24,45,87,146

Fudge 3,4,5,6,7,9,14,24,27,35,37,42,46,48,50,53,60,61,70,71,74,75,81,101,103,105,107,108,112,118,119,125,126,127,129,137,138,143,144,146,147,150,153

G

Gin 69

H

Hazelnut 4,5,7,47,69,92,143,147

Herbal tea 80

Honey 4,6,48,74,122

J

Jus 58,63,88

L

Lemon 88

M

Macadamia 4,7,62,66,147

Macaroon 4,38

Margarine 118

Marshmallow 4,6,7,48,49,103,104,105,109,148

Marzipan 13

Meringue 4,57

Milk 6,105

Mint 4,5,6,7,50,51,75,82,106,107,112,137

N

Noodles 99

Nougat 7,97,153

Nut 3,4,5,6,7,26,27,36,45,47,49,50,51,52,56,58,70,83,87,94,101,108,110,111,112,138,139,146,154

O

Oatmeal 7,151

Oil 48,76

Orange 3,4,5,6,25,52,70,88,113

P

Peanuts 4,6,61,122

Pecan 3,4,6,7,10,55,61,123,124,133,154

Peel 87,89,97,145

Pepper 3,5,6,7,11,50,87,88,124,125,149

Pie 75,92,132,134,140

Pistachio 4,6,7,37,69,126,145,154

Pizza 4,5,49,98

Popcorn 3,4,5,6,34,49,54,61,83,129

Potato 4,6,55,126

Pulse 11,66,100,136

Pumpkin 3,6,16,129,130

R

Raisins 4,59

Raspberry 4,6,7,56,82,128,129,143

Rice 11,18,27,29,41,52,77,81,98,102,150

Rum 4,6,59,88,112

S

Salt 3,7,10,33,132,133,134,140,149

Savory 7,139

Squid 7,136

Sugar 7,137,138

Sweets 4,38,104

T

Tea 5,80

Toffee 3,4,5,29,31,39,60,84

Truffle 3,4,5,6,7,15,30,45,47,51,52,56,57,58,59,62,63,66,67,68,69,73,82,83,85,86,88,91,92,98,101,104,112,114,115,116,123,126,130,139,143,147,149,151,152,155,156

W

Walnut 3,4,7,35,60,149

White chocolate 146

White sugar 60,85

Z

Zest 91

Conclusion

Thank you again for downloading this book!

I hope you enjoyed reading about my book!

If you enjoyed this book, please take the time to share your thoughts and post a review on Amazon. It'd be greatly appreciated!

Write me an honest review about the book – I truly value your opinion and thoughts and I will incorporate them into my next book, which is already underway.

Thank you!

If you have any questions, **feel free to contact at:** *author@bisquerecipes.com*

Shani Moore

bisquerecipes.com

Made in United States
North Haven, CT
02 December 2021

11883280R00089